B₇T 12.10

British Poetry since 1970
a critical survey

British Poetry since 1970
a critical survey

Edited by Peter Jones and Michael Schmidt

PERSEA BOOKS, Inc., New York

821.914
J 78 b
1980

Contents

BRITISH POETRY SINCE 1970 does not attempt — as its predecessor *British Poetry since 1960* did — to be comprehensive. The earlier volume included too many catalogues and general essays: subtitled 'a critical survey', it was more survey than criticism. Here we tend to the other extreme. Most of the essays are on individual writers. There is an anthology of poems to indicate where we, as editors and publishers, place our emphasis. Including new poetry in a book of criticism is part of our strategy: the book is intended to be of value to the general poetry reader. It addresses not a 'subject' but a living art.

Criticism clears a certain space around the work it describes or explores, sharpening response and facilitating judgment. The juxtaposition of critical essays reveals prevalent themes and technical concerns. We commissioned most of these essays from writers who themselves emerged during the 1970s. It was our general policy to seek out advocates.

We must acknowledge with gratitude the work of three colleagues who helped us with this, as with so many other, Carcanet projects: Helen Lefroy, Margaret Hutchinson and Helen Ramsbotham.

P. J. and M. S.

Introduction

DECADES acquire in retrospect a distinctive character. Some of them attract adjectives: 'gay' nineties, 'roaring' twenties. Some *become* adjectives: when one speaks of a 'thirties' poet, specific names and qualities come to mind; and we know what a critic means when he says a poem is 'fifties'. Decades that become adjectives are often dominated by a group or school (the Auden group, the Movement). Those that remain substantives may do so for a number of reasons. The decade of the 1940s, for instance, included too many events and changes to distil itself into a descriptive word. The 1960s were spoiled by excess of opportunities and choices and by the paucity of generously stringent critics.

A London publisher has a theory that good and bad decades alternate. The 'teens were good, the twenties bad; thirties good, forties horrid; fifties so-so, sixties disgusting. We have yet to seek his verdict on the seventies. From so short a perspective it is hard to predict whether it will prove a substantive or an adjective decade. We rather expect it to be the former, unless 'seventies' comes to denote a new and attentive approach to traditional formalism, no longer disabled by the strategic ironies of the 1950s; a period of 'unillusion' (to use a Hardyesque term), when young writers began to find their way home from the euphoria and betrayed optimism that characterized much of the 1960s. Neil Powell, a writer who grew up in the sixties, evoked the period as 'that low dishonest decade... which splintered and shattered cultural criteria, turning serious writers into madmen and frivolous writers into pop stars'. The young writers found their way home to a Britain that *is*. The overdue recognition of Geoffrey Hill's uncompromising work, the emergence of C. H. Sisson and, from another part of the wood, the rediscovery of Edgell Rickword, indicate a change in the quality of seriousness of some readers and writers.

There were several positive developments in the 1970s. Charles Tomlinson's work began to be justly appraised; Donald Davie's long labours as poet, critic and teacher began visibly to pay off; W. S. Graham was 'discovered' to be writing his best poems. Because no new poet dominated the scene and the legacy of the 1960s—disorder and uncertainty—had made critics wary of the present, attention was paid to what had been passed over before. Michael Hamburger, Roy Fisher, J. H. Prynne, Elaine Feinstein, Christopher Middleton, John Heath-Stubbs and David Gascoyne were among the writers who found themselves with unexpected advocates. The achievement of older poets — Elizabeth Daryush, Frances Bellerby, Sylvia Townsend Warner, Adrian Stokes, F. T. Prince, Padraic Fallon and, among the Americans, HD, Delmore Schwartz and Yvor

Winters — was acknowledged. The deaths of W. H. Auden, David Jones, Hugh MacDiarmid, Austin Clarke, I. A. Richards, Stevie Smith and — at a tragically early age — of John Riley were marked with critical and publishing activity. Perhaps 'seventies' will come to mean 'pluralistic', a positive diversity by contrast with the negative disorientation of the decade before. Judging from the *spirantia exta* of the 1980s, the omens are not good for the survival of this discriminating pluralism.

These reflections will strike critics who found the 1970s 'the bleakest decade since the 1920s' as altogether too sanguine. No major movements, no dominant new poets, no serious literary debate in the public arena: such facts are for some disheartening. Worse was the absence until the last three years of the decade of estimable new critics of contemporary poetry. The critics who have now surfaced are, for the most part, poets of merit as well.

We do not wish to suggest that the 'general standard' of poetry improved in the 1970s. Our claim is more modest: that a number of good (not just 'promising') new poets appeared and that several established writers added significantly to their work. We are concerned with the general 'poetry scene' only as it touched and influenced the serious writer. The state of publishing and criticism, the quality of the audience, the availability of books and magazines: these are important secondary factors in the literary environment. As for the 'poetry scene', it was riven and inconstant as it always has been and — to the poet who obeys a Muse rather than an audience — peripheral.

As publishers we are from time to time asked: where is the Ted Hughes, the Philip Larkin, the Thom Gunn of the new generation? We can list the many imitators each has spawned — but this is hardly to the point. Success can be emulated: it cannot be duplicated. It is worth bearing in mind that those poets who established their reputations in the 1950s and who continue to loom large were in many respects fortunate. They attracted their first public at about the last moment when a residual literary consensus existed. Promoted by a distinguished publishing house, championed by established poets and critics, they satisfied with their genuine merits the post-war hunger for a 'new generation' of writers. What is more, they were leading contemporary writers when it became fashionable to teach contemporary literature. Their work became familiar in selection to school-children and university students. They were part of the curriculum, and there they have remained. Curricula have a tendency to ossify.

Today the very factors that made their emergence possible — even inevitable — have changed. If, as we believe, talents comparable to theirs have appeared in the seventies, they have not — apart from Seamus Heaney — come to the surface as those poets did. The audience is now different from the one that welcomed them. Publishing and reviewing patterns have altered. Earlier groups of writers have broken up. London itself, with its media, editors and publishers, its concentration of resources, has lost much of its magnetism and energy. Writers who gravitated there in the 1960s, whether from Aylesbury or from the Antipodes, put down roots in shallower soil than they might have done. Forty years ago George Orwell spoke of 'the bleaching-tub of London "culture" '; and as we look from our provincial vantage point, we are tempted to say, *plus ça change*. A London-based contributor to this book provides an example of the characteristic cosmopolitan perspective. As evidence of 'homogeneity' among some young poets he adduces the fact that 'most were based in the provinces'. Outside the city walls, you have the bleak, equal provinces, while inside (the unstated bias is) you have variety, exchange, vitality. But Tomlinson in Gloucestershire, Bunting in Newcastle, Sisson in Somerset, Hughes in Devon, Hill in Leeds, Finlay in Lanarkshire, Graham in Cornwall, Larkin in Hull: the provinces do not, of themselves, seem to homogenize poets. London critics have a soft-spot for Ulster: the Ulster poets, our contributor tells us, are 'not in any sense a group'. And yet, as another of our critics, Andrew Waterman, demonstrated in his notorious essay 'Ulsterectomy' *(PN Review* 3), that is precisely what they are. The metropolitan enthusiasm for Ulster has been rewarded of late by two poets — Seamus Heaney and Tom Paulin. Otherwise the province remains, like any other, and like the capital itself, a hive of essentially local activity, locally interesting, which does not transcend locality. The infla- tion of the 'Ulster school' has occurred for quite understandable extra- poetic reasons; but for the serious reader, there is no reason to re-draw the map of English *poetry* around the six counties.

Another common journalistic assumption (evident in one of our contri- butor's essays) is that an Oxbridge education is a homogenizer. If this were the case, there would be other *useful* categories: polytechnic poets, red-brick poets, eleven-plus poets, W.E.A. poets. Homogeneity and individuality are not so simply matters of accidental circumstances. When they exist, the causes lie deeper in the age than that.

Despite the development of provincial centres of activity, the centrality of London remains, for the dissemination of poetry and criticism, a fact. Manchester, Newcastle, Cambridge and other cities publish magazines and books with national readership, but there is not the concentration of resources in these places to offer a serious challenge to London. This is why the health of London is a matter for concern: its media are primary sources of public information; its publishing houses and magazines are the best-established and distributed. This poetry capital is susceptible to conquest by determined groups. The groups rise and fall. The seventies was a period of transition between such group efforts; there was no dom- inant force, and this helps to account for the diversity of work published and evaluated. We are currently witnessing the consolidation of a new orthodoxy in London. It can only be hoped that it will be broader in perspective and have a longer historical reach than the one that preceded it. Donald Davie, describing the achievement by *The Review* group in taking the commanding heights in the 1960s and early 1970s, wrote:

> Precisely because the positions [of editorial responsibility] that matter are so few, it is entirely feasible for a group to secure one or two sub-editorial chairs and a few reviewing 'spots', so as to impose their shared proclivities and opinions as the reigning orthodoxy for a decade. It is altogether fatuous to cry out at this as scandalous: it is inevitable, given the smallness of England, and the economic advantages of metropolitan consolidation. *(Poetry Nation* II).

The 1970s notably lacked defining and unifying social issues with 'imaginative content'. Inflation and oil-crises did not have the force that, a decade earlier, Vietnam had had or, two decades before, the CND rallies, the unfolding of the blue-print for the Welfare State, the still-echoing proximity of the Second World War.

In an end-of-decade interview, George Steiner suggested that we had reached the end of 'the long list of solid dreams' — the Russian Revolution, China, Cuba, Czechoslovakia, Chile. Now, 'even the young have the strong intuition that every hope goes wrong'.

> Why did we let ourselves be seduced by the great dreams? They were, I think, enormously creative mistakes, enormously creative fantasies. What really scares me at the moment is: how do we operate without such windows? What happens when there is the insight or the conviction or the instinct that, whatever you do, you'll get it wrong? *(Listener,* 3 January 1980)

Some of the best poets since the war have been working in a world without such windows. Donald Davie's 'Remembering the Thirties', Charles Tomlinson's 'Prometheus', C. H. Sisson's 'Over the Wall' and 'Carmen Saeculare', Geoffrey Hill's *Mercian Hymns,* and many other outstanding poems (which also happen to be 'political poetry' of a high order, durable because not useful) focus on the world Steiner describes. So too in a different sense does Philip Larkin. It is not so much disillusion as afterthought on illusion, with a nostalgia for illusion savagely held in check. Hardy's poem 'The Oxen' is a grandfather of such poems: a past not idealized but shown as unrealized, impoverishing by its effect or by sheer contrast the present. Recent history has made ideology, as well as religious faith, a vexed province.

Casting about for something solid to get its teeth into, conscience began to gnaw at particulars. Some new poets turned to their own historical and cultural experience and began to value those writers who had been doing so before. George Steiner says, 'we're turning inwards'. The young poets we most value and their immediate predecessors have been doing quite the opposite. Betrayed by the forward dreams of ideology, some of them set out to explore that betrayal. Others looked in history for confirmation of it. This was not a strategy of passivity or self-dramatization. Confessionalism had had its day in the 1960s. It was more a matter of finding new bearings, of action *in* poetry rather than action *with* poetry. The political matter in the work of poets such as Jeffrey Wainwright, Roger Garfitt and Jeremy Hooker is contained. The poems have value but no use. History, no longer arranged in a satisfying millennial pattern, became again a dimension through which the poet could move with doubt and fear and therefore in the hope of discovery. Unreason — a vogue of the 1960s — gave way not to programmatic reason, as it had done when in the 1950s some poets deliberately rejected the excesses of the loudest of their predecessors; it gave way instead to particularism. Poetry was a discipline once more, but without prescribed strategies: a discipline for exploration, 'process' (a popular word throughout the decade), not a quest for precise and finite statements. There may have been too much of the 'dying fall', poems ending in gestures of impotence or defeat; but irony was less a matter of strategy, more an aspect of theme. The elegiac tone dominated, but the elegist seemed often to be speaking for a community or for a place, not simply for himself. Hardy was back, in a manifestation different from that which haunted Auden and different too from the one that cured Larkin of Yeats. Edward Thomas was magnified and anatomized. He appears to have been the presiding spirit of the decade. The great modernists — especially Ezra Pound — seemed (but only seemed) to withdraw into the shadows.

One genre in particular answered many poets' need to avoid 'turning inwards' and to address, albeit obliquely, themes of general pertinence. If we are 'habituated to nightmare', as George Steiner suggests, the poet who goes back to the time before we went to sleep and seeks there the sources of the dream can help to clarify, if not alleviate, our situation. His poem may be an imaginative analysis and a kind of exorcism. During the trip into the past, he may relearn old and serviceable prosodic skills, rediscover a now neglected 'nature' as Robert Wells and Dick Davis have done.

But principally we have in mind the historical sequence, practised by a wide range of poets, of various political complexions and with diverse prosodic means. 'The past that is relevant is the one that also speaks to one's contemporaries', the Marxist poet and critic Edgell Rickword said. It is such a past that many poets have sought. Some have cast their poems as dramatic monologues. One of the outstanding poems of the decade is the 'Thomas Müntzer' sequence by Jeffrey Wainwright, which takes the German radical priest for its subject and realizes his experience with remarkable evocative thrift. Several of Wainwright's poems are sequences, observing events or recounting them through the voices of participants. One senses in each poem the centrality for the poet of the issues: but it is the external facts that shape the process through which the poet works his lines. He avoids the detached or independent lyric as inadequate for his complex and unindividualistic purposes.

Jeremy Hooker follows a similar course. His poems are organized in such a way as to be read sequentially. History and pre-history are forces as strong as the present seen and felt reality: they make demands as his own experience does.

Andrew Motion, Roger Garfitt, Peter Scupham, James Fenton and Brian Jones are among the poets who have developed this genre in the 1970s. Well-established poets — who may have helped to direct their approach — have gone before them. Jon Silkin's dramatic elegies for the Jews of Medieval York, Geoffrey Hill's historical sequences and Seamus Heaney's bog poems are part of this concern: to see places and events in their full human complexity, to re-imbue with human warmth facts which have turned cold, to make earlier lives and earlier struggles part of a present which they illuminate.

Those poets, new and established, who are developing this genre — not itself new, of course, but now common — are more numerous than those we have named. The genre has been most useful to poets politically on the left but dissatisfied with the 'popular' socialist poetry of the 1960s. Their work constitutes an impressive contribution to the *literature* of the left, but more pertinently, a renewal of interest in verse narrative which incorporates, by means of prosodic freedom and sequence order, the suggestive intensities of lyric poetry with a variety of perspective and voices which strictly qualify the individuality of the speaker.

As we enter the 1980s, the spirit of the 1960s is still with us in various disguises: in liturgical reform, in outmoded political rhetoric, in popular poetry anthologies, even among some surviving poets and critics. In literature as in liturgy, the spirit of the sixties is often fuelled from America, and the most savage American assaults on British poetry as an entity have come during the 1970s. The plausible virulence of our native critics can be stimulating and helpful; the virulence of *some* American critics — even when it is articulate — often misses the target, either because it has not acquainted itself with the target area or because it has ulterior motives. Still, it has an effect: a few readers and writers become dispirited. British poetry retains, of course, a number of American champions. But enemies can be as fascinating as friends, especially when they help (even if by reaction) to reveal our nature to us. A look at the case against British poetry will help to define what it isn't and what it is.

The Review, Ian Hamilton's sporadic magazine, ceased publication in the 1970s. It was an important loss: it had long been a valuable critical magazine, provocative and consistent, and has not been — nor could it be — replaced. In a 1971 issue, the American poet Louis Simpson contributed an 'Opinion' article which set out a few typical prejudices about British poetry and was a catalyst to our publishing *British poetry since 1960*. In 1977, Simpson's prejudices and a few besides surfaced decisively in the American journal *Contemporary Literature*. Professor Marjorie Perloff guest-edited a special issue sub-titled 'The Two Poetries: the Postwar Lyric in Britain and America'. The 'two poetries' which Anthony Thwaite (*Listener*, 5 April 1973) had tried to identify within British poetry itself were now segregated and given *national* homelands. It was not a matter of 'ground' and 'underground' but 'Britain' and 'America'. Professor Perloff is more extreme than Mr. Simpson. If her evidence strikes us as a little bizarre, even caricatured, we must remember how short her perspectives are and how narrow her view of contemporary British poetry. There are sins of omission which many British critics, too, commit when they regard American verse.

For her and her contributors, post-war British poetry is Philip Larkin, Charles Tomlinson, Donald Davie, Ted Hughes, Thom Gunn, Jon Silkin and — almost — Geoffrey Hill. Her contributors are all academics. It does not alarm us that they study poetry, or even that they teach it; only that some of them seem keen to *use* it to curious ends.

Professor Perloff herself sets out (as Simpson less blatantly did before her) to demonstrate the superiority of American to British poetry and criticism. Few dispute that some American poets (though not all those featured in her introduction) are outstanding; few deny that some American critics (not, perhaps, those she has enlisted) have genuine powers. But it is one thing to rate poets and critics, quite another to rate poetry and criticism.

The academy — schools and universities alike — has modern poetry by the throat. The market for books of poems is now pre-eminently academic. No new poet is safely established until he is on a syllabus. The market for *teachable* poetry is the readiest one — a subject to which we shall return. The author of unteachable poetry risks the loss of market and of publisher. Perhaps this is why much good old and new work is published by small non-profit presses whose programmes are unworldly and who flower and perish with almost seasonal regularity. The market for poetry has never before been so clearly identifiable or so patently influential on the sort of poetry and criticism that get into print among the commercial houses. *British Poetry since 1970*, though it addresses the 'general reader', will be purchased primarily by that identifiable, essentially academic market. Most of its contributors are teachers.

British and American markets differ. The American academic market is more diverse, for one thing. Professor Perloff might usefully have ex-

plored to what extent there are 'two markets', 'two academies'. At such a
level generalizations are possible and, in a limited way, useful. There are
at least 'two criticisms'. To risk our own admittedly dubious generaliza-
tion, we would suggest that the characteristic British critical procedure is
to pass from text to context, in good Coleridgean fashion. Another sort of
critic, common in America but by no means unknown in Britain, moves
from presuppositions that properly derive from disciplines of a philosophical, scientific or pseudo-scientific nature, to the text which is examined in terms strictly alien to it. Both sorts of criticisms have advant-
ages and shortcomings. As editors we are drawn to the former school
(though not all the essayists in this book agree with us); Professor Perloff
belongs, with some of her critics, to the latter.

In the past, American writers who have asserted the independence of
American literature have done so in a spirit of independence — not
attempting to kick what Poe called 'our British Grandmamma' down-
stairs. Some recent critics are more ambitious: they seek to reverse the
colonial role. They are no longer in rebellion against a dominant tradition;
its dominance in most corners of the United States is no longer felt. They
wish to point up the bankruptcy of the British tradition, to identify that
bankruptcy in the very *weight* of tradition.

Emerson has had a decisively liberating effect on his countrymen. He
did not polemicize: he suggested. His prose is a sea of aphorisms, many of
which sound wise because his prose rhythms are so persuasive. As words
changed meaning, so his writings seemed to change. To American surrealists and to confessional poets, a sentiment such as 'the whole of nature
is a metaphor of the mind' could mean almost anything they wished,
'mind' and 'nature' not being tied by context to specific implications.
'The reliance on authority measures the decline of religion, the with-
drawal of the soul.' The enthusiast might take this to mean that the rejection of the authority of tradition and precedent leads to creative freedom and originality. There is an older argument: that creative freedom
comes, in literature, only with the closest possible attention to and knowledge of precedent. Originality is a process of growth and extension, not of
discontinuity. Radicalism has to do with roots, and when poetry is stifled
by convention, it is a return to, not a breach with, tradition that is required. That is, after all, the lesson of the Anglo-American 'modernists'.

Less humanly sanguine than Emerson was Poe; but he was equally keen
to 'snap asunder the lead-strings' that bound American to British culture.
His stock is low now in the reputation exchanges, but his critical tact
deserves to be recalled, especially what he wrote about 'originality'. 'It is
by no means a matter as some suppose' (including Emerson and Professor
Perloff) 'of impulse or intuition,' he said. 'In general, to be found, it must
be elaborately sought, and although a positive merit of the highest class,
demands in its attainment less of invention than negation.'

Poe was not heeded: Emerson's plausible call to independence was taken up. What might worry British and American readers is the recent rhetoric not of American cultural independence but of victory — a crowing over the defeated, a habit of self-congratulation. It is salutary to bear in mind the words of Octavio Paz: 'A writer's nationality is his language.' It is also worth reflecting on the conclusion of a wryly disaffected essay by C. H. Sisson, 'Some Reflections on American Poetry' (1978). He wants to

> raise the general question of the *separateness* of American poetry, which seems now to be widely assumed though I have not seen it anywhere persuasively argued. Richard Ellmann begins his introduction (to the *New Oxford Book of American Verse*) with a categoric 'American poetry, once an offshoot, now appears to be a parent stem.' It sounds as if it would cause something worse than the Boston tea-party if one tried to overturn this piece of dogmatism. None the less, it seems to me to be essential, for the health of literature on both sides of the Atlantic, that it should be overturned. Anthologies now properly begin with Anne Bradstreet, but it is of course absurd to regard her as the beginning of anything, except possibly of the geographical habit of writing English verse on the North American continent. She is a tiny, engaging figure in the literature of the seventeenth century. And what is Philip Freneau apart from the literature of the eighteenth century? It could only be a political fury, not a care for letters, which taught that these people were initiators.
>
> At what point did the situation become different? And the answer must be, It never did. And it never will, as long as the language spoken on the two sides of the Atlantic — and in how many other places! — is such as to permit more or less unimpeded conversation. This is not a matter on which the immense international role of the United States, and the diminished and dependent role of the United Kingdom, has any bearing. (*Parnassus*, Autumn 1978)

He draws a Roman analogy: we do not think of St Augustine as an African writer, of Seneca or Martial as Spanish writers, of Ausonius as a French writer. Sisson, of course, overstates the case in order to make it audible above the orthodox hubbub.

The article by Louis Simpson in *The Review*, which provided one of the pretexts for our earlier volume, was written, we later guessed, at about the time that he was working on the poems gathered together in his mid-1970s collection *Searching for the Ox*. There he snapped asunder the strings that had bound him to a definably English tradition. His generalizations about British and American poetry, viewed from the perspective of his disappointing book, come to seem personal, schematizing his own crisis. Mr Simpson, pushing the imaginative frontiers of poetic language outward (and westward) asserted that the best poets should be active *at* the frontiers: and he defined the frontiers. Such arguments were already familiar, most influentially advanced by a British critic, Al Alvarez, in the introduction to his anthology *The New Poetry* (1962), a book which, though the poetry is no longer very new, remains widely in evidence. In the 1960s there was much frontier work and brinkmanship — linguistic, emotional and psychological. But even then, at less fashionable frontiers, important work was being pursued as usual. The reaction against the 'extremism' advocated by the more apocalyptic sixties critics was best expressed in Charles Tomlinson's poem 'Ars Poetica', published in 1972 and bearing the dedication 'In memoriam A. A.' — evidently addressed to Mr Alvarez (previously — but there obliquely — answered in the 1969 poem 'Against Extremity'). Tomlinson did not include 'Ars Poetica' in his 1978 *Selected Poems*. It is one of his 'Bagatelles', and it was worth including in that volume:

> What is it for
> this form of saying, truce
> with history in a language
> no one may wish to use?
>
> Who was it said
> 'a form of suicide'? — meaning
> you drive yourself up to the edge
> or as near as you can ride
>
> without dropping over.
> Some drop, wit-
> less — and we
> are to praise them for it?
>
> Well, if mourning
> were all we had,
> we could settle for a great simplicity,
> mourn ourselves mad.
>
> But that is only half
> the question: blight
> has its cures and hopes
> come uninvited.
>
> What is it for? Answers
> should be prepaid. And no Declines
> of the West Full Stop
> No selling lines.

It is hardly surprising that the third stanza has the tone and cadence of Donald Davie's angry poem 'Pentecost'. Davie has been a severe critic of the 'extremist' dogmas of the 1960s.

Professor Perloff takes up Donald Davie's statement that American readers cannot *hear* the tones and rhythms of British poetry any more than the British can hear those of American poetry. Davie qualifies his statement by his context, but Professor Perloff takes it as axiomatic. She recalls how the great modernists 'transcended national boundaries'. Eliot affected the British, Auden the Americans. This happy cross-pollenization by the genius-bees culminates for her symbolically in Sylvia Plath and Ted Hughes who 'quite literally made a marriage between American and British poetry, absorbing, at least for a time, the same influences and domesticating the same myths'. She thus drains a particular relationship of human content and assigns to it an emblematic literary significance it never had. Plath and Hughes hardly represented the *aurea mediocritas* of American and British poetry. Nor were their imaginative procedures radically similar at any stage of their development. Both are unique. They can be followed only at a distance and at considerable peril. The symbolism of the marriage, satisfying as it may seem to the critic, is illusory.

Since Sylvia Plath's death, almost *because* of it, Professor Perloff suggests, British and American poetry have gone their separate ways. Lowell came to England but not to become a British writer; Davie and Gunn went to America but are not American writers. It may be that they did not wish to exchange metaphorical passports — any more than Robert Graves desired to become a Spaniard — but such considerations do not occur to Professor Perloff. Davie has written consistently for a British readership ever since he left Britain, and he returns home frequently. His exile has sharpened his perspective, not changed his allegiances. If anything, it has intensified them.

American poetry, Professor Perloff continues, has more in common with French, Latin American and East European poetry than with British. It is probably vain to point out how much Hughes has learned from East European poetry (and how much he has told us about it); or Tomlinson from French, Spanish and Russian; or Sisson from French, German, Italian and Latin; or Hamburger and Middleton from German and French; and all these writers have learned from American poets as well. Vain also, perhaps, to indicate how close Robert Lowell, John Berryman, Elizabeth Bishop, Richard Wilbur, and in a younger generation John Peck, Robert Pinsky, Robert Hass and others are to the long English tradition (nationality apart). There is considerable direct and indirect communication still, much 'audibility' for those with attentive ears. It is inevitable, and serious British poets in the seventies have not been as myopic as the old 'insular' stereotypes suggest.

It is, however, the case that much American *criticism* has a great deal in common with continental criticism. And certainly some American poets side-step London *en route* to Paris and places East (and West). Where American writers used to like to talk in terms of 'generations', there is now a fashion for schools, systems, trends, nationalities. 'Generations' suggest developments in time. The new terminology, the new dogmas, free themselves of the long perspectives and for succession substitute spatial categories. Professor Perloff likes American poetry better than British because it is more susceptible to interpretation by the methods she finds most up-to-date. She is well up in her French criticism.

This is the heart of her case:

> I would argue that the modesty, what Calvin Bedient calls, with reference to Larkin, the 'imaginative barrenness' of contemporary British poetry, has much to do with the poets' persistent and perhaps burdensome sense of tradition, a tradition their American counterparts dismiss with what is all too often a frightening insouciance.

We doubt the truth of her statement as it relates to the best American writing being produced today. But we note how firmly in the sequel she comes down on the side of those who dismiss tradition. She offers no analysis of what that tradition is. Calvin Bedient is more generous: he has emerged as one of the most perceptive critics of British poetry in the 1970s — a sensitive American reader who finds no difficulty in hearing the British patois. The Second World War, he reflects, 'stunned' British poets (its aftermath continues to do so), 'And yet the genius of British poets has lain in getting around their own knowledge, around in it, creating original poetry despite their lucidity.' His adjectives are: 'alert', 'lean', 'austere'. They suit much of the best new writing of the seventies as they do the surviving work of the two previous decades.

In evidence of the health of American poetic thought Professor Perloff calls on the magazine *Boundary 2: A Journal of Postmodern Literature.* The title gives away at once its sixties antecedents and its academic pretensions. We are here at 'boundaries' or 'frontiers' again, places where the writer is so busy looking over the edge (of language or of life) that he may lose touch with what is bounded. MacNeice wrote the memorable lines: 'A centre needs periphery,/And each event implies the world'. One might say now that periphery needs a centre. The word 'boundary' in the title is qualified by the subtitle, dragged back from the emotional or confessional brink and sanitized by the word 'postmodern'. Professor Perloff doesn't like the word, and nor do we. It has certain academic uses, but when it appears in the title of a magazine which features the work of poets as well as academic critics, we begin to smell a class-room.

Despite the title, Professor Perloff praises the magazine for 'a series of essays that attempt to define "postmodernism" in relation to "mod-

ernism" (and other -isms)². She quotes Edwin Brock's lament that,
though British poetry is getting along quite well, 'What is sadly lacking in
Britain is the kind of attention that poetry receives in the States.' Receives
from whom? It is the academy he has in mind and those journals which
Professor Perloff claims 'have served a real function' in America,
'stimulating discussion about "the new poetry", whether in Heideggerian
or Derridean terms, or within the framework of ethnopoetics, or with
respect to such other arts as painting and film-making'. A criticism that
rejects 'tradition' and the perspectives provided by precedent cannot but
seek alternative perspectives, 'frameworks', outside the discipline of
poetry. Such perspectives may well alert us to qualities in a work which
might otherwise have remained latent; but we believe that the most valuable contexts — the *primary* ones — in which to assess and interpret
poetry (after having responded to it without such mediation) are those of
human experience and our common poetic tradition. Regarded from the
angle of film-making, explicated in Derridean terms, the poetry of, for
example, Frank O'Hara may loom large; but set within the tradition
represented by (to go no great distance) Pound and Williams, Crane and
Lowell, it looks a little pale, surely. It is possible to transvalue poetry if it
helpfully conforms to one of the poetically extraneous disciplines.
Professor Perloff would deliver criticism, and that criticism would deliver
poetry more and more exclusively into the hands of 'professionals',
exegetes and theorists.

When Professor Perloff introduces David Antin, a contributor to
Boundary 2 and a poet who speaks, tape-records his extempore words, has
them typed out and printed by New Directions, a prestigious New York
house, our hearts sink. Some have the temerity to dismiss these
'improvisatory lectures' as 'mere talk'! Find, she seems to say, a definition
of poetry which will exclude this work. It is really for her to find a definition that will *include* it. Antin's book, *Talking at the Boundaries,* is
'selling well'. That proves something. Mrs Wilson's poems are selling
well, too.

David Antin's work is no doubt an example of the 'insouciance'
Professor Perloff mildly chastises in passing on to her main target, British
poetry. The target is less vulnerable than she thinks.

In Britain there are critical tendencies destructive of poetry as well, but of
quite a different nature. The journalistic trivialization of the art, the tendency to personalize (also common in America) in order to market work,
and the habit of over-reaction whether to inflate or deflate a reputation,
are all unfortunate and prevalent. Though it can be argued that reviewers
and critics don't affect poetry, they can affect readership and help to
determine the market. Also, undeniably, they do seem to set a tone for a
period and they can establish among new writers certain attitudes. We do

not doubt that Mr Alvarez's formulation of the 'gentility principle' in the early sixties, quite as much as the rugged example of Ted Hughes's verse, led even quite naturally genteel young poets to a kind of rugged ventriloquism. To feel uncomfortable, there were writers who put some grit in their shoes and imagined this was suffering. Other critical formulations have had their effects. When Louis MacNeice spoke of his and his colleagues' sharing 'the Greek preference for information or statement' he was helping to deflect the challenges of modernism.

There is pressure first for change and then for orthodoxy. Reaction against an earlier generation or movement clears a little space and then tries to increase the space with elbowing negatives. Kingsley Amis's rather notorious cry in the 1950s, 'Nobody wants any more poems about foreign cities', was eloquently refuted in 1960 by Charles Tomlinson in his poem 'More Foreign Cities':

> . . . There is Fiordiligi, its sun-changes
>   Against walls of transparent stone
>   Unsettling all preconception. . .

All the same, the statement had an effect, a narrowing one. In the seventies a few metropolitan critics took up a similar cry: nobody wants any more poems about the countryside. They seem to say, 'The majority lives in the city and must be addressed in terms of its own subject-matter.' As well to say, 'I live in the city and sheep and moors bore me silly.' The positive formulations of the modernists and, among contemporary poets and critics, of Davie, Middleton, and a few others, retain creative force among attentive writers; but the negative formulations and catch-phrases help to shape general taste and prejudice.

There is — and has been since the beginning of the century — a journalistic instinct which makes a bee-line for the second-rate. The survival of this instinct matters a great deal more today than it has done in the past. As Roy Fuller wrote in the *Listener* (6 December 1979):

> Today the evaluation of authors is especially important, for several reasons. One is that contemporary literature has been brought into the school and university curricula. There, set books, available books, cheaper books and the inertia of teachers tend to elevate and prolong reputations which might otherwise have had a humbler and briefer life.

One cannot expect such evaluation from academic critics. And the seventies were years in which, as we have said, the academy ingested contemporary poets and poetry with a real appetite. So complete a meal did it make that even the Chair of Poetry at Oxford was, for the first time in many years, snatched away from poets and returned to academics. John Jones was elected Professor. In various newspapers and magazines poetry has become the prerogative of academics: critics such as John Carey, John

Bayley and Christopher Ricks (to name but three) pronounce in the places where once T. S. Eliot, Edwin Muir, Edgell Rickword, W. H. Auden and others were accustomed to chart the course of poetry, an art they practised and which their successors teach. Coleridge in *Anima Poetae* raised the question which our recent experience answers:

> The question should be fairly stated, how far a man can be an adequate, or even a good (as far as he goes) though inadequate critic of poetry, who is not a poet, at least *in posse*. Can he be an adequate, can he be a good critic, though not commensurate? But there is yet another distinction. Supposing he is not only not a poet, but is a bad poet! What then?

What indeed! The academic poet-reviewer too is a treacherous friend of the muse and a prevalent figure in the reviewing media.

Here one must go warily, for there are poets who work in schools and universities and who write reviews and essays who are not 'academic' poets. It is those who are in school and form poetic schools that do most harm, while poet-teachers such as Davie, Middleton, Hooker, Tomlinson, Hill, Wainwright, Gunn, Scupham and others are interested in poetry as an art in all its manifestations — so long as they are excellent — and not as a competitive trade within a market. They are inward with the art and are not easily dazzled by mere novelty, the way a young critic or a mature academic, bored with his discipline, may be.

The academy has a hold, however, even over these emancipated poets. Few poets are not, in one way or another, affiliated with or attached to the educational establishment. Those whose hands are, as it were, clean or only faintly dirty are easier to number than those who have earned or augmented a livelihood in teaching either the academic syllabus or 'creative writing' at some time. Special fellowships, lectureships and the like grew quite common in the seventies. They have been common in the United States since the 1940s and even earlier. Many poets without academic qualifications for the jobs found and find themselves in academe. Others with qualifications enter the attractive and tenured life on a more regular basis.

It would be perverse to suggest that such developments have not affected the poetry these writers have produced. The study of poetry, the continual interplay between poet-tutor and audience-class, help to identify what 'goes' and what fails. The 'well-made poem', with a discussable or teasing image structure, dramatic progression and climax, paraphrasable meaning and thematic 'relevance', is a common classroom commodity, and very useful it is to the pedagogue. David Wright calls the genre 'identikit poem'.

The experience is analogous to that sense of audience which some poets developed during the public reading epidemic of the 1960s, though perhaps it is more intensive and potentially rewarding. A sense of audience affected the style and manner of some genuinely talented writers. In America, Robert Lowell witnessed to this fact:

> I went on a trip to the West Coast and read at least once a day and sometimes twice for fourteen days, and more and more I found that I was simplifying my poems. If I had a Latin quotation I'd translate it into English. If adding a couple of syllables in a line made it clearer I'd add them, and I'd make little changes just impromptu as I read. That seemed to improve the reading.

There is no evidence that a heightened sense of audience improved the poems. It may indeed have contributed to Lowell's nervous habit of revising his poems, distrusting each draft, continually re-casting them in later years. Poets smaller than Lowell went astray on the road or in the classroom. Philip Larkin's reflection on the Beatles can stand as an epitaph to those for whom poetry became a performing art or a teaching aid: 'I doubt whether their own fancies and imagination are strong enough to command an audience instead of collaborating with it.'

In the 1960s, almost *because* of the existence of an audience and a market for popular poetry and the 'spin-off' by way of readings to poets without thespian aspirations, the negative spirit was at work, if only in the excess of production — books, magazines, readings and happenings — that glutted the market almost as soon as it was identified. The disorientation of the 1960s came with the apparent disappearance of traditional barriers against the 'foreign', including the American, in poetry. We had never had so *much*. In 1970 Thom Gunn noted that American poetry 'from Williams to Duncan and Snyder' was all there, and all there *at once*. No wonder America seemed dauntingly active. In the space of five or six years the work of fifty years became available. Now most of those books — including Williams, Duncan and Snyder — are out of print in their British editions. They came like visitors, turned the house upside-down, and went away. For English writers and readers it was like a feast at which all the courses were brought on at once. Some had to excuse themselves after a few confused mouthfuls. Imitation, fits of ventriloquism — and on a few poets a positive and lasting impact. What was damaging was the rapidity of the appearance of so much work, so ill-assorted, and its inevitable, brisk disappearance. Gunn, Davie and Tomlinson remain important advocates and guides to the American work most likely to survive the Atlantic crossing and speak to British writers and readers, yet often the very work they advocate, so recently available, is no longer to be found.

Translations, too, proliferated in the 1960s. In the 1970s the rate of publication decreased (though there is strong evidence that there are more poets more intelligently translating contemporary and classical poetry than ever before). The availability of translations, encouraged by the magazine *Modern Poetry in Translation* which Daniel Weissbort and Ted Hughes founded in the early 1960s, added to the rich confusion of the decade. Standards of translation were extremely varied. Much work was translated for other than poetic reasons, some of it for political reasons (the vogue for dissident literature sharply distorted our perception of the character of East European and Latin American poetry, for example). Some poets look like surviving their stay here — the Russian Acmeists, a few East European poets such as Vasko Popa, Zbigniew Herbert, Miroslav Holub, Janos Pilinszky; Latin American writers such as Pablo Neruda and Octavio Paz, to name a few — on their merits and the virtues of their translators. But for each who stays perhaps a dozen have vanished from sight. Some remain — and remain influential — because they have found British poets to champion them. Michael Hamburger's skilful advocacy of German writers, Hughes's of Popa and Pilinszky, Feinstein's of Tsvetaeva, and so on — such advocacy has made a few important foreign poets part of the general English diet. Those great foreign writers who were published in bad translations have suffered badly; the market for their work was killed for a generation.

The quantitative decline in poetry publishing in 1970 as compared with 1960 was rather greater than a return to earlier levels of activity. In the 1960s a number of new lists and small publishing ventures got under way. Many of those lists and imprints closed down during the 1970s. Long-established poetry publishers ceased or reduced their 'poetry commitment' in the 1970s in response to commercial exigencies. A few commercial houses swam against the tide — Secker & Warburg most dramatically, issuing a wide range of work by new and established poets as well as poetry in translation and American work. By contrast, Chatto, Cape and other once very active lists became cautious. Some lists which were relatively quiet during the 1970s came awake in the last years of the decade. Among the larger commercial houses, Oxford University Press is — in the area of contemporary poetry — comparable with Faber & Faber. By contrast, Macmillan, once vying with Chatto as among the most active lists, has fallen almost silent, along with Cape. They have a residual commitment to be sure, and this is heartening; but expediency has made poetry, always a poor sister, poorer still. It is like the parable of the talents.

The continued success of the Oxford and Faber lists must be allied to the market forces we mentioned earlier. A fine imprint guarantees library sales, and the presence of Faber and Oxford poets on school and university syllabuses, not to mention the export capacity of both firms, means that their books of poems are printed in longer runs than are normal for poetry publishing in general and they can — if they do not count overheads too closely — publish modestly-priced poetry at a profit or at break-even levels, even despite the inflation in printing and paper costs. Successful books will subsidize the slower sellers; a rational and dispassionate remaindering or pulping policy will keep stocks at manageable levels, and the great lists survive the forces which have winnowed their competitors.

Small presses, however, have had an important role to play. In the 1960s, when there was less need for them, there were more active small presses than in the mid-to-late 1970s. The demise of Fulcrum Press, the leading small house of the 1960s, much impoverished the 'little presses' scene. Other presses of varying 'smallness' have survived the decade. Notable among them are Ferry Press, which publishes in brave disregard of the market; Grosseteste Press, which grew out of the *Grosseteste Review* and is similarly uncompromised; Enitharmon Press, with an interesting, rather more conventional list; the always unpredictable and interesting Anvil Press, which grew out of the magazine *New Measure* and has, under Peter Jay's editorship, survived the bad squalls of the early 1970s; Mandeville and Menard Presses, both very small and inventive, run by poets with strong individual tastes; and — largest of the small presses — Carcanet itself, which publishes the work of new and established poets. In the 1960s the small presses were active but, with a few exceptions, only marginally important. Now, though there are fewer of them active on a national scale, they have assumed much larger importance due to the changes in the economic climate in general and the publishing climate in particular. Because the print-run of 750-1,000 copies cannot (except for the 'fine printer') be remunerative, the Arts Council has become crucial in supporting publishing of an exploratory kind. It may not be desirable, but it is a fact that subsidy has kept the work of many established writers in print and helped towards the production of the work of many of the best new poets, a situation which would never have arisen in the 1950s nor, to the same degree, in the 1960s.

It was in the 1960s that good money began to be made available to poets for readings, fellowships and fees. The primary source was the Arts Council and the Arts Associations which began to proliferate then. The poetry boom of the sixties and the echoes of it in the seventies would hardly have persisted as long as they did without funds from some source. Though performing poets might expect to draw audiences and pay their way, other poets with less draw still wanted — or came to want — paying. Many poets decided they had something to sell and sell again. We remember a 1969 reading in Newbury where four poets and an Arts Association Director at a cost of £80 in fees and a little more in expenses read to a hall filled with three ladies and one child. We remember still the horror we felt in the early 1970s when a literary agent referred to William Carlos Williams, whose work we wished to re-issue as it went out of print, as a 'very valuable property'. We are no longer so innocent, such terminology is familiar to us. The Arts Council word for those who seek grant aid (i.e., money) is 'client'. The 1979 Scottish Arts Council Report spoke of the arts 'cake' which it divided between hungry clients. The culmination of this movement by writers to get their 'rights' was the Pyrrhic victory of the Public Lending Right Act and, some believe, the debasement of vocation.

The ascendancy of the academy over poets and poetry in the 1970s may also be seen as — at least potentially — a debasement of vocation. But this depends, of course, on the poet himself, the academy in which he lands, and the terms on which he lands there. Many poets in the past have been teachers. Today, however, the majority of poets are; and 'being a poet' may qualify them for a post. The secondary-school teacher, the university lecturer or professor, usually achieve their prominence on their academic strengths, while the creative writing fellow is in a different position, untenurable and often funded not by the institution where he or she works but by an outside body (the Arts Council, a bequest, a Gulbenkian Foundation Grant, etc). The creative writing fellow is, in every respect, in an exposed position. His duties are likely to be few and ill-defined. He is supposed to 'create' in a congenial habitat, to meet and talk about his work, and theirs, with students, teachers and 'the wider community', sharing his skills (on the strength of which he was appointed) as best he can. He is a guest, the institution is his host. Many writers have functioned successfully in this ill-defined role—a tribute to their imaginative acumen — and have been valued by those among whom they have worked. Most have suffered a certain strain upon 're-entry' into the quotidian world after one, two or three years.

Different though academic environments and terms of employment can be, they have this in common: the poet is presenting poetry (his own or that of other writers), discussing, interpreting, extending it. He has a class, pupils, seminars. The art becomes a subject to be taught. The subject may have its place in a curriculum beside Maths and Home Science or Anglo-Saxon and Bibliography. The poetry instructor's vocation may seem more exalted than that of the metallurgy instructor, but in the levelling curriculum it counts equally with metallurgy.

The very fact of 'presentation' and its consequences for the primary art may mean that the poet-instructor comes to borrow his energies from literature and criticism, to write out of the subject rather than out of the world which is his. He may compose from, or for, a seminar. Undeniably, the academy may feed the poet. In return, and quite as undeniably, the poet may come to feed the academy. This is the possible effect of the ingestion of poetry by the academy. The writer becomes a servant rather than a master — a sort of civil servant. George Orwell wrote in his 1945-6 essay 'The Prevention of Literature': 'Everything in our age conspires to turn the writer, and every other kind of artist as well, into a minor official, working on themes handed to him from above and never telling what seems to him the whole truth.' It is a peril, certainly, even — or especially — today. Before praising too warmly the arrangements of our age, it is worth reflecting how much the publication of poetry and the material survival of poets have become a matter of dependence on state and institutional patronage. These are relatively rich patrons; also, relatively powerful ones. Increasing dependence on such patronage is not necessarily a desirable, though it may be an inevitable, development.

When we look forward into the 1980s, the prospect is not entirely promising. The disorientation of the 1960s produced, even in some well-established writers, worrying uncertainties. Take, for example, two poets who took their early bearings from Patrick Kavanagh: R. S. Thomas and Seamus Heaney. In mature work, Thomas suddenly succumbed to the influence of a younger poet, Ted Hughes, rather as George Crabbe, late in life, succumbed to the influence of Wordsworth. Though Thomas recovered his balance and has written fine poems since, the mark of Hughes remains upon him as an unassimilated influence, a borrowed energy. Heaney in *Field Work* (1979), his fifth book, shows a similar susceptibility to the mature voice of Lowell, a poet temperamentally remote from the Irish writer. Also, Heaney appears to have discovered, but not yet assimilated, Dante. Like Kavanagh, both writers appear to have become disaffected with their native virtues and to have resorted to imitation, even ventriloquism, in an effort to escape an imaginative rut. Yeats, in his transition from his early to his great work, examined (with the help of Pound) the quality of his language, learned the power of transitive verbs and the strength of nouns unencumbered by adjectives. He progressed painstakingly through a regeneration of technique and did not take the short-cut through imitation of another's style. Influence or affinity is — in the work of serious writers — normally evident in apprentice-work and early collections. When poets, striving consciously to change course, resort to borrowed strategies, they can harm their art, however considerable it is.

The vice of the age may well be this sort of deliberateness, this chafing against the bondage of a formed style and an exhausted subject-matter. It is a deliberateness evident in generic choices (including the historical sequence), in forms, in diction. It is not always an imaginative deliberation, something we expect from the highest poetry, but more a sense that the poems are constructed and have not the sanction of the pulse or of the discovering intellect. There is a kind of poetry which seems to be the fruit of analysis rather than forceful synthesis, following from rather than preceding critical thought. It is a poetry patently *aware* that it is poetry; it lacks inevitability, urgency, it is poor in world. It is praised by academic critics and by critic-poets, while the work of what we take to be mainstream English poets, in touch with an imaginative rather than a critical tradition, is undervalued.

A case in point is the poet Craig Raine whom Blake Morrison in this book, and several critics elsewhere, have highly applauded. Peter Porter attributes to him the founding of a new school of 'metaphor'; John Bayley compares him with Donne and the early Pasternak; John Carey recommends him in the same breath with Seamus Heaney. In 'Not Playing the Game' Edwin Morgan writes,

> — Although a poem is
> undoubtedly a 'game'
> it is not a game.

The deft use of quotation marks alerts us. Against the general poetic gloom of our best writers, a game rather than a 'game' appeals to some critics. It alleviates the tedium of the severe witness of such writers as Larkin, Davie, Thomas, or the serious levity of Graham. But what if the game is not worth the candle, lacks Auden's formal tact, the warmth of Causley; what if it reduces style to technique and makes of technique a self-generating system of 'transformations'? Dr Morrison recommends Raine's mixed metaphors as an aspect of alert vision. To us they seem more to display confusion or, worse, *mere* levity. Raine's disciple Christopher Reid makes 'poetry out of what is essentially a misreading of signs'. In such terms we might recommend even Swinburne, though Swinburne was a prosodist and understood the rudiments of poetic syntax. No one has, to our knowledge, praised the prosody of this particular breed of new writers: they have none. Interest in and understanding of prosody have not characterized the 1970s. Morrison contends that such poetry requires that we look; it seems to us that it provokes puzzlement, rather. What we are supposed to *see* becomes more remote: when a gardener stands 'tired as a teapot', do we see gardener, teapot, or some steam let off by the connection? Or is it a gratuitous gesture, or a dig at the pathetic fallacy? The essential limitation of the 'movement' represented by Raine and Reid, a limitation Dr Morrison acknowledges, is the mechanical nature of its means. Technique can dictate a great deal of verse (MacNeice's *Autumn Sequel* is a particularly dull example of verse dictated by a formal and technical predisposition). Remote metaphors are 'no more poetical than anagrams; such pleasure as they give is purely intellectual and is intellectually frivolous'. The words are Housman's and they refer to the excesses of the Metaphysical poets: 'their object was to startle by novelty and amuse by ingenuity a public whose one wish was to be startled and amused.' This is hardly true of Donne or Herbert; it may be true of these particular young contemporaries. Their public — the public that has praised them — is the public that has most assiduously sponsored their success: professors, lecturers and dons, the modern arbiters, who do not realize that their entertainers degrade the reality they pretend to illuminate.

There are several points at which we as editors would differ from our contributors; but having solicited advocacies, we are glad to let them stand. The tone of the volume is perhaps *too* optimistic, despite the downbeat and the challenge of the Middleton, Davie and Sisson contributions. We have not in the 1970s experienced a 'major decade'. Though in retrospect decades acquire a character, they remain for the critic at best a convenience, a slice of time through which writers born seven decades ago and writers born two decades ago have lived and written. In the end decades are best characterized by what first surfaced in them. Which will be seen to have been the outstanding new poets of the decade? As editors, we put our money on Peter Scupham, Andrew Waterman, Dick Davis, Robert Wells, Michael Vince, Andrew Motion, Jeremy Hooker, Jeffrey Wainwright, Tom Paulin, Paul Mills, and. . . we might add five or six more names. Enough to be going on with.

The poetry of R. S. Thomas

OVER A PERIOD of some forty years of writing, R. S. Thomas has published fourteen volumes of poetry and two selections, *Song at the Year's Turning* (1955) and *Selected Poems: 1946-1968* (1973). None of the separate collections is very large, but each uncompromisingly defines the poet's attitude to his subject matter. And it is the subject matter which counts with R. S. Thomas; it is what the poems draw attention to: not to the poet nor the poetry, but to the scrupulous concern to record faithfully what has been thought, seen or experienced in a language which, though not foregoing change or development, preserves throughout a distinctiveness gained remarkably early in the poet's career. The most striking change from one volume to the next occurs between *Not That He Brought Flowers* (1968) and *H'm* (1972), but the latter volume's emphasis on the definition of man's relationship to God had already been prepared for in the context of two of Thomas's preoccupations of the preceding years.

One of these, and perhaps the most compelling for the general reader, is that which has to do with Welsh hill-farming life as it is epitomized in a particular figure:

> Iago Prytherch his name, though, be it allowed,
> Just an ordinary man of the bald Welsh hills,
> Who pens a few sheep in a gap of cloud . . .

The physical description is unsparing: Prytherch has a 'half-witted grin', his clothes are 'sour with years of sweat'; yet, even though the poet declares 'there is something frightening in the vacancy of his mind', Prytherch is seen as embodying man's fortitude. But R. S. Thomas did not begin with such poems. His distinctive stance is identifiable only from the moment when, under the influence of Patrick Kavanagh's *The Great Hunger* (1942), Thomas turned from merely descriptive verse like 'Cyclamen' (published in the *Dublin Magazine* in 1939 and collected in *The Stones of the Field*, 1946) and found both subject and theme in his native Wales. While the impact of Kavanagh's poem, which Thomas readily acknowledges, has not gone altogether unnoticed in Ireland, it has been overlooked by Welsh and English critics alike. Kavanagh's slap in the face of Yeatsian idealism about the Irish peasant was in places couched in terms that were intended to shock, and perhaps the debunking of that myth called for extreme measures; it is, however, the less sensationally ironic aspects of Kavanagh's peasant farmer, Maguire, which impressed the Welsh poet. Here is an extract from Kavanagh's commentary near the end of *The Great Hunger:*

> The peasant ploughman who is half a vegetable—
> Who can re-act to sun and rain and sometimes even
> Regret that the Maker of Light had not touched him
>   more intensely.
> Brought him up from the sub-soil to an existence
> Of conscious joy. He was not born blind.
> He is not always blind. Sometimes the cataract yields
> To sudden stone-falling or the desire to breed.

But if this is where Thomas found his subject, his theme already goes beyond Kavanagh's blunt statement of the deprivation and frustration caused by the tyranny of the small farmland and the matriarchal traditions of the Irish peasantry. Maguire, dead, '... can neither be damned nor glorified ... The tongue in his mouth is the root of a yew'; Thomas's Prytherch, on the other hand, is described as one who

>   ... season by season
> Against the siege of rain and the wind's attrition,
> Preserves his stock, an impregnable fortress
> Not to be stormed even in death's confusion.
> Remember him, then, for he, too, is a winner of wars,
> Enduring like a tree under the curious stars.

Thomas's early poems contain numerous analogies between earth and man which imply a relationship which the themes specifically declare does not exist. This opposition between image and meaning provides for an irony which is sometimes harsh, as in 'A Thought from Nietzsche' *(The Stones of the Field),* where the body, 'Lean acre of ground', is described as:

>   ... dry sand
> In whose bare banks the blood stream bickers in vain.
> You are betrayed by the wilderness within,
> That spreads upwards and outwards like a stain.

But more often the irony yields a compassion, as in these lines from the title poem of *Song at the Year's Turning:*

> ... Lost in the world's wood
> You cannot stanch the bright menstrual blood.
> The earth sickens; under naked boughs
> The frost comes to barb your broken vows.
>
> Is there blessing? Light's peculiar grace
> In cold splendour robes this tortured place
> For strange marriage. Voices in the wind
> Weave a garland where a mortal sinned.

Winter rots you; who is there to blame?
The new grass shall purge you in its flame.

The compassion comes precisely from the implication that the Wordsworthian link between man and spirit through Nature ought to be there
but is not; or only rarely. One of the starkest assertions of the 'neutrality
of [Nature's] answers' is found in 'That' (*Not That He Brought
Flowers*):

> ... the germ finds its way
> From the grass to the snail to the liver to the grass.
> The shadow of the tree falls
> On our acres like a crucifixion,
> With a bird singing in the branches
> What its shrill species has always sung,
> Hammering its notes home
> One by one into our brief flesh.

There are further developments of this theme from a poem like 'The Cry'
(*Poetry for Supper*, 1958) through to 'The Bright Field' (*Laboratories of
the Spirit*, 1975), except that progressively as the analogy gives way to
statements of personal vision, the ironic effect is lost. One of the reasons
for the different texture of the poetry written after 1970 is that the subject
matter rarely allows for more than one viewpoint to be taken at the same
time.

Thomas's poetry about the Welsh peasantry swings from the sympathy
expressed in 'Affinity' (*Stones of the Field*) to the almost vindictive attack
in 'Valediction' (*Song at the Year's Turning*). Here he is less generous to
his Welsh farmer than Kavanagh had been to his Irish counterpart:
'Unnatural and inhuman, your wild ways/Are not sanctioned; you are
condemned/By man's potential stature'. This characteristic method of
pushing each line of enquiry and response to the limit may risk the tedium
of mere repetition, but it intimately prepares the reader for whatever
resolution of the extremes is achieved.

The most significant move towards such a resolution occurs in *Poetry
for Supper* where in two poems Thomas asks forgiveness of Prytherch,
(that '... dark figure/Marring the simple geometry/Of the square fields
with its gaunt question'), yet at the same time points out that his words
sprang neither from mockery nor mere compassion. In 'Dark Well', the
opening poem of the next volume (*Tares*), the poet recognizes that his
emphasis on the animal vacancy of the peasant's mind was a necessary
exaggeration in order to imply spiritual need:

> There are two hungers, hunger for bread
> And hunger of the uncouth soul
> For the light's grace. I have seen both,
> And chosen for an indulgent world's

> Ear the story of one whose hands
> Have bruised themselves on the locked doors
> Of life; whose heart, fuller than mine
> Of gulped tears, is the dark well
> From which to draw, drop after drop,
> The terrible poetry of his kind.

In both 'Absolution' (*Poetry for Supper*) and 'Servant' (*The Bread of Truth*) Thomas concedes that the peasant's struggle with the land represents a fidelity of purpose and identity, in bone and blood, which the poet's mental strivings after truth have failed to achieve. But it is in 'He', from the latter volume, that Thomas finally defines his attitude towards Prytherch:

> He has become part of me,
> Aching in me like a bone
> Often bruised. Through him I learn
> Emptiness of the bare mind
> Without knowledge, and the frost
> Of knowledge, where there is no love.

In this self-identification with the persona, the errors of both extremes are acknowledged. And when in *Not That He Brought Flowers* that persona is finally dropped, the theme of spiritual enquiry more and more takes the form of a monologue with God.

A second persistent theme throughout Thomas's work concerns the lonely and often barren predicament of the priest, who is as isolated in his parish as Prytherch is on the bare hillside, 'Ploughing cloudward, sowing the wind/With squalls of gulls at the day's end'. And as late as *Not That He Brought Flowers* (1968), in a poem with the appropriately oblique title, 'They', the same basic questions persist:

> Daily the sky mirrors
> The water, the water the
> Sky. Daily I take their side
> In their quarrel, calling their faults
> Mine. How do I serve so
> This being they have shut out
> Of their houses, their thoughts, their lives?

The priest's frustrated desire to serve requires the sustenance of solitary meditation, and this subject becomes increasingly prevalent throughout the published work up to *Frequencies* (1978). It is first expressed in 'Country Church' (*The Stones of the Field*) with a simple description of the place of meditation. *An Acre of Land* also contains a poem, 'Maes-Yr-Onnen', which merely describes the chapel. But in the next volume, *Song at the Year's Turning*, 'Kneeling' vividly evokes the pause before, and then the moment of, vision:

> To one kneeling down no word came,
> Only the wind's song, saddening the lips
> Of the grave saints, rigid in glass;
> Or the dry whisper of unseen wings,
> Bats not angels, in the high roof.
>
> Was he balked by silence? He kneeled long,
> And saw love in a dark crown
> Of thorns blazing, and a winter tree
> Golden with fruit of a man's body.

Later, it is precisely this pause before vision which is the centre of the poetry. 'In Church' (*Pietà*), for example, describes the vigil

> ... of a man
> Breathing, testing his faith
> On emptiness, nailing his questions
> One by one to an untenanted cross.

And in 'Kneeling' (*Not That He Brought Flowers*), the poet enigmatically declares that 'The meaning is in the waiting'. The change rather startlingly announced by the next volume's title, *H'm,* thus had its thematic source in the work of the preceding two decades; but the fact that the new title is not biblically metaphoric like that of so many of the previous volumes has some important bearings on the ensuing shift in language and tone.

If there were any doubts before about whether R. S. Thomas should be called a religious poet—though there should have been none—they must have been resolved during the past decade with the appearance of *H'm* (1972), *Laboratories of the Spirit* (1975), *The Way of It* (1977) and *Frequencies* (1978). There are some beautiful love poems to be found here, and each volume continues, though sometimes in a new style, some of the subjects of the poetry published up to 1968. The main preoccupation, however, is with questions concerning the nature of spiritual reality; and the territory to be explored is no longer the natural setting of the Welsh hills but the mind itself. 'Groping', an early poem in *Frequencies,* states that 'The best journey to make/is inward'; the volume ends with:

> ... Was the pilgrimage
> I made to come to my own
> self, to learn that in times
> like these and for one like me
> God will never be plain and
> out there, but dark rather and
> inexplicable, as though he were in here?

Such a question is a long way from the Herbert-like assurance of: 'Yet living souls, a prodigious number/Bright-faced as dawn, invest God's chamber', from Thomas's translation, 'The Cry of Elisha after Elijah', in his first volume, *The Stones of the Field*; nonetheless, it has been prepared for in the nagging ironies of the Prytherch poems, and more specifically by the sequence of poems concerned with personal meditation, which lead directly to an intensification of that subject in all four of the volumes published since 1970. The outcries of dismay with which many of Thomas's faithful readers greeted *H'm* were, however, not so much caused by a failure to see the development of themes as by the change of form that volume represents. In the early poems the shift from what is observed to what is felt by the poet requires that the peasant in the field, or the parishioner in the street or at prayer, be seen by the reader, whether the description carries metaphoric meanings or not. When, on the other hand, the poet turns from observation to introspection, from what can be seen (as so often in the early volumes we are enjoined to see) to what cannot, the language becomes more abstract; concepts replace images. The idiom employed in the opening of 'Petition' *(H'm)* merely emphasizes the lack of the visual which is so common in the poetry of the 1972 and 1975 collections:

> And I standing in the shade
> Have seen it a thousand times
> Happen: first theft, then murder;
> Rape; the rueful acts
> Of the blind hand. . . .
> . . . I am eyes
> Merely, witnessing virtue's
> Defeat; seeing the young born
> Fair, knowing the cancer
> Awaits them.

Up to 1968 R. S. Thomas relies upon a syntax which, because its purpose is descriptive, remains basically that of straightforward statement:

> The fox drags its wounded belly
> Over the snow, the crimson seeds
> Of blood burst with a mild explosion,
> Soft as excrement, bold as roses.

The qualifications made are phrasal or adjectival, as befits the visual effects the poet wishes to achieve. As an observer, a reporter of the world about him, he does not need the kind of syntax which is built on qualifying clauses whose investigative logic helps evoke feeling. The trouble is that at first when the poet moves from exterior to interior, to the examination of the self in what becomes almost exclusively an enquiry about the purpose of existence, the syntax does not change in kind. It becomes more bare, freer of adjectival definition, but it remains poetry of statement; and because it is no longer descriptive, abstract nouns play an increasingly weighty role in the meaning. Not that there is anything wrong with noun strength in a poem—Yeats's 'Leda and the Swan' is crammed with nouns, but they are either drawn from nature or, allusively, from literature and legend. What happens in some of Thomas's verse is that in the effort to express thoughts about thought, the syntax becomes clogged with phrases built out of nouns linked by the preposition 'of', a pattern particularly prevalent in *Laboratories of the Spirit*. In 'Emerging', this usage is all the more strikingly hobbled in contrast to the casual colloquialism which introduces this section of the poem:

> . . . It begins to appear
> this is not what prayer is about.
> It is the annihilation of difference,
> the consciousness of myself in you,
> of you in me; the emerging
> from the adolescence of nature
> into the adult geometry
> of the mind . . .

The last three lines also point to the change in imagery from physical to mental, from natural to scientific, which is carried in the titles *Laboratories of the Spirit* and *Frequencies*. Fortunately, the transition is never quite complete. In 'Relay', however, from the former volume, we get the worst of both worlds when the ideas are imprisoned in a substantival syntax which is prosaic as well as lacking in imaginative kinesis:

> I switch on, tune in—
> the marvellous languages
> of the peoples of the planet,
> discussing the weather! Thousands of years
> speech was evolving—that line of trees
> on the hill slope has the illusion
> of movement. I think of man
> on his mountain; he has paused
> now for lack of the oxygen
> of the spirit; the easier options
> surround him, the complacencies of being
> half-way up. . .

The criticism which R. S. Thomas made in his Introduction to *A Choice of George Herbert's Verse* (1967) could well be levelled at a number of his own poems published since 1970: 'There is too often the impression that the verse is being made subordinate to an idea'.

Another element in both the 1972 and the 1975 volumes which gives the reader pause is the poet's view of 'the machine' as an evil force obliterating man's relationship with God and even having the power to challenge God himself. This attempt at a kind of mythologizing is a large step from the anger directed against the constraining effects of mechanization in many of Thomas's poems about Wales; and it fails not only because it is unrealistic to imply that man would be better off in a pre-industrial civilization, but principally because the threat of 'the machine' is never made vividly real. 'The Gap' (*Laboratories of the Spirit*), for example, presents the innocent genius of the paleolithic cave-dwellers as an Eden of art; but the contrast with modern man is given in the following list of abstractions:

> This was before
> the fall. Somewhere between them and us
> the mind climbed up into the tree
> of knowledge, and saw the forbidden subjects
> of art, the emptiness of the interiors
> of the mirror that life holds up
> to itself, and began venting its frustration
> in spurious metals, in the cold acts of the machine.

Similarly, when Thomas talks about the instrument which enables man to build his own destructive world, the references are at best awkward in sense, and sometimes inappropriately ambiguous:

> . . . It put out a hand
> as though to implore
> wisdom, and a tool
> gleamed there. The alternatives
> of the tree sharpened. God
> spoke to him out of the tree's
> wholeness, but the sound
> of the tool drowned him . . .

The word in this poem's title, 'The Tool' (*Laboratories of the Spirit*), is never used in that volume with the deftness which up to now the reader has come to expect of the poet, but it is worth noting that his reputation for fastidiousness and exactness of expression came from the telling combination of adjective and noun. In the 1975 volume, the unadorned ugliness of the term 'tool' may be deliberate, but it impedes effect rather than contributes to it.

Thomas's evocation of 'the machine' as responsible for the break in what should be a natural link between man and God invites comparison with Ted Hughes's recent work. The picture of mockingly destructive energies in *Crow* (1970) and of a world governed solely by sexual aggression in *Gaudete* (1977) constitute an attempt to create a mythology as negative as Thomas's. There are some stylistic parallels as well. In the mid 60s Hughes's verbal power presented a striking contrast to Thomas's spare restraint in language, but the latter's *H'm* contains lines which could easily be mistaken for a recent Hughes poem, as in 'Repeat':

He touched it. It exploded.
Man was inside with his many
Devices. He turned from him as from his own
Excrement. He could not stomach his grin. . .

In *Crow* and *Gaudete* Hughes's images of anatomical distortion or of the body's animal functions so blatantly draw attention to themselves that the effect is frequently opposite to that intended, a risk which Thomas also runs in these lines from 'Rough' (*Laboratories of the Spirit*):

. . . God took a handful of small germs,
sowing them in the smooth flesh. It was curious,
the harvest; the limbs modelled an obscene
question, the head swelled, out of the eyes came
tears of pus. There was the sound
of thunder, the loud, uncontrollable laughter of
God, and in his side like an incurred stitch, Jesus.

In 'Welsh Summer', from the same volume, there is a marked change in Thomas's treatment of the old topic of a countryside defaced by mechanization:

. . . .Places that
would have preferred peace
have had their bowels opened; our
children paddle thoughtlessly there in the mess.

As with Hughes, the image here does not work because it is excessive, if not vain. Each poet, too, uses the same kind of fragmentary opening. Compare, for example, the number of poems in Hughes's *Crow* which begin 'There was. . . .(this grin, this terrific battle, this man)', with Thomas's 'There was a background of guns and bombs' (*H'm*), 'There was this problem' (*Laboratories of the Spirit*). Despite the loose colloquialism, 'this', which appears often in Hughes, the biblical echo of such openings is of course meant to support the mythologizing. At the same time it foreshortens and dislocates the normal view of reality. It is merely a device for introducing a subject, and, like all devices, its effect is soon lost if it is used too often. Parallels of a more occasional nature appear between the two poets in phraseology or idea, sometimes in poems totally different in mood, as between 'Crow's First Lesson' and Thomas's title poem, 'H'm', both of which deal with the articulation of love; the former in a grotesque, surrealistic picture of voracious sexuality, the latter with a taut irony derived from the inferred biblical text:

and one said
speak to us of love
and the preacher opened
his mouth and the word God

> fell out so they tried
> again speak to us
> of God then but the preacher
> was silent reaching
> his arms out but the little
> children the ones with
> big bellies and bow
> legs that were like
> a razor shell
> were too weak to come

How far Thomas is able to go beyond Hughes thematically is demonstrated by 'The White Tiger' (*Frequencies*). In this poem, with an exactness of physical description which Hughes might envy, and a profound irony Hughes has not yet shown he can match, Thomas at the same time reveals the unavoidable limitations of man's view of the eternal, and recognizes what restrictions are thereby imposed on God.

After *Laboratories of the Spirit* Thomas drops the features which temporarily identify him with Hughes. One of the many distinctions between the two poets over the period from 1970 to 1975 is that while the latter's mythologizing relies on rhetorical tricks which soon become boring (and whatever else myth may be, it cannot be that!), Thomas constantly refers to the topography of a Christian imagination. And although he fails to create a new myth out of 'the machine', he revitalizes the old one by his insistence on the enormous gaps in man's understanding of spiritual reality.

The difficulty has precisely to do with language, with the means of communication. Thomas declares his position in 'The River' (*H'm*), where he describes the natural scene with consummate deftness: 'the cobbled water... the trout's indelible/Shadows... the weed's branches...', but states that he is merely revisiting 'the sources/That are as near now/As on the morning I set out from them.' As the poem makes plain, what he sets out for is the territory of the mind, where 'the chemistry/of the spirit' ('Dialogue', *Laboratories of the Spirit*) is discoverable in numbers, equations and the angles between stars. Whereas the irony and compassion of the Prytherch poems came from the linking of man and nature through interdependent images of the physical world, the exactness of Thomas's new vocabulary provides not so much for irony as for the religious paradox of 'this great absence/that is like a presence' which is defined in 'Absence', from the 1978 volume whose title takes as metaphor those frequencies which load the invisible air with language. But there is no diminution of compassion: the poet makes it clear that although the terminology of science (see 'They', *The Way of It*) may be the means of defining this 'God of form and number' ('Emerging', *Laboratories of the Spirit*), it does not explain the predicament of the sentient

man in a universe beyond both his control and his understanding. 'At It'
(*Frequencies*) contrasts 'the eloquence/of the abused heart' with

> the verdict
> of (God's) calculations, that abstruse
> geometry that proceeds eternally
> in the silence beyond right and wrong.

In 'The Absence', Thomas finally admits:

> ... My equations fail
> as my words do. What resources have I
> other than the emptiness without him of my whole
> being, a vacuum he may not abhor?

This tentative hope that God may not be indifferent to man who cannot
live without the concept of his existence represents an attempt to articulate the nature of belief. Inevitably it involves a conflict between reason
and imagination which can only be resolved in either faith or doubt, and
Thomas's poetry explores both states, but in very different ways. The
theme of doubt often takes the form of a series of questions which at times
run the risk of being just rather turgid prose, as in these lines from
'Perhaps' (*Frequencies*): '... To suffer himself to be persuaded/of
intentions in being other than the crossing/of a receding boundary which
did not exist?' In 'Balance', on the other hand, from the same volume,
images of isolation and fear prefigure the questions which end the
poem:

> ... I have abandoned
> my theories, the easier certainties
> of belief. There are no handrails to
> grasp. I stand and on either side
> there is the haggard gallery
> of the dead...
>   Is there a place
> here for the spirit? Is there time
> on this brief platform for anything
> other than mind's failure to explain itself?

The resolution which the 'seeker/In time for that which is/beyond time'
('Abercuawg', *Frequencies*) finds in faith is expressed in poems which
develop naturally from the pre-1970 sequence about personal meditation.
The culminating recognition there that 'The meaning is in the waiting'
leads directly to the understanding of presence in absence, a concept
which first appears in 'Via Negativa' (*H'm*), then in 'Sea-Watching'
(*Laboratories of the Spirit*), in 'Nuclear' and 'They' (*The Way of It*), and
in at least half a dozen poems in *Frequencies*. And it is this state of mind
which allows for both praise and vision. Here the concrete images

Thomas uses repeatedly link religion and nature, either through allusion to a biblical text, as in 'The Bright Field' *(Laboratories of the Spirit)*, which concerns a Wordsworthian moment in time:

> I have seen the sun break through
> to illuminate a small field
> for a while, and gone my way
> and forgotten it. But that was the pearl
> of great price, the one field that had
> the treasure in it. I realize now
> that I must give all that I have
> to possess it . . .

—or in direct sacramental reference, as in 'The Moon in Lleyn' *(Laboratories of the Spirit)*: 'Why so fast/Mortal? These very seas/are baptized. . . .'; or as in these lines from 'In Great Waters' *(Frequencies)*:

> . . . There is
> a sacrament there more beauty
> than terror whose ministrant
> you are and the aisles are full
> of the sea shapes coming to its celebration.

None of the books published since 1970 lends itself to a reading through at one sitting because the poet's method is to exhaust all the avenues of enquiry into a particular topic. Since Thomas does not revise a poem once it is finished, the various approaches to the same subject are in a sense re-writings; but the fact that there is never a revising of exactly the same material may in part explain why there are few poems which are perfectly wrought throughout. When Thomas's subject matter was visually identifiable, a change in the way of seeing it brought pleasurable familiarity; when, however, the poetry is largely conceptual, as in the 1972 and 1975 volumes, the repetition of theme can be stultifying to the point where subtle differences of method and purpose are missed. But *Frequencies* clearly shows that the experiments of *H'm* and *Laboratories of the Spirit* have been worked through to a more assured handling of the new forms and mode. References to 'the machine' are dropped; there are fewer abstractions and a greater integration of metaphor and allusion with the new vocabulary; there is, too, a wider list of subjects, some of which hark back to the poet's earlier concerns but are expressed more succinctly than before.

The last thing R. S. Thomas's poetry does is draw attention to itself as poetry: from the beginning his hallmark has been the unity of manner and meaning; and this is as true for the lighter lyric verse, which shows a highly developed skill in language and tone, as it is for the urgent and tortuous questionings of the mind about the spirit. His basic limitations have to do with narrowness of range and style, but the choice on Thomas's part is deliberate. It is his conviction that one of the important functions of poetry is to embody religious truth, and since for him as poet that truth is not easily won, his poems record the struggle with marked honesty and integrity, thereby providing the context for the necessarily infrequent moments of faith and vision which are expressed with a clarity and gravity rarely matched by any of his contemporaries.

The strict temperature of classicism:
C. H. Sisson

'IT WAS HARD FOR HIM', Joyce writes of Stephen Dedalus, 'to compel his head to preserve the strict temperature of classicism'. It was hard for all the heroes of 'the Pound era' to do this, and has been harder still for the writers who have followed them. Why, we should ask ourselves, has the most unfashionable of contemporary English writers, C.H. Sisson, found it comparatively simple to 'preserve the strict temperature of classicism'? And why, we should go on to ask, has he achieved celebrity at a time when we are being asked to accept that 'the Pound era' was really 'the Stevens era' or 'the Hardy era' or 'the Lawrence era' or almost, it seems, anyone's era as long as Pound is kept firmly in the background? To answer such questions is, in some measure, required of us by the generous reception accorded to *In the Trojan Ditch*, Sisson's collected poems and selected translations, published five years ago, the somewhat less than generous reception of his most recent volume of poems, *Anchises* (1976), and the recent publication of his collected essays, *The Avoidance of Literature*. The fact that it is possible to answer such questions at all indicates that, unlike many more modish and popular figures, Sisson has been painstakingly putting together a body of work that may be said to constitute, in the fullest sense, an *oeuvre*, a self-consistent and self-sustaining literary output that, for all its variety, is finally, to quote Dryden in *The Secular Masque*, 'all of a piece throughout'.

The mention of Dryden may serve to remind us of exactly how unfashionable Sisson's affiliations are. 'I, at any rate, and of all men', Pound wrote in 1934, 'don't want Johnnie Dryden dug up again.' Sisson is, charateristically, more temperate: 'I have come in the end to have great sympathy with Dryden, who. . . at the end of his days took pride in being able to do a translation better than any one of them.' Of course, in Sisson's case, it is not merely a sympathy with Dryden that distinguishes him from his contemporaries. What other modern poet of comparable stature, for example, could be found who would express sympathy with any one of the following: the life and writings of Charles Maurras, the spirit of British administration as manifested by the Civil Service, the necessity of *clercs* and the viability of Coleridge's 'clerisy', the close connection of Church and State, the undesirability of 'freedom of ex-

pression', the irrelevance of liberalism in 'life-and-death con-
frontations', and finally, the lasting importance of such neglected
writers as Hooker, Filmer, William Barnes, Clough and Charles Péguy?
Add to this such pronouncements as 'one should not pride oneself on
oddity', 'the avoidance of literature is indispensable for the man who
wants to tell the truth', and 'we live in a system of force modified. . . by
traditions as ancient as our race', and it is clear that, with Sisson, we are
confronted by a very rare bird indeed, someone for whom 'the intoxi-
cations of publication and reputation' are easily resisted in favour of the
sobriety which is the indispensable prolegomenon to 'plain speaking' and
'congenital truthfulness'.

One reason, it seems to me, why Sisson has been able to realize the
consonantia, claritas and *integritas* that ultimately eluded those writers
who, at the turn of the century, were intent on cultivating 'the classical
temper', is that he has gone back, as they did not, to Augustan models and
not been seduced by other versions of classicism. There is a big difference
between going back to Catullus, Lucretius, Horace, Virgil and Ovid and
going back to Provence and Confucius (as Pound did), to Aquinas (as
Joyce did) and to Dante (as Eliot did). The gap only widens when this is
consolidated by a taste for such resolutely English writers as Chaucer,
Raleigh, Campion, Cranmer, Swift and Johnson rather than Villon,
Corbière, Laforgue, Cavalcanti and Vico. Not that Sisson denies the
importance of familiarity with foreign cultures; his book on *The Spirit of
British Administration* is indeed informed, as its sub-title hints, by 'European comparisons' that are not always flattering to the English. The
longest and most important note to his translation of Horace's *Ars Poetica*
goes so far as to say that 'some foray into one or more other European lit-
eratures is almost indispensable for a critical sharpening of one's appreciation of work in one's own language.'[1] The epigraphs to Sisson's books
are, in fact, predominantly French: La Bruyère, Barbey d'Aurévilly,
Rabelais, René Crevel. But Sisson's respect for the English tradition is
clearly dominant: 'it should be clear', he continues in his note on Horace,
'that no range of eclecticism can excuse or compensate for a lack of solid
knowledge of the literature of the tongue to which one was born—an
initial fatality to which every writer is subject.' It is, indeed, this 'solid
knowledge' that makes him, in *English Poetry 1900-1950*, such a stimulating critic of modern poetry.

There are obviously other reasons, theological and political (Sisson
regards these two areas as essentially one), why he should have evolved a
corpus of belief that he is honest and self-deprecating enough to recognize as 'a reactionary bucketful'.[2] And it is important here to remember
that he did not, like Pope, 'lisp in numbers' (not numbers that saw the
light of day, at any rate) until he was over forty, and did not become in any
sense well-known until he was sixty. Both the strengths and the weak-

nesses of Sisson's work may be said to stem from this, since it is only to be expected that ideas will be modified in the cut-and-thrust of debate, and that poets usually alter their particular procedures, whether well or badly-received by the public. There is a massive consistency about Sisson's work that makes one doubt whether greater notoriety would actually have affected him at all, although it may, in time, come to seem symptomatic that the poems after *Metamorphoses* (1968) show him altering his procedure quite radically. Sisson's consistency is of the kind that would make his poems difficult to date without his authority, but is obviously something much desired, as his remarks in the first foreword to *In the Trojan Ditch* about 'the continuity of statement' in the volume make abundantly clear. The apparent perversity of placing his most recent poem at the beginning and his earliest at the end of that collection—compare the novel *Christopher Homm* which begins with Homm's death and ends with Homm's birth—is obviously calculated to upset the academic obsession with development which he summarily dismisses in the essay 'Natural History',[3] and to remind us that it is not the poet's originality that should impress us, but rather his ability (in the words that Goldsmith used of Swift, quoted—from Herbert Read—by Sisson) 'to describe nature as it is' and has always been. 'If there is one lesson of history which is of certain validity', writes Sisson in *The Case of Walter Bagehot*, 'it is that a new age is never so new as it imagines', a sentiment no less bluntly, though more dramatically, expressed in the poem 'Anacreon' ('Nothing is new', *In the Trojan Ditch*, p 63).

Sisson's idea of the poet is predicated upon ideas that, though no longer fashionable, held sway for a thousand years and more, namely that the poet is a 'maker' and worker in words, and that the poem is, when completed, as much a natural object as wind or waves or trees. The poet is, indeed, 'the man who wants to tell the truth' and who must therefore avoid 'literature' and 'the profession of letters' (as the first essay in *Art and Action* caustically describes it). It is the desire to tell the truth that distinguishes the poet from the civil servant who is 'not a man of ideas' and the Civil Service which is 'not a discipline of the truth.' The same compulsion marks the poet out from a 'dilettante' such as Walter Bagehot, a figure who, in Sisson's mind, could not be further removed from the appallingly thorough sincerity of Swift, for example. The truth-telling function of the poet, Sisson believes, has been dissipated by the false inflations of Romanticism, which, after originating in the idea of 'a man speaking to men' in Wordsworth's phrase, moved further and further into esoteric sublimities. Ideally, in other words, the poet should be close to the impersonal figure of which Eliot speaks in the essay 'Tradition and the Individual Talent' (1919) and the 'horror' of his 'truth'[4] should be such that he 'cut[s] the air with scimitars'. Sisson is not, in truth, an unemotional poet and acknowledges that 'my unrecognized style was made by sorrow'. But he certainly prides himself on the fact that he has been engaged in 'plain endeavours' with an 'instrument. . . .untuned'. This does not so much absolve the poet from having a personality, as Eliot's theory seems to require, as allow the poet to speak in his own voice so long as it remains close to other people's. There is certainly nothing desiccating about Sisson's idea of poetry; 'it needs a poet', he states categorically in *The Case of Walter Bagehot*, 'rather than a mathematician to realize vividly the shadowy and elusive connection between word and fact.' The poet is only contingently a maker of epigrams and epitaphs (Sisson is a brilliant exponent of these); but he is fundamentally a moralist. The stone must be made to speak; the word must become flesh.

Much of the anguish in Sisson's poetry, expecially in his more recent work, derives directly from the Eliotic paradox that the impersonal truth requires a personality to enunciate it. For a poet whose mode is so anachronistic as to seem to him 'a dead language' like the Latin he admires, it is only natural that he should have moments when he feels that 'there is no I in me.' But it is important to distinguish Sisson's anguish from the prevailingly solipsistic climate of modern literature, and to see that, for all his fears about not being 'crystalline' enough, he is more crystalline than any of his more celebrated contemporaries. Sisson's voice is, in fact, quite unmistakable, whether at the beginning of poems:

> I was born in Bristol, and it is possible
> To live harshly in that city
>
> ('Family Fortunes')

at the middle of poems:

> Young men are fools
> And now I am old
> I am a fool.
>
> ('The Regrets')

or at the end of poems, where he is especially powerful:
> It is the waning of the year.
> A death in spring-time is the best.
>
> ('Metamorphoses')

> Iago was an honest man;
> I have that reputation too.
>
> ('Virgini Senescens')

Sisson's uniqueness is particularly evident in those poems of the middle period which deal with themes of age and lechery and which are bound to remind us of the later Yeats and also, to some degree, of the 'aged eagle' T. S. Eliot.[5] Those of us who might have felt that there was little to add to Yeats's analysis are bound to be stopped in our tracks by such a passionate and objective attack as that which opens 'The Regrets':

> Beware of age.
> For I have learned
> An old man should
> Be kept in chains.
> He is a gentle
> Psychopath. . .
> I tell you mark
> This leper well
> And send him forward
> With a bell.

And even when the subject-matter is gentler, and more nostalgic, Sisson sounds more like himself than he sounds like Yeats:

> I saw five hares playing in the snow.
> That was only a winter ago
> Yet they dance in my eyes and are as wild
> As if I were old and had seen them as a child.

The key to Sisson's mastery at moments like this is his uncanny ear for rhythm, and readiness to exploit un-English (usually classical) rhythmical patterns. His concern for rhythm is perhaps the most basic element in his attitude to poetry, and fairly obviously derives directly from Pound. 'Rhythm is the ligament', he writes in a short essay on Pound, 'that binds together the body of a poem' and in the first foreword to his collected poems, he again says 'the proof of the poem—any poem—is in its rhythm.' Sisson's passion for rhythm over against any of the other 'ligaments' that might bind a poem together—the complexity of the thought, for example, or cunning structural patterns—is what keeps his best poems close to the accents of the speaking voice when it has something compelling or inevitable to say. But his comparative disregard for structure, especially in longer poems, is in many ways a weakness, and makes one sometimes wonder whether what he calls 'the inevitable facility' of a practised poet may not, ultimately, lead to poems which are flaccid. There are brilliant moments in his longest poem 'The Discarnation', where his virtuosity in handling a difficult metaphysical stanza can hardly be faulted, but the whole work ultimately seems to add up to something less than the sum of its parts, and the variations of tone, though clearly intentional, do not seem to have an unerring logic behind them. Even the greatest poets have had difficulty in bringing octosyllabics to their appointed end, and no doubt part of the pleasure to be derived from octosyllabics is the way the form seems to be perpetually self-generating. But we only have to compare Sisson's 'Metamorphoses' with, for example, Swift's verses on his own death to see that Sisson's octosyllabics are not really binding enough, even admitting that the poem is a sequence of transformations as the title suggests, to offer us anything more coherent than isolated statements.

There are also times, as almost never in his prose, when his rhythmical sense seems to desert him and bring him too close to 'plain speaking' for the poetry to survive. We are all much indebted to Marianne Moore for reminding us that 'there is something beyond all this fiddle', and yet it may be that, when verse becomes indistinguishable from prose, the 'fiddle' seems not so much superfluous as out of tune. Sisson's instrument is, as he himself admits, predominantly 'untuned' but he has his music, as any poet must, and he conjures melody from it even at his most acrid and acrimonious. It is the careful management of sounds that makes his gloss on Shakespeare's 'Phoenix and the Turtle' more than an instance of clever appropriation. The context is Pygmalion and Galatea:

> To his surprise the girl grew warm;
> He slobbered and she slobbered back
>
> —This is that famous mutual flame.
> . . . .
> May Venus keep me from all hope
> And let me turn my love to stone.
>
> ('Metamorphoses', iii)

And the third section of the poem that gives its title to his collected volume, 'In the Trojan Ditch', is again as much a matter of sound as of meaning:

> Excoriate
> Exaggerated, near dead
> Racked, ripped
> Uncovered, dismembered
> The ribs
> Cracked in a nut-cracker. . . .

It is precisely Sisson's ability to play new melodies on an old instrument that saves him from the charge that in his poetry (where it may be presumed to matter more than in his prose) he is monotonous. He is only monotonous when his ear for measure and cadence fails him, and prevents him from doing what he has identified as the poet's primary task, 'making a poem which will not be the same as the last one' (compare the first foreword again, where he speaks of 'the rejection of whatever appears with the face of familiarity'). One says this fully conscious that it is pointless to speak of his vision as other than extremely bleak, conscious of the gap between effort and achievement and between the transcendent and terrestrial worlds as only a troubled Anglican can be. (The 'Sevenoaks Essays' collected in *The Avoidance of Literature* are the best illustration of this aspect of Sisson's thought.) For it is precisely in his refusal to be comforted and his unsparing awareness of cultural malaise (whether or not we agree with his Eliotic idea that after the death of Charles I 'the intelligence of England deteriorated') that his 'bitter mind' finds what solace it can, since there is 'no remedy but death'. For all his pessimism (which is so thoroughgoing in the novel *Christopher Homm* as to seem almost wilful), he is a kind of humanist. In a recent essay on Wyndham Lewis, in one of the many remarks about others that one cannot forbear from applying to Sisson himself, he says: 'There was lurking under Lewis's much-advertised carapace not merely a humanism, but a humanity, without which, after all, there is no great work in literature, however much one may be tempted to keep silent on the subject by the slop which generally passes for humanity'.

It may seem, at such moments as this, as if Sisson is experiencing as much difficulty as Stephen Dedalus in preserving 'the strict temperature' of his classicism, and it may be that one of the reasons for his celebrity in this resolutely un-classic age is that such remarks offer us a *frisson* that more flatulent writers cannot emulate. But if one considers Sisson's *oeuvre* as a whole, it would be difficult to find much evidence of a Swiftian *saeva indignatio* irrupting from a language that is almost uniformly sober and chaste and controlled. However much he may believe that 'The passions are the shape of man' ('The Shape') and however many poems (from 'The Body of Asia' onwards) take the body as a paradigm of the mind, his subject, whether it be couched in verse, literary criticism, or discursive prose, is government and polity, and there is no more classical a theme than that. It would not, perhaps, be too much to see his practice as a translator—he is certainly one of the finest in contemporary literature—as conditioned by a precisely similar concern with 'the problem of form, a reading of the originals so that they *make sense* in our time'. Certainly, the craft of translation offers, for Sisson, as perhaps no other intellectual exercise quite can, a regulative influence upon one's 'temperature' and a continual illustration that 'the writing of poetry is, in a sense, the opposite of writing what one wants to write.'

References

1   *The Poetic Art*, p 53. Cf. *English Poetry 1900-1950: an assessment*, London, 1971, p 116: 'One cannot have much awareness of what the English language is like until one has some acquaintance with a Latin and purely Germanic language.' The editorial from *Poetry Nation Review*, 6, reprinted in *The Avoidance of Literature*, shows Sisson returning to this topic.

2   *Art and Action*, p x. Sisson relates his Toryism to that of Dr Johnson (*The Avoidance of Literature*, pp 222, 530) and considers it a 'doctrine of opposition'.

3   The essay on Yeats in *English Poetry,* reprinted in *The Avoidance of Literature,* proceeds retrograde, exactly as the novel *Christopher Homm* does.

4   'Loquitur Senex', *In the Trojan Ditch,* p 116. Cf *English Poetry,* p 215: 'A man is an artist only so far as he restricts his writing to the area within which, for him, the rules and the truth coalesce'.

5   It is not, however, surprising to find Sisson, in *English Poetry,* preferring Donne to Yeats and speaking with some asperity of Yeats's 'dogmatics of lust' (p 164). Sisson also criticizes the Eliot of the religious poems but clearly prefers Eliot to Yeats. Michael Schmidt's introduction to the collected essays is most helpful on the declining influence of Eliot and Pound (and Maurras) on Sisson.

Walls of glass:
The poetry of W. S. Graham

I

W. S. GRAHAM has published seven books of poetry in over thirty years, and is unquestioningly acknowledged by his select audience as one of the most rigorous and rewarding British poets; but he has never been popular or even widely known. This may partly be due to the fact that he has been 'somewhat unlucky in his timing', in that (as Edward Lucie-Smith once noted) his demanding volume *The Nightfishing* appeared the same year as Philip Larkin's more accessible *The Less Deceived*. But the intrinsic reason lies in the difficulty of his poems, especially his early poems; a point which has always been conceded in the little criticism that has appeared of Graham's work. On the appearance of *The White Threshold* in 1949 Edwin Morgan remarked how Graham had 'moved into the front rank of those who are striving to light up the imaginative dialogue of poet and reader without resort to well-laid fuses of moral or social response', and applauded the integrity, the 'undeviating and dangerous singlemindedness' of his determination to 'remain undistracted and unwooed'. Reviewing *Malcolm Mooney's Land* twenty years later, Robin Skelton said that 'W. S. Graham resolutely avoids the public stance; his poems are directed to individual listeners and not to crowds'. Calvin Bedient contrasts Graham with the poet who would 'wear the common language like a consecrated robe': 'Graham wants to cut his own cloth, show by his style that he is *not* the public. His cultivated eccentricity argues the right to stand alone'.

And he has stood alone; the negative evidence is there to confirm these observations. Graham's poems have never been widely anthologized, imitated, or (mercifully) set for examinations. *Collected Poems 1942-1977* have now (1979) appeared from Faber, who have never before published a selection. The only representative selection from his work appeared in volume 17 of the Penguin Modern Poets in 1970 (a volume which also featured David Gascoyne and Kathleen Raine). His poems continue to make their rare appearances in magazines; but he is almost like the ghost of a poet, whose visitations are perceived by a few initiates but pass unnoticed by the majority — even the majority of the readers of poetry. One of Graham's finest poems, 'Johann Joachim Quantz's Five Lessons', concludes with this sober injunction from the musician to his pupil:

> Do not be sentimental or in your Art.
> I will miss you. Do not expect applause.

It would seem then that Graham has been prepared to do without applause for most of his career. The purpose of this essay is not to set the echoes ringing with combative assertions, but to offer an interpretative introduction to Graham's work for the reader who may well (and quite excusably) have missed one of the rarest talents in English poetry. The opportunity is provided by the fact that Graham's last two volumes, *Malcolm Mooney's Land* (1970) and *Implements in their Places* (1977), were both published in the 1970s.

II

W. S. Graham's first book of poems *Cage Without Grievance* was published by David Archer's Parton Press in Glasgow in 1942 when Graham was twenty-four. There followed *The Seven Journeys* two years later; *2nd Poems* in 1945. A pamphlet poem *The Voyages of Alfred Wallis* was published in 1948 by a small press in Cornwall, where Graham (who had left his native Scotland first for London and then for New York) was shortly to make his home, and where he still lives. These early poems show Graham drunk with words and prodigal of images; dazed with Dylan Thomas (whom he had met in London, among the poets who congregated in Soho) and blown about with the windy rhetoric of the New Apocalypse:

> This flying house where somewhere houses war
> World of the winding world hands me away
> Hauls at my tugging blood for words to wear
> Like rose of rising in the mercury counting sky
>
> ('Warning Not Prayer Enough', *2nd Poems*)

And so on. The excitement is purely verbal, the 'lonely energy' of the poetry (as Graham was later to call it) runs to earth without discharging its meaning. On the technical side, one notices especially the enfeebling fondness for what one might call the poetic participle: for the much-abused -ing (and also the agent -er) forms, which set up an easy rocking rhythm without making much demand on the syntax.

But nevertheless these poems do clearly initiate some of Graham's permanent themes (the drama of identity, in the multiplying of the self; the paradoxes of communication, with particular reference to the mystery of the poem; the metaphoric voyage; time) and also introduce us to his favourite contrastive images of land and sea, tree and wave, owl and gull, voice and silence. The successful poem 'My Glass World Tells of Itself' (*2nd Poems*) presents us with the image of a ship in a bottle, which (as we shall see) is to recur throughout Graham's work as his personal symbol of the timeless and motionless world of art: his Grecian Urn.

Graham's first important book was *The White Threshold*, published by Faber in 1949. This is still disfigured by the influence of Dylan Thomas (indeed, the influence of Thomas on both the language and the imagery of many of these poems is if anything more marked) but it was also now apparent that Graham had a voice of his own. In poems like 'Listen. Put on Morning', 'The White Threshold', and the 'Three Letters' with which the volume concludes, one recognizes a poet of authority and rigour, the assurance of whose style and the finished beauty of whose poems could not fail to attract the reader—despite his frequent and uncompromising obscurity. One important technical advance in this volume was the development of a short, three-stressed line (Robin Skelton informs us that Graham 'studied the three-stress line over a long period by keeping a journal whose every entry was written in this form'), which certainly helped Graham to pare down his rhetorical excess and allowed for that verbal precision and rhythmical originality which have since become the hallmark of his mature style.

The Nightfishing appeared in 1955, when 'it became immediately apparent that we were in the presence of a master'; then, strangely, there was a gap of fifteen years before the publication of *Malcolm Mooney's Land* in 1970—a volume which reminded older readers of Graham's existence and as it were announced him as a new poet now in his fifties to others. *Implements in their Places* followed in 1977, confirming the fact that Graham had earned what John Berryman celebrates in his elegy for William Carlos Williams,

> the mysterious late excellence which is the crown
> of our trials & our last bride.

It is this 'late excellence' which must be the main subject of this essay; but it is essential I feel to spend a little time with *The Nightfishing* before proceeding. One is not surprised to learn that W. S. Graham doesn't like to think of himself as having 'improved' as a poet if this means that his early work should therefore be neglected, if not entirely forgotten. Many of the early poems, one must agree, do present more difficulty than many readers will be prepared to encounter without better assurance that the effort will be rewarded. But the title poem 'The Nightfishing', and the 'Seven Letters' which relate to it, besides providing a basis for the understanding of Graham's later work, and clues to his subsequent development, are also important poems in themselves which will reward our attention.

'The Nightfishing' is an accomplished and beautiful poem, but even so one of formidable difficulty. Michael Schmidt has rightly remarked that Graham's poems resist prose paraphrase; but it is necessary at least to indicate the area of exploration of the poem, however inadequate an idea this may give of its final effect. At one level the poem is about a fishing trip. The central section describes how a fishing boat sets out from Greenock, trawls for herring, and returns to the port at dawn. And simply as description it works magnificently—illustrating how a debt to Hopkins has been repaid:

> Over the gunwale over into our deep lap
> The herring come in, staring from their scales,
> Fruitful as our deserts would have it out of
> The deep and shifting seams of water. . . .

But the outer sections of the poem confirm the fact that this description is densely metaphoric, and functions as part of a larger meaning. Calvin Bedient has written, rather portentously, that the poem 'is a profound experience; its nineteen pages put us amid Being'. However one chooses to express it, certainly the poem works at the deepest and dumbest levels of our selves, among our own 'deep and shifting seams'. Section I introduces the poet confronted with the mystery of being, hinging as it does on the determination of the self:

> Now within the dead
> Of night and the dead
> Of my life I hear
> My name called from far out.

He is called, uttered, born. The second section provides some vivid, surreal images of birth (still reminiscent of Thomas's obstetric imagery) and then we move into the third and longest section, where in fact the underlying metaphor frequently surfaces:

> The steep bow heaves, hung on these words, towards
> What words your lonely breath blows out to meet it.
> It is the skilled keel itself knowing its own
> Fathoms it further moves through, with us there
> Kept in its common timbers, yet each of us
> Unwound upon
>
> By a lonely behaviour of the all common ocean.

The boat is the physical vessel of the self, the body which is common to all humanity ('its common timbers') yet distinct in its own individual activity, its 'lonely behaviour'. The vessel is white-rigged with thought (like Keats's 'branched thoughts' in the 'Ode to Psyche'); the nets trailed in the sea are nerves. The sea itself is the great inclusive, inexhaustible image of all life, all time, all consciousness, on which and in which each individual must venture all he has and is. The caught herrings (possibly) are words, articulated moments rescued from the wash of time—but also killed. But to separate out the symbolism too thoroughly is also to kill or at least denature the poem. We notice that the sea itself is frequently described as a 'mingling element', mingling our own multiple selves, our separate selves (as it does in Virginia Woolf's *The Waves*), mingling all the living and all the dead (as does the falling snow in Joyce's story *The Dead*).

The sea is also an agent of change; there is submerged reference to *The Tempest* ('Pearled behind my eyes') and the idea of a 'sea-change' remains strong.

The fourth section finds the poet returned to 'that loneliness' which was 'Bragged into a voyage', and which is not assuaged by the ambiguous phrase 'There we lay/Loved alone'. In the fifth the poet attempts to locate the self in a place, 'fastened with movement'. But the self is never stable; the consciousness which determines identity is itself a mingling element:

> This is myself (who but ill resembles me).
> He befriended so many
> Disguises to wander in on as many roads
> As cross on a ball of wool.

The self is in fact the first of our necessary fictions. The sixth section is crucial, presenting as it does man as poet and poem as object, both beyond change; through the image (once more) of the ship in a bottle:

> The rigged ship in its walls of glass
> Still further forms its perfect seas
> Locked in its past transparences.

Graham is a deftly allusive poet, and I would think there is a strong possibility that he means us to recall here the beautiful image of permanence invoked by Shakespeare in sonnet number 5:

> Then were not summer's distillation left
> A liquid prisoner pent in walls of glass. . .

The last section is valedictory; the restless self is committed (like Tennyson's Ulysses) to another journey, 'Out into the waving/Nerves of the open sea'; while the poem of the self comes to rest in its 'breathless still place'. The reader new to and curious about Graham would do well to go back to 'The Nightfishing' and to the 'Seven Letters' which accompany it. But meanwhile we must move on to consider the work which Graham has published during the present decade.

III

Despite the fifteen-year silence, there is a clear continuity between Graham's earlier and his later work. He takes up his themes and images in *Malcolm Mooney's Land* exactly where he left off:

> Language swings away
> Before me as I go
> With again the night rising
> Up to accompany me
> And that other fond
> Metaphor, the sea. ('The Dark Dialogues')

But it would be a mistake to conclude that nothing has changed, or that Graham is simply repeating himself. The whole process or pretence of communication has become more problematical, beset with more obstacles and even dangers than formerly. Instead of the fish-rich seas of the earlier work, the title poem introduces us to an Arctic world of ice and snow where words themselves have frozen, and from which he can look back almost nostalgically to 'old summers/When to speak was easy'. Now it is a glacier rather than a boat that drives its keel; now he is in a tent rather than a room, words are 'buried under the printed snow' (we note the characteristic pun) rather than swarming like herring in the sea. Language has become more resistant, more dubious as a means of communication:

> Out at the far off edge I hear
> Colliding voices. . .
> Tomorrow I'll try the rafted ice.
> Have I not been trying to use the obstacle
> Of language well? It freezes round us all.

The growing blizzard is 'filled with other voices' than Mooney's (which is itself a projection of the poet's own voice); he can no longer distinguish him, 'Becoming shapeless into/The shrill swerving snow'. And if contact with himself is threatened, the poet has also lost confidence in the connection between word and thing, which must hold as the hinge of all adequate communication. 'Sit/With me between this word/And this. . . Yet not mistake this/For the real thing'. Graham leaves us to resolve the paradox that his language is actually more than adequate to detain the 'real thing' in words:

> Tell him I came across
> An old sulphur bear
> Sawing his log of sleep
> Loud beneath the snow.
> He puffed the powdered light
> Up on to this page
> And here his reek fell
> In splinters among
> These words.

The effect is similar to that achieved in Ted Hughes's poem 'The Thought Fox', where the animal is persuaded to leave its prints on the page. Mastery of the language does not alter the fact—or the irony—that language mocks itself; like a recurring decimal, it can never be *exact*. And there is another sinister enemy. The poet is now almost morbidly conscious of the ultimate silence that overlooks and overhears all that we try to do and say.

> From wherever it is I urge these words
> To find their subtle vents, the northern dazzle
> Of silence cranes to watch.

Although the poet has tried to commune with himself and with others in the poem, writing a diary and telling stories, he ends with the inevitable admission of his loneliness:

> I have made myself alone now.
> Outside the tent endless
> Drifting hummock crests.
> Words drifting on words.
> The real unabstract snow.

It is typical of Graham's orientation towards reality—and also of the way his enclosing metaphor controls his material—that the poem actually alludes in many of its details to the voyage of the Norwegian explorer Nansen towards the North Pole in 1893-6. Nansen deliberately had his ship the Fram become locked in ice, on the theory—which proved correct—that ocean currents would carry it safely northwards. (Could this provide another appropriate meaning for Graham's 'walls of glass'?). I have suggested several parallels with other writers already in this essay, parallels which help I think to establish the scope as well as the seriousness of Graham's work. But this seems a good point to remark upon the most important and illuminating parallel, which is with Samuel Beckett. According to Michael Schmidt, Graham has acknowledged a debt to Beckett, but even without this the reader could not fail to be struck by the close correspondence between the ideas, themes, and literary technique of the poet and those of the prose writer and dramatist. The revolving obsession with identity, consciousness, and articulation; the telling of stories to create the fiction of the self, and the creation of voices and personae to evade the implosion of the self; the reliance on pun and allusion as a literary method; the deepening pessimism (which this implies) as to the possibility of communication with our kind, and the admission of loneliness as one's ultimate condition, are all themes of Beckett's Trilogy (especially of the last piece, *The Unnamable*); and it is these same themes which move Graham to his most memorable utterance. If Beckett has insisted that 'art is the apotheosis of solitude', Graham likewise once wrote that the poet

> is concerned with putting into words those sudden desolations and happiness that descend on us uninvited there where we each are within our lonely rooms never really entered by anybody else and from which we never emerge.

The obsessions of both writers converge in the relentless questioning of language itself, whose capacity to redeem us from this solitude turns out to be largely an illusion. Language is conceived now as a kind of double agent which both serves and betrays, revealing us to ourselves (and others) and at the same time disguising the fugitive self which can never be known. Robin Skelton has observed that Graham uses language 'as a metaphor for the human condition'; this is an essential point to recognize if we are to respond to the passion of Graham's exhaustingly reflexive mode of expression:

> I stop and listen over
> My shoulder and listen back
> On language for that step
> That seems to fall after
> My own step in the dark
> ('The Dark Dialogues')

Beckett's Unnamable is unable to establish 'what I am, where I am, whether I am words among words or silence in the midst of silence' (392). He is 'made of words' but they are 'others' words' (390), he is 'made of silence' but the silence is continually invaded by voices and cries (417). Language diffuses his identity, he can never confidently say 'I'. Three things he says have conditioned his existence, three things which we can see are really one and the same, a kind of existential trinity: 'the inability to speak, the inability to be silent, and solitude' (400). Now the fifteen sections of Graham's poem 'Approaches to How They Behave' (which clearly looks forward to the title poem of Graham's more recent volume) reflect very similar concerns. Speaking has the same ambiguous relation to silence:

> Having to construct the silence first
> To speak out on I realize
> The silence even itself floats
> At my ear-side with a character
> I have not met before. (XV)

His words are not under his exclusive control; they derive a life of their own from the silence that surrounds them, and which is also inhabited by other people:

> What does it matter if the words
> I choose, in the order I choose them in,
> Go out into a silence I know
> Nothing about, there to be let
> In and entertained and charmed
> Out of their master's orders? (I)

The words he sends out 'In roughly your direction' (III) may freeze, become hazardous 'floating bergs to sink a convoy' (IV). Because one is conscious all the time that 'Speaking is difficult', 'one tries/To be exact' (II); but despite our efforts, what we naively call communication can never be said to have occurred:

> The words are mine, the thoughts are all
> Yours as they occur behind
> The bat of your vast unseen eyes.

But despite the defensiveness of these assertions, the poem includes an interesting explicit metaphor which gives us a clue as to how Graham attempts to cope with an apparently insuperable problem.

> The inadequacy
> Of the living, animal language drives
> Us all to metaphor and an attempt
> To organize the spaces we think
> We have made occur between the words. (II)

The recalcitrant animal has to be exercised, the unreliable spaces organized in whatever ways we can discover. These may include direct confrontation, the method Graham prefers to metaphor in the searching poem 'The Dark Dialogues'. Here he asks the direct question 'Who are you?', and confesses the need 'to say/Something and to hear/That someone has heard me', only to be driven back on himself by the language

> And whoever I meant
> To think I had met
> Turns away further
> Before me blinded by
> This word and this word.

Adapting Marvell's 'Dialogue of Self and Soul' (to which there may well be an implicit allusion here) Graham is blinded by a word, deaf with the drumming of a word: eye and ear enclose rather than liberate. Even the self he falls back on is indistinct, unutterable in words: 'There is no other place/Than where I am, between/This word and the next'; the voices and identities of his father and mother usurp his own, 'As I sit here becoming/Hardly who I know'. He can assert that 'always language/Is where the people are', but neither language nor people can be detained. I try (he says) 'To clench my words against/Time or the lack of time', but always 'Language swings away/Further before me'. In a minimal, reductive definition of his function, he is trying to teach his ears and eyes 'to observe/The behaviour of silence': a peculiarly Beckettian pastime.

In 'The Fifteen Devices', similarly, the experience of psychological decomposition ('When who we think we are is suddenly/Flying apart') is paralleled by 'the prised/Open spaces between the flying/Apart words'. The self is a place, nameless and unlocatable; the poem is a space, an arena where potential meanings are released and then left to themselves. This last idea is developed in the beautiful and lucid poem 'The Constructed

Space', whose opening word 'Meanwhile' breaks in as it were on the continuous dark dialogue of one:

> Meanwhile surely there must be something to say,
> Maybe not suitable but at least happy
> In a sense here between us two whoever
> We are.

The poem he goes on to define as 'a public place/Achieved against subjective odds and then/Mainly an obstacle to what I mean'. The 'obstacle' lies in the fact that the meaning received need not be the same as that conveyed. The poem presents us with a sudden realization of this fact:

> Or maybe, surely, of course we never know
> What we have said, what lonely meanings are read
> Into the space we make.

After such a realization the meaning of the poem can only be described as an approximation:

> I say this silence or, better, construct this space
> So that somehow something may move across
> The caught habits of language to you and me.

'Habit is a great deadener' is another Beckettian axiom; Graham too recognizes the danger, and there is continuous evidence of his precautionary measures against the hardening of habitual phrases in the way he often indulges as a kind of exercise in puns and other word-games, subverting or reforging the conventional expression. Thus he describes himself with Joycean alertness as 'lying wordawake', and expresses the wish to 'be out of myself and/About the extra, ordinary world'. It is with such a punning phrase that Graham concludes this poem: 'Here in the present tense disguise is mortal'. Disguise is both human and deadly; we can avoid neither our humanity nor our sentence of death. And disguise in this sense, referring to the inevitable opacity of the self, the 'quick disguise' (another pun) which life condemns us to, is a theme to which Graham often returns.

'The Constructed Space' is a very explicit, almost literal statement of the theory that lies behind many of the poems. Elsewhere this theory is more richly caparisoned in metaphor. The beast in 'The Beast in the Space' for example is a mythical monster that 'lives on silence' and 'laps my meaning up'; it is this beast that now possesses the arena of the poem.

> I am not here, only the space
> I sent the terrible beast across.

And the seven sections of the fine concluding poem 'Clusters Travelling Out' develops very imaginatively the metaphor of the self as confined in a prison cell, trying to establish some kind of communication with his fellow-prisoners. He never knows if his message is being received:

> Are you receiving those clusters
> I send out travelling? Alas
> I have no way of knowing or
> If I am overheard here.

At the end of the poem (and the book) he is left 'waiting for/A message to come in now', much as Vladimir and Estragon wait hopelessly for Godot. We notice that here too the metaphor has more than one level. The tap on the wall is also the tap on the typewriter:

> I tap
> And tap to interrupt silence into
> Manmade durations making for this
> Moment a dialect for our purpose

—and also making the poem: 'It is our poetry such as it is'.

  Another way in which Graham makes his theme more concrete is to consider the problem of communication with particular people. There are half a dozen poems in *Malcolm Mooney's Land* (and more in *Implements in their Places*) addressed to friends and to his wife which—although still oblique and difficult—are very moving. Here we have Graham's more personal expression of the need to find 'a way/Of speaking towards you' (in 'Wynter and the Grammarsow'): 'I mean there must be some/Way to speak together straighter than this,/As I usually say': his need 'to be by another aloneness loved' ('Hilton Abstract'), which line speaks straight enough to anyone. The fine elegiac poem 'The Thermal Stair', for Peter Lanyon, is the most direct of all: 'Remember me wherever you listen from'. 'I leave this at your ear for when you wake' is the first and last line of the poem to his wife. But he is older, death is nearer (it has overtaken some already), and so there is due acknowledgement of the power of time. 'I stand in the ticking room' he says to his wife; 'The times are calling us in' he reminds Wynter, calling us towards 'the real sea' where the rest of the dead await our coming. But the consolation seized in these poems—perhaps surprisingly—is the traditional one that the poem can itself stand against time; we are back to the Shakespearean 'walls of glass'. From this perspective the artist's task may after all be simply expressed:

> His job is love
> Imagined into words or paint to make
> An object that will stand and will not move.
>   ('The Thermal Stair')

IV

The first thing to remark about Graham's last collection, *Implements in their Places,* is that it is more accessible than any of his earlier work. (It is for this reason that the reader new to Graham might be well advised to begin with this last book, and read him backwards). Never before has Graham written as simply and directly as in the dozen or so personal poems included in this volume. The strenuous syntactical effort of the earlier poems is replaced here by a restrained authority, a certainty of utterance which is characteristic of that 'mysterious late excellence' wherever it is encountered. 'Loch Thom' is a beautiful example. The poem describes a visit made by the poet to the watery 'stretch of my child-hood':

> And almost I am back again
> Wading the heather down to the edge
> To sit. The minnows go by in shoals
> Like iron-filings in the shallows.
> My mother is dead. My father is dead
> And all the trout I used to know
> Leaping from their sad rings are dead.

'It is a colder/Stretch of water than I remember': the poignancy of the experience is finely captured in the contrasted physical descriptions of past and present; there is no importunity on the part of the poet himself. In the poem addressed to his father ('To Alexander Graham') the emotion is controlled by the use of the dream situation:

> Lying asleep walking
> Last night I met my father
> Who seemed pleased to see me.
> He wanted to speak. I saw
> His mouth saying something
> But the dream had no sound.

The visual images are sharp, the atmosphere of Greenock 'As real as life. I smelt/The quay's tar and the ropes'. Only in the last line of the poem is the feeling alluded to—tentatively, and in the perfect rather than the present tense: 'I think I must have loved him'. 'Lines on Roger Hilton's Watch' ('Which I was given because/I loved him and we had/Terrible times together') and 'Dear Bryan Wynter' ('This is only a note/To say how sorry I am/You died') are in the same direct idiom, moving elegies in Graham's most spare and essential style. 'Do not be sentimental or in your Art', said Johann Quantz to his pupil; and if Graham has avoided sentimentalism in these fine poems it must be largely due to his expert use of his characteristic three-stress line, on which we have commented earlier. The short line encourages a strict economy of word, breaks up familiar collocations of words into new groupings, and above all gives Graham the opportunity of setting up a tense rhythm, which is at the same time tightly controlled but fluent and expressive:

> Of course, here I am
> Thinking I want to say
> Something into the ghost

> Of the presence you left
> Me with between the granite
> Of my ego house. . .

But despite the excellence of these 'private' poems, one cannot help
feeling that it is still in the more exploratory, reflexive mode that
Graham's true distinctiveness as a poet is discovered; in the poem of the
self, and the poem of the poem itself: what Wallace Stevens called 'The
poem of the mind in the act of finding/What will suffice'. One could
suggest that there are two groups of poems in this broad category, plus
the unclassifiable title poem. Graham has always been fascinated by the
implications for literature of the other arts, and there are three poems
here that reflect this continuing interest. The masterful 'Johann Joachim
Quantz's Five Lessons' takes the example of music. The celebrated
musician is teaching the flute to his student Karl; the teaching is partly in
words, and so we have the formula: 'It is best I sit/Here where I am to
speak on the other side/Of language'. But the object of the lesson is
music, the playing of the flute; and so a different kind of silence is
invoked, a different kind of concave world:

> Now we must try higher, aware of the terrible
> Shapes of silence sitting outside your ear
> Anxious to define you and really love you.
> Remember silence is curious about its opposite
> Element which you shall learn to represent.

One thinks inevitably of Blake's great humanistic consolation: 'Eternity is
in love with the productions of time'. Graham here more specifically
dwells upon the mysterious correspondence between the convex world of
musical art and the concave world of silence, which create the same curve
from opposite sides and confirm each other with the exactness of an
equation. The syntax in this poem has the perfect tautness of music; the
movement and the sheer control of meaning is a positive pleasure for the
reader:

> Karl, I can still put on a good flute-mouth
> And show you in this high cold room something
> You will be famous to have said you heard.

In the Fourth Lesson Quantz becomes more personal. Master and pupil
pass beyond technique ('I think you are good enough/To not need me
any more') to the philosophy of music: with the musician as demi-urge.

> What we have to do
> Today is think of you as a little creator
> After the big creator.

The last lesson is a kind of Master Class in artistic conscience.

> Do not intrude too much
> Into the message you carry and put out.
>
> One last thing, Karl, remember when you enter
> The joy of those quick high archipelagoes,
> To make to keep your finger-stops as light
> As feathers but definite. What can I say more?
> Do not be sentimental or in your Art.
> I will miss you. Do not expect applause.

This (as we have seen) is equally applicable to music or poetry, and contains lessons which Graham himself has scrupulously observed throughout his career.

There isn't space unfortunately to explore all these poems in the way they deserve: poems like 'The Found Picture' and 'Ten Shots of Mr Simpson', although I must at least note the fact that this last poem includes once again Graham's personal symbol: 'a white-rigged ship bottled sailing'. If Mr Simpson is a prisoner of art he joins the liquid prisoner in its walls of glass.

The other poems confront the perennial themes—language, consciousness, identity—with Graham's home-made metaphors. The interrogative structure of the opening poem 'What is the Language Using Us For?' brings a new urgency to what before was meditation. Malcolm Mooney returns as the perplexed questioner, 'moving away/Slowly over the white language', his regular habitat; and in his usual role:

> He is only going to be
> Myself and for you slightly you
> Wanting to be another. He fell
> He falls (Tenses are everywhere.)
> Deep down into a glass jail.

The glass jail is the image of art once more—an art which kills (as Mr Simpson was 'shot') as well as eternizes:

> The point is would you ever want
> To be down here on the freezing line
> Reading the words that stream out
> Against the ice?

The touch of the Muse, we remember, the touch of the White Goddess, is a freezing touch; a fact which was dramatically illustrated in Graham's poem 'Five Visitors to Madron' in *Malcolm Mooney's Land*. The second part of the poem is more explicit: 'What I am making is/A place for language in my life/Which I want to be a real place/Seeing I have to put up with it/Anyhow'. This recalls Beckett's resigned answer to the question as to why he still used words: 'Parce-qu'il n'y a rien d'autre'. We have to accept that it is through language that we perform as well as we are able

the human function of art: 'we want to be telling/Each other alive about
each other/Alive'. The third part resumes the seafaring metaphors of *The
Nightfishing*, to coincide with a challenging series of rhetorical questions:

> What is the weather
> Using us for where we are ready
> With all our language lines aboard?
> The beginning wind slaps the canvas.
> Are you ready? Are you ready?

Once again, there are several other poems that require more careful
analysis than there is space for here: poems like 'Untidy Dreadful Table',
'Enter a Cloud', and 'The Secret Name'. This last is a beautiful if chilling
poem, one of several in which Madron Wood appears as an image of the
absolute, and presumably death. Like Beckett's Unnamable, the persona
of this poem listens for his own name in order to know and situate himself, but this 'hurries away/Before you in the trees to escape' leaving him
in the terrifying solipsist enclosure:

> To tell you the truth I hear almost
> Only the sounds I have made myself.
> Up over the wood's roof I imagine
> The long sigh of Outside goes.

The self is divided again: 'I leave them there a moment knowing/I make
them act you and me'; and the poem is the wood, the uneasy place where
these selves take refuge. 'Under the poem's branches two people/Walk
and even the words are shy'. But this is no 'rosy sanctuary', like that
provided by Keats for Psyche. Madron Wood is more sinister, and there
is obviously more threat than promise in the concluding section of the
poem:

> The terrible, lightest wind in the world
> Blows from word to word, from ear
> To ear, from name to name, from secret
> Name to secret name. You maybe
> Did not know you had another
> Sound and sign signifying you.

Which brings us finally to the title poem, about which I must confess to
feeling a certain uneasiness. 'Implements in their Places' is not one poem
but a gathering of 74 fragments of from one to nineteen lines, a curious
mixture of impersonation and self-mockery along with some genuine
Graham. We know where we are for example when the Muse breathes
'her rank breath of poet's bones' (4), or where Graham protests: 'Terrible
the indignity of one's self flying/Away from the sleight of one's true
hand' (56). Loch Thom reappears 'in place' of number 57 (was this I

wonder the poet's age when he wrote it?):

> There is no fifty-seven.
> It is not here. Only
> Freshwater Loch Thom
> To paddle your feet in
> And the long cry of the curlew.

And Quantz's lesson on the impersonality of art is beautifully recapitulated in the two lines: 'It is only when the tenant is gone/The shell speaks of the sea' (48). The most interesting group, however, is the fifteen or so (24-40) which revolve round the poet's permanent struggle with words and meanings. Language is chastised as 'constrictor of my soul' and as 'you terrible surrounder/Of everything' (30,35). Even the contemporary idiom is put to good use in this context. The poet is 'Commuting by arterial words/Between my home and Cool Cat/Reality' (28), he is 'Sad to have to infer/Such graft and treachery, in the name/Of communication' (29); in a moment of punning frustration he can exclaim: 'I want out of this underword' (42). Another four-line fragment gives us a description of Graham as he may see himself now, at the end of his last volume; a less heroic and more self-conscious version of Malcolm Mooney:

> Only now a wordy ghost
> Of once my firmer self I go
> Floating across the frozen tundra
> Of the lexicon and the dictionary. (27)

V

Seven years elapsed between *Malcolm Mooney's Land* and *Implements in their Places*. I don't know how long we shall have to wait for Graham's next volume. No shorter time, I imagine; I know of only one poem which has been published since the last book, although some more have been broadcast. Meanwhile, we have now the *Collected Poems* from Faber. This is a matter for satisfaction since the early volumes are now unobtainable and even *Malcolm Mooney's Land* is out of print. Graham himself may well be able to dispense with our applause, but that does not mean that we should have to dispense with Graham. The publication of his collected poems will at last enable a wider readership to get to know and begin to appreciate a profound, humane and generous poet now at the height of his powers; a poet who was not the victim (as many are) of excessive praise when he was described in the *Malahat Review* on the publication of his last volume as 'clearly one of the finest, if not *the* finest, poet now writing in English'.

Note

Chapters devoted to Graham in Calvin Bedient's *Eight Contemporary*

Poets (1974) and Michael Schmidt's *50 Modern British Poets* (1979) represent the only extended criticism of his work. Edwin Morgan's review of *The White Threshold* in *Nine* (vol 2, 1950) is well worth reading, as is Robin Skelton's review of *Malcolm Mooney's Land* in the *Malahat Review* (no 15, 1970).

Donald Davie, dissentient voice

DONALD DAVIE's substantial *Collected Poems,* which appeared in 1972, covered the years 1950-70; and anyone unacquainted with the oddities of English literary reputations might have supposed that by then Davie's position as a writer of considerable importance would have been secure. Apart from the poetry, there were the critical works—among them, *Purity of Diction in English Verse* (1952), *Articulate Energy* (1955), and *Ezra Pound: Poet as Sculptor* (1965)—and a prolific, provocative output of essays and reviews. Yet Davie's reputation was by no means secure then; nor is it now, at the end of the decade; and any account of his work since 1970 must be at least partly concerned with the tension (at best a creative tension) between Davie and his English audience or, more bluntly, between Davie and England.

It has been a momentous decade for Davie but not, I think, primarily for him as a poet. It is almost framed by two controversies: the extended row with Larkin in the pages of the *Listener* over the *Oxford Book of Twentieth-Century Verse* in 1973; and a no less fiery debate with Jon Silkin and others in 1979. In both controversies, central issues are pursued with characteristic seriousness and an exasperated candour. Between them come four more critical books: *Thomas Hardy and British Poetry* (1973); the Fontana Modern Masters volume on *Pound* (1975); *The Poet in the Imaginary Museum* (1977); and the 1976 Clark Lectures, *A Gathered Church* (1978). And then there have been, of course, the essays, the reviews, and the editorial presence in *Poetry Nation Review.* Together, these various activities tend to overshadow the poetry; but, as Davie himself once admitted, 'The poet-scholar cannot keep apart/The gift and the investment'. Thus, for instance, the title of Davie's Clark Lectures will send us back to the poem of the same name in *A Winter Talent* (1957), the fourth of a quartet called 'Dissentient Voice'—an apt enough phrase in more than one sense:

> So here I take the husk of my research,
> A form of words—the phrase, 'a gathered church',
> A rallying cry of our communions once
> For you* perhaps still stirring, but for me
> A picturesque locution, nothing more
> Except for what it promises, a tang.
> * The poem is dedicated: 'In memoriam A.E.D. ob. 1939'.

'Except for what it promises. . . ': so, in the first poem, 'Bedfordshire', of his 1974 collection *The Shires,* we find Davie contemplating

> Dissenting nineteenth-century demureness
> In a brick chapel. I have never known
> What to do with this that I am heir to.

That is the right sort of problem for a poet. The restless, ruminative sense of a mind moving among half-understood echoes and associations informs the poems in *The Shires*—a far richer book than it at first appears—as well as many of the pieces at the end of the *Collected Poems* and in Davie's most recent collection, *In the Stopping Train* (1977). The circumstances surrounding Davie's emigration to California in 1968, and the poems written at that time, are outside the chronological scope of this volume; but the perplexed and unresolved tensions with England continue to reverberate:

> 'Brain-drain' one hears no more of,
> And that's no loss. There is
> Another emigration:
> Draining away of love.

With these half-truthful lines, Davie concludes the bitterly and reflexively ironic 'Sussex', a poem in which he insists upon his adopted Americanness by styling himself a 'transatlantic visitor' and in which, most tellingly, the central image is a village cricket match:

> We had to pinch ourselves
> To know we knew the rules
> Of cricket played on the green.
> Our boy will never learn them.

The reflexive allusion—and the reason why *we* know he knew the rules—is to a magical poem from *Events and Wisdoms* (1964) called 'Barnsley Cricket Club':

> 'A thing worth doing is worth doing well,'
> Says Shaw Lane Cricket Ground
> Between the showers of a July evening,
> As the catch is held and staid hand-clappings swell.

There, in the warmer tone of Davie's earlier writing, is the source of his more recent angularity: for it is precisely because he is so sensitively aware of his roots that he is compelled to record the anguish of deracination.

The responses to England contained in *The Shires* are far from comfortable but they are glancingly, and therefore the more sharply, affectionate: if 'love' has not 'drained away', it has become infinitely complicated. In 'Leicestershire', the Leicester Poetry Society is remembered and a footnote to Malcolm Bradbury's *Eating People is Wrong* thus inadvertently provided. In 'Cheshire', Davie experiences 'A lift to the spirit, when everything fell into place!' Here again, the response to landscape is complex, modulating into an eloquently simple and memorable tribute to another poet:

> And Mr Auden, whom I never knew,
> Is dead in Vienna. A post-industrial landscape
> He celebrated often, and expounded
> How it can bleakly solace. And that's true.

Behind *The Shires*, inevitably, is 'Essex', at whose university Davie was Professor of English and which

>   merits
> Better than I can give it
> Who have unfinished business
> There, with my own failures.

The paradox (not, after all, such an unusual one) is that Davie's 'failures' at Essex produced some strikingly successful poems: the pared-down lucidity of his *Essex Poems* (1969), a poetic flavour which has been called American but which might equally be described as East Anglian, continues to influence his work. Alongside this, however, is a more disturbing development which becomes clear from a comparison of the excellent *Essex Poems* with the section of the *Collected Poems* called 'More Essex Poems': a slackening of control and, at times, a descent into almost hysterical rancour. *The Shires* is almost (and perhaps surprisingly) free of this, but it disfigures the less successful pieces in *In the Stopping Train* and among Davie's uncollected poems.

The basic problem concerns Davie's relationship with his audience: and this means Davie's relationship with England for, as Michael Schmidt has pointed out, 'Davie's work, all of it, is beamed towards England. He is writing to us and of us. We are his principal concern' (Michael Schmidt, ' "Time and Again": The Recent Poetry of Donald Davie', *Agenda*, 14:2, 1976). Many of Davie's poems of the late sixties and early seventies chart a loss of confidence in the English audience, exacerbated by the Essex experience and the prevalence of modish, superficial subcultures. One might expect Davie's fury to have abated, given the widening geographical and temporal distance, but if it has (and a poem like 'St Paul's Revisited' suggests that it hasn't) there remains as a residue an irritating stylistic mannerism. Davie has always tended to be an exclamatory writer: since *Essex Poems*, though, much of his work has been peppered with obscure and frequently incomplete exclamations: 'They see his face!' ('The Departed'); 'Rancour! Rancour!/Oh patriotic and indignant bird!' ('St Paul's Revisited'); 'This West! this ocean!' ('Seeing her leave'); 'Now this!/Earthquake!' ('Gemona-del-Friuli, 1961-1976'). Such fragments (shored against his ruins, perhaps) seem intended to shut the reader out; and I think that this defensive exclusion, as it seems to be, of the reader is in fact at least as damaging to the poems as the widely-noticed bitterness which goes along with it. Yet, in an obvious sense, this objection of mine is a naive one: I have just, after all, alluded to *The Waste Land* and in the same breath complained, like early critics of Eliot, that Davie's work has become obscure and fragmented. My unease stems from the suspicion that Davie is inclined to give his readers a bumpy ride because he feels that they deserve it and that it will be somehow salutary for them: but the effect of this may be to isolate from the poet just that consensus of intelligent readers which he actually seeks to address. There is, as if acknowledging this difficulty, 'A Wistful Poem called "Readers" ' in *In the Stopping Train* which, far from being wistful, is a laboured joke: Davie admits as much in his laboured title.

A solution to this problem of audience is to talk to oneself. That is partly what seems to be happening in the title sequence of *In the Stopping Train,* where the tension is between the 'I' of the poem and the 'he', 'the man going mad inside me'.

> I have got into the slow train
> again. I made the mistake
> knowing what I was doing,
> knowing who had to be punished.

Larkin, one recalls, 'was late getting away' and, presumably as a consequence, took the slow train in 'The Whitsun Weddings': that ironic parallel—two poems could hardly be more different in tone and manner—cannot have escaped Davie. Nor can the punning possibilities of the situation have eluded a poet who, later in the sequence, teases the pain/pane pun so mercilessly: the train, stopping and starting, is also a train of thought; the poem is linear and is made of lines ('It's not, I explained, that I mind/getting to the end of the line.'); 'the man going mad' is going off the rails. It is the inner linguistic aspect of the subject which interests Davie: the poem, unlike Larkin's, contains almost no external description. Indeed, one of the preoccupations here is the way in which language can become divorced from external realities:

> Jonquil is a sweet word.
> Is it a flowering bush?
> Let him helplessly wonder
> for hours if perhaps he's seen it.
> Has it a white and yellow
> flower, the jonquil? Has it
> a perfume? Oh his art could
> always pretend it had.
>
> He never needed to see,
> not with his art to help him.
> He never needed to use his
> nose, except for language.

'He' taunts himself with the way in which art falsifies, obliquely regrets that he has lost (if he ever had it) the ability to look simply at things. Flowers are reduced to words; 'And he can name them all,/identify hardly any.' Yet the process of naming, of conferring a meaning, eliminates the external reality of the flowers and transforms them into linguistic counters which he 'turns. . . .around in his head'. The paradox infuriates him: 'his' stanzas are full of impotent panic; this is why, or at any rate how, 'he' is going mad.

The 'I' persona is altogether more calm, knowing about the initial and deliberate 'mistake', juggling in a more relaxed way with ideas of stopping and starting, commenting on 'him' in a tone of resignation:

> I have travelled with him many times
> now. Already we nod,
> we are almost on speaking terms.

But the relationship between the 'I' and the 'he' is continually shifting, like the equally ambiguous relationship between the 'I' and the 'you' in 'Prufrock'. Perhaps with this model in mind, Davie, like Eliot, astonishes the reader with an abrupt change of perspective at the end of the sequence:

> He knew too few in love,
> too few in love.

> That sort of foolish beard
> masks an uncertain mouth.
> And so it proved: he took
> some weird girl off to a weird
> commune, clutching at youth.

> Dear reader, this is not
> our chap, but another.
> Catch our clean-shaven hero
> tied up in such a knot?
> A cause of so much bother?

> He knew too few in love.

That is how 'he' would behave if he were really going mad? Or that is a genuinely external third-person 'he'? The suggestion is perhaps that there is a kind of external social madness which is quite distinct from the internal personal madness. The cunningly ambiguous conclusion (does 'in love' apply to 'him' or to the 'too few' others or to both?) seems to echo the equally enigmatic conclusion of 'July, 1964' from *Essex Poems:*

> A man who ought to know me
> wrote in a review
> my emotional life was meagre.

'He', in the context of this sequence, is also 'a man who ought to know me': and *vice versa*.

'In the Stopping Train' may well by now appear to be baffling, so I had better insist that this is not the case. Its sparseness of syntax and imagery, its angularity of thought do in fact produce a frightening lucidity. The sequence frightens in its cannibalistic ability to devour its potential subject-matter as it goes along: it becomes an extraordinarily and designedly *impoverished* piece of writing about lacks, gaps, needs. It is undeniably impressive — and properly the focal point of the book which is built around it—but it is not the kind of thing one would wish Davie to attempt too often.

In the Stopping Train, the collection, is a worried and worrying book, reaching out in its skeletal fashion to various antecedents: to Christopher Smart, for instance, in one of the most vivid and successful poems, 'Morning'; or, once again, to Pasternak; or to Davie's own earlier work, as when 'A Spring Song' reshapes the mode of 'Time Passing, Beloved' only to be reshaped—or 'read'—itself in the adjacent 'A Wistful Poem Called "Readers" '. In the final poem, 'Townend, 1976', Davie is at his best—at once topographically accurate and thoughtful, relating the inner and outer worlds so mercilessly wrenched apart in the title sequence. Here, at last, the tension between Davie and his English subject-matter does become creative:

> When does a town become a city? This
> That ends where I begin it, at Townend
> With Wright the Chemist (one of the few not changed),
> Grows cityfied, though still my drab old friend.
>
> Thanks therefore for the practical piety
> Of E. G. Tasker, antiquarian;
> His *Barnsley Streets*. Unshed, my tears hang heavy
> Upon the high-gloss pages where I scan
>
> What else, though, but remembered homely squalor?
> Generations of it! Eldon Street
> Smells of bad drains of forty years ago
> Ah sweetly. But should penury smell sweet?
>
> An end to it then. An end to that town. Townend.
> A Tetley's house, the Wheatsheaf, holds its station
> Since 1853, where Dodworth Road
> Stars into five streets, 'major intersection'.

These are the opening stanzas of a fairly long poem, and they clearly demonstrate how concrete detail and introspection can work profitably with rather than against each other; they show, too, how successfully Davie's ironic, questioning tone can build upon a clearly visualized starting-point.

Despite this, and despite other distinguished recent poems, Davie's most notable and memorable poetic achievements so far seem to belong to the fifties and the sixties rather than to the seventies. No doubt this is partly a matter of distancing: poetry needs to settle into familiarity before it can be properly judged. But it is also, I think, a matter of Davie's recent preoccupations finding their appropriate expression in his stylish and energetic prose: ideas which can be worked *out* in prose may prove too intractable to work *into* poems. This is not to suggest that poems shouldn't contain ideas—far from it—but to wonder whether the rough edges and fragmented syntax of some poems in *In the Stopping Train* really do justice to the ideas they try to embody. Where the ideas are linked to a clear external subject—as in much of *The Shires* or in 'Townend, 1976'—the resulting poetry is coherent and moving. The poet should indeed stand, as Forster said of Cavafy, 'at a slight angle to the universe'; but with Davie the angle sometimes seems to grow uncomfortably wide.

Being different from yourself: Philip Larkin in the 1970s

BOOKS and articles about Philip Larkin have often begun by discussing his connections with 'the Movement', the group of poets whose work appeared in Robert Conquest's 1956 anthology *New Lines*. By 1970 the 'Movement' poets had long taken their separate ways and it now seems strange that such different writers could ever have seemed to have much in common. Elizabeth Jennings has gone on to develop the strength and quiet individuality of a basically contemplative poetry; Thom Gunn has moved to California, and to a delicate, mythically-and socially-aware lyricism not unlike that of Gary Snyder, with whom he shares a tendency to wander dangerously close to whimsy; Donald Davie (also via California) has come to an appreciation of Pound and is now the leading British interpreter of that poet who above all others epitomizes those things against which the 'Movement' tried to take a stand.

As a movement, the 'Movement' finished long ago, and it can be argued that Larkin has changed as much as any of the poets so far mentioned. On the other hand, during the 1970s a number of like-minded writers, several of them former 'Movement' poets, have quietly taken over many of the symbolically important positions in the outer world of public poetic business. One might say that a certain generation of poets—or a certain phase of poetry—has come into its inheritance. John Wain, for example, was Professor of Poetry at Oxford from 1973 to 1978; a friend and admirer of Larkin's, he devoted his fifth lecture to Larkin's work. Another friend and former 'Movement' poet, Kingsley Amis, as well as remaining one of the leading English novelists, was entrusted with the editing of a *New Oxford Book of Light Verse* to replace Auden's 1938 anthology. Oxford Books of this and that are felt to have a kind of canonical status, embodying the doctrine of their generation on whatever genre they represent, and Larkin was honoured in his turn by an invitation to edit the *Oxford Book of Twentieth-Century English Verse,* which appeared in 1973. His predecessor in this exercise was Yeats, whose *Oxford Book of Modern Verse* appeared in 1936. That glittering booby-prize the Laureateship fell to John Betjeman in 1972, leaving Larkin himself in the far safer and happier rôle of 'The *other* English Poet Laureate, even more loved and needed than the official one', as Calvin Bedient expressed it. As if to demonstrate the precise significance of this rôle, Larkin was commissioned to write a 'public' poem: the 'Prologue' for *How Do You Want*

To Live, a report on the environment published by HMSO in 1972. The poem appeared printed in the grey sky above a photograph of a Teesside chemical works, a panorama of industrial mess not without picturesque qualities of a cluttered, bristling sort: cooling towers, chimneys, massive thickets of metal piping. A slightly revised version of the poem appeared as 'Going, Going' in *High Windows*.

Thus the 1970s for Larkin have been a decade of consolidation. Previous achievement has been crowned. Alone of his four small books of verse *High Windows* had from the start a large, expectant public. It was reprinted twice in 1974, its year of publication, and had reached a fourth printing two years later. There are good reasons for a certain mellowing in the tone of Larkin's work. Not surprisingly, *High Windows* contains fewer of the depressive or suspicious poems, of experience examined and found wanting, that characterized *The Less Deceived* and *The Whitsun Weddings*. More unexpected is the fact that it shows the re-emergence of tendencies kept carefully out of sight since Larkin's first collection, *The North Ship* (1945); and most startling of all, that poem after poem takes us towards a symbolist vision of the kind which the earlier poems were determined to exclude.

High Windows is not Larkin's sole publication of the decade; 1970 saw the collection of his *Daily Telegraph* jazz reviews in book form as *All What Jazz: a record diary 1961-68,* which carried an entertainingly polemical introduction announcing his antipathy to modern jazz as just one more aspect of a general objection to modernism in the arts, a tendency which he personified in the alliterative trio of Parker, Pound and Picasso. How far this essay represented a stage in the careful construction of an anti-intellectual 'man-in-the-street' persona is anyone's guess. But it seems likely that Larkin wanted people to think that the 'sullen fleshy inarticulate men, stockbrokers, sellers of goods, living in thirty-year-old detached houses among the golf courses. . . . fathers of cold-eyed lascivious daughters on the pill. . . .and [of] cannabis-smoking jeans-and-bearded Stuart-haired sons', the 'men whose first coronary is coming like Christmas; who drift. . . .into the darkening avenues of age and incapacity' for whom his jazz criticism is purportedly written, represent also his notion of the ideal readers of his poetry.

The Introduction to *All What Jazz* contrasts amusingly with the absence of any such 'argufying' in the Preface to the *Oxford Book of Twentieth-Century English Verse* (1973). Larkin's anthology was, in its way, as controversial as Yeats's had been thirty-seven years before, and for somewhat similar reasons. It amazed by its resolute bias towards minor poets and traditional poetic forms, away from the aggressively modern and experimental. Yet it is hard to see how the task of selection could have been performed better. No one needed another *Faber Book of Modern Verse,* and by consulting his own taste and prejudice Larkin produced a thoroughly enjoyable book full of delights all the better for being unexpected. Yet those who looked for strident denunciations of modernism were disappointed. Knowing full well the turbulent sea of controversy that awaited the launching of his book, Larkin kept his preface low-key, modest, almost bureaucratic in its blandness. He defined his scope and offered his acknowledgements: no more.

To discover Larkin's poetic, therefore, we must look at the poems themselves, which is as it should be. The Larkin of the 1970s is the Larkin of *High Windows*, and one of the most striking features of that book is its preoccupation with the past. There is much nostalgia, and seen in context 'Going, Going' appears as one of a group of poems about the English past whose loss Larkin fears. This anxiety is justified, although certain reviewers were right to point out how little in the way of a living England is implied by the catalogue of loss in 'Going, Going':

> The shadows, the meadows, the lanes,
> The guildhalls, the carved choirs,

are lines that would do as caption for an English Tourist Board poster. The selection of snapshot detail is too perfectly decorative.

The book begins with 'To the Sea', an evocation of the day-at-the-seaside which has been an English tradition since the end of the last century, and ends with 'The Explosion', whose timeless theme—the violent death of peaceful, unremarkable human beings and its baffling impact on those who survive them—is set by a careful reference to detail (men wearing 'moleskins', coins still made of gold) at a historical distance from us, somewhere before the First World War. 'Show Saturday', a poem closely related to 'To the Sea', calls up another English custom, 'half an annual pleasure, half a rite',—the country agricultural show—and prays for its continuance ('Let it always be there') just as 'To the Sea' comments, with mingled wonder and relief, 'Still going on, all of it, still going on!'

A more detached fascination with the past is evident in sections I and III of 'Livings'—one the soliloquy of a commercial traveller set, specifically, in 1929, the other a glimpse of High Table at an Oxbridge college as it might have been on almost any evening from the late seventeenth to the early nineteenth century. The mood of 'Livings' III is explored further in 'The Card Players', which conjures up and gently parodies Dutch and Flemish genre-painting (Teniers, perhaps, or Hobbema). Both poems describe a world grotesque, uncouth and yet radiant with an aura of the marvellous which is felt so strongly just because of the entirely uninhibited behaviour and talk of the figures before us. The dons of 'Livings' III, like Jan van Hogspeuw and Old Prijck, are elemental beings. Jan 'pisses at the dark', Dirk Dogstoerd 'holds a cinder to his clay with tongs', Old Prijck 'snores with the gale'; the dons, arguing with bibulous gusto about religion, money, sex, death, diseases, politics and food, are as secure, as untroubled by self-doubt (and, one feels, as little concerned with the shivering 'sizar' sitting late over his books) as the bells which 'discuss the hour's gradations' at the prompting of numerous more-or-less accurate clocks all over town, or the 'Chaldean constellations' overhead. In both poems a sense of immense cosiness—'The secret, bestial peace!'—is communicated. The scenes are sealed in by the cold and dark of the night, but far more by their distance in time. Such worlds never existed, we know; but approximation to them was possible, we feel, in a simpler world long since annihilated.

In a less interesting way, 'Dublinesque' also places its subject in the past, with its 'leg-of-mutton sleeves,/And ankle-length dresses'. Given the funeral which is its subject, its economical use of unexpected detail—the dancing, and someone clapping time—and its conclusion, enigmatic yet adding a touch of sentimentality with its final cadence:

A voice is heard singing
Of Kitty, or Katy,
As if the name meant once
All love, all beauty

—the poem could be a tribute to the early Joyce, a new story for *Dubliners*. 'How Distant' likewise implies a story, and takes a similar period, around 1900, to give resonance to its subject. These poems—numerically one-third of the collection—contribute a very strong ingredient to the overall flavour of *High Windows*. In no previous collection has a concern with the social and historical past played so large a part, though Larkin has of course written numerous important poems which make full use of history: 'MCMXIV', for example, 'Deceptions', and 'An Arundel Tomb', to name those that come instantly to mind.

Of the other poems in *High Windows* three are satirical squibs. 'Posterity' and 'Homage to a Government' are forceful in a rather limited way, and 'This Be The Verse' is a splendid exposure of facile pessimism. The latter reads like a parody of Housman and if intended as such it beats well into second place Pound's 'Mr Housman's Message'. The remaining poems are of the kind most often associated with Larkin: wry, self-critical, not hopeful but conscious of the lure of hope and of the other fine prospects which to varying degrees cheat us in life.

Yet important and surprising developments are seen at once when these poems are compared to the earlier work. The title poem, 'High Windows', takes on a characteristic Larkin subject—the ageing observer regarding the sexual behaviour of the young first with a touch of prurience ('I see a couple of kids/And guess he's fucking her'), next with envy ('this is Paradise/Everyone old has dreamed of all their lives') and then, seeing a parallel between their apparent sexual freedom and the re-

ligious freedom he perhaps appeared to have when he was young, getting
the whole business of the human expectation of happiness into perspective. But the final resolution, if such it can be called, is not directly
stated and the poem explicitly emphasizes the fact:

> Rather than words comes the thought of high windows:
> The sun-comprehending glass,
> And beyond it, the deep blue air, that shows
> Nothing, and is nowhere, and is endless.

This, perhaps, is the ultimate void in which human life is lived. Not altogether an unfriendly void; indeed, it sounds attractive, though dizzying.
The young, who are expected by their elders to go, in an oddly mixed
metaphor, 'down the long slide/Like free bloody birds' will be pitched
out into that void some day, and if they really are birds they should fare
well enough. But they seem not to be, and endless nowhere sounds rather
like death. These and many other less identifiable notions are evoked, but
the lines remain enigmatic. The image itself seems related to that which
ends an earlier poem, 'Water', and there are verbal echoes:

> I should raise in the east
> A glass of water
> Where any-angled light
> Would congregate endlessly.

Both poems refer to religion, and one feels that the 'high windows' might
be the clerestory of a church: where else do we see, from inside, high
windows? (Admittedly the phrase occurs in *A Girl in Winter*, Larkin's
novel of 1947, where the windows are those of a library.)

  But the striking development is the turn to symbolism rather than discursive statement. The earlier poems tend to offer stated judgements:
'how we live measures our own nature'; 'Never such innocence again';
'Life is first boredom, then fear'. But poem after poem in *High Windows*
refuses to give us anything so consolingly tangible. The three 'Livings'
are presented without final comment: we make of them what we please.
'Friday Night at the Royal Station Hotel' evokes a mood of curious, alert
loneliness and ends on a cryptic note reminiscent of the early Auden:

> The headed paper, made for writing home
> (If home existed) letters of exile: *Now*
> *Night comes on. Waves fold behind villages.*

'Money' ends, again, with windows, but this time we look out from them
to a landscape which represents only in the most tenuous and oblique way
the 'singing' of money. Always Larkin seems to be aiming for the symbol
which will resonate in the mind, calling forth harmonies that have
nothing to do with the carefully limited, scrupulously precise resolutions
of most of the earlier poems. The most notable instance is probably 'The

Card-Players', which ends with a line of exclamation—
     Rain, wind and fire! The secret, bestial peace!
as if the poet is suddenly awed to silence by his own subject.

'The Card-Players' is a fascinating poem in several ways. There is something factitious about it; yet it remains interesting after many readings. It suffers from a problem which besets most poems which describe pictures, in that the imagined picture communicates a static quality which is out of place in a poem. Enumerating details which we know would fit together in a pictorial composition does not produce a satisfying poetic structure. Larkin conscientiously makes his figures move and perform actions, but there remains something arbitrary about the scene. Nothing really happens, nor do the figures relate to one another in any way. There are details which seem to imply some special meaning but yield nothing. Why, for example, does Jan hit the Queen of Hearts when he 'gobs at the grate'? The gesture is the most decisive and surprising action of the poem. Its crude slapstick, and the particularizing of the card, have the air of making a point and providing a climax to the poem. But what do they mean? Can the line really be a rhetorical flourish, a meaningless shock-effect? It seems so.

At the same time the poem seems to embody symbolic patterns of a kind untypical of Larkin's mature work. Great play is made throughout with the four elements, but the final line mentions only three. 'Rain, wind and fire!'—there are water, air and fire but where is earth? The answer, clearly, is that earth is represented by the men themselves. When Dirk 'holds a cinder to his clay' something more than the lighting of a pipe is implied. Once alert to such patterns in *High Windows* one notices a surprising number. Is it without significance, for example, that 'Sad Steps' and 'Solar'—a moon poem and a sun poem—are on facing pages? That 'Livings' III ends with a reference to astrology, or that the speaker of 'Livings' II sets out 'divining-cards' after dinner, for all the world as if he expected a visit from Mrs Equitone or Madame Sosostris? Can one conceive of the Larkin of *The Less Deceived* so much as mentioning astrology or the Tarot without obvious irony?

Larkin has said on radio (in 1972) that he would like to write '*different* kinds of poems, that might be by different people. Someone once said that the great thing is not to be different from other people, but to be different from yourself' (I quote from David Timms' *Philip Larkin*, Edinburgh 1973) and this is what he has done. But these aspects of *High Windows* should lead us to think again about his relationship with Yeats, under whose influence his early poems were so obviously written. Yeats can be a powerful and dangerous influence—'pervasive as garlic', in Larkin's words—but in *The North Ship* Larkin's submission to his style was quite exceptionally thorough. Most commentators have been surprisingly eager to accept Larkin's apparently ingenuous account of his early poetic development, in which chance plays so large a part and choice such a small one. In the Introduction to *The North Ship* Larkin beguilingly portrays himself first as 'isolated in Shropshire with a complete Yeats stolen from the local girls' school', then as landing in 'digs' where the early sunlight in his east-facing bedroom compelled him to read something in the mornings, which something happened to be the poems of Hardy whose impact provoked an 'undramatic, complete and permanent' reaction against Yeats. Was ever a professional librarian and dedicated poet so mercilessly pushed about by a couple of stray books? Really, the story won't stand a great deal of scrutiny. After *High Windows* it begins to look, rather, as if the poetry of Larkin's 'middle period' had been a conscious, disciplined attempt to throw off the Yeatsian stranglehold: a criticism of all Yeats's attitudes and techniques as the price of poetic independence. Now, at last, something of the earlier style has been allowed to return to the surface, revealing that Larkin was never really either the narrow-minded, self-pitying moaner of his hostile critics or the hard-headed 'poet for the common man' of his admirers. The mask was meticulously constructed, but a mask it was.

Larkin's finest achievement of the 1970s, however, has been a group of poems which eschew both symbolist experiment and the limitations of satire and social criticism. A small number of poems, in particular 'The Building', 'The Old Fools', and the uncollected 'Aubade', have confronted the things we can hardly bear to face—sickness, old age and death—with a degree of nervous honesty rare even in poetry and virtually unknown in common life.

'The Old Fools' approaches its subject in a deliberately heartless manner which shocks in a rather superficial way until we admit that we ourselves have inevitably at some time held, even if only briefly and guiltily, some such attitude to senility. The poem moves on to attempt a sympathetic understanding of the disoriented inner world of the aged. Larkin's conjecture that

> Perhaps being old is like having lighted rooms
> Inside your head, and people in them, acting.
> People you know, yet can't quite name. . . .

is neither novel nor especially convincing; indeed, the poem is not remarkable for strength of thought. What is truly admirable is the fiendish cunning with which it lures the reader into a detached, mildly patronizing curiosity about the very old, who are assumed to be safely over there in the third person, before springing its hideous trap:

> Can they never tell
> What is dragging them back, and how it will end?
>
>   . . . Well,
> We shall find out.

And the last line is not a mere punch-line, for our instinctive reaction is to start again at the beginning and re-read the poem with a new sense of urgency. The old fools are our future selves.

'The Building' adopts a rather similar strategy, avoiding the word 'hospital' so that the truth closes in on us slowly and with menace as we read. The Building becomes the embodiment of a sort of religion: its patients are 'white congregations. . . set apart above'; its purpose is

> a struggle to transcend
> The thought of dying, for unless its powers
> Outbuild cathedrals nothing contravenes
> The coming dark.
> Illness is its equivalent of original sin, for
> something has gone wrong.
> It must be error of a serious sort,
> For see how many floors it needs, how tall
> It's grown, and how much money goes
> In trying to correct it.
> The building cannot succeed in its purpose, for, entering,
> All know they are going to die.
> Not yet, perhaps not here, but in the end,
> And somewhere like this.

Death itself is the subject of the uncollected 'Aubade', which appeared in the *Times Literary Supplement*, 23 December 1977. Traditionally the *aubade* is a dawn-song; its medieval and Renaissance exemplars are mostly love-poems regretting the dawn that separates lovers. Larkin's poem, however, adds one more to the group of fine twentieth-century *aubades* which have more to do with the thoughts that besiege unquiet modern sleepers when they awake, tired and defenceless, in the small hours. Empson's 'Aubade' ('Hours before dawn we were woken by the quake') and MacNeice's ('a precise dawn/Of sallow and grey bricks, and newsboys crying war') are exceeded in bleakness by Larkin's, which circles again and again about its subject, turning back each time to come at the incomprehensible horror, trying one escape-route after another (religion, metaphysics, courage, company and alcohol) and finding them all securely blocked. As an exercise in facing the fact of death—'plain as a wardrobe'—'Aubade' is effective above all because it resists the pressure poetic form exerts towards resolution. Refusing to reach a point of security, transcendence or consolation as a means of rounding off the poem, Larkin closes by allowing the speaker's sense of desolation to leak out, as day breaks, into the objects of waking life: the telephones, the offices, the postmen.

Poems like these, finding their terrible subjects at the heart of mundane daily experience and presenting them with an authority almost bardic and yet quite free from romantic trappings, form a substantial achievement, and one earned by the discipline of working, during previous decades, within the limited poetic of *The Less Deceived* and *The Whitsun Weddings*.

Charles Tomlinson

MANY who assent to the proposition, poetry is the best that language can do, are reluctant to concede its corollary, that poetic thought is the best thought. It would be fruitless to argue the case, but its most persuasive illustration, the poet among contemporary poets writing in English whose work might convince a sceptic of its truth, is Charles Tomlinson. Volume by volume his poetry has broadened its experiential, emotional and technical range, but most remarkable has been the continuity and coherence of its thinking. Coherence rather than consistency is the word for the intellectual achievement of major poetry (for this is major poetry): it allows for the different emphases which in a work of systematic thought would be ruled out as contradictions. Tomlinson's successive remakings of his poetic world, unlike Yeats's, have involved no dismantling of the past: it is a major *body* of work, a continuous process of thought. All the poems comment on each other, adding to the total structure, and each poem means more by its relation to the whole. The new poems are not merely additions but have the same modifying effect on the order formed by the preceding poems as Eliot says the truly new work has on a whole tradition of literature; as the body of his poetry grows, one's conception of it as a whole and relative evaluation of the constituent parts must constantly be readjusted.

The customary division of Tomlinson's work into two groups, poems of the natural world and poems of the human world, is a misleading one. It has been inferred that, cutting his teeth on natural phenomena—he is, after all, also a painter—his poetry 'took on' human subjects to enlarge its range. It was noted that some of the things described in the early volumes—houses, cities, walls, humanized landscapes—were, in any case, already saturated in human presence and traditions. Blurb-writers and reviewers have continued gratefully to record the appearance of poems on social, political, and historical themes. Though these poems deserve their high regard, the singling of them out for special mention perhaps intimates an only partial appreciation of the human meaning in what is still the larger group of his poems. Tomlinson has commented that the world of natural fact—of space, heights and distances, forms and patterns—entered by so many of his poems, the world of air, clouds, trees, water, in which the actions of cold, heat, wind, snow, light and shadow are re-created and analysed, contains human images or has human implications. Even this, arousing, as it might, suspicion of something arbitrary in the metaphorical process, could be misleading. For what these poems prove is that the relation between sensory and mental experience is one not of analogy but identity. 'Perception' is a word that assumes the identity. When the poet casts 'a glance. . . .into the depths of distance' ('The Greeting'), obviously the language of sight is also the language of understanding; the phrase tells us without analogy the human meaning of such seeing: it is the distanced, impartial, total, self-exceeding view. Eye and mind have the same potential for clarity and stability, the same aspirations to accuracy, wholeness, and perspective. The eye's participation in the life of space affords the same range of satisfaction, too, as does the mind's entry into a social and temporal world. In 'Witnesses', 'Hillside woods. . . dense with summer. . . the profusion, the protrusion of leaves', are 'an aerial city' because the eye's and mind's release into the complex relations of their 'jostled surfaces. . . nudging. . . Beckoning, bridging the underdeeps', and their enjoyment of the way the dense foliage, blocking out further distances and filling the air with an assertion of crowded life, articulates space by giving it boundaries and three-dimensional depth, are also the mind's enjoyment of an earth enriched with human meaning and its release from self into a world of others.

In 1979 Tomlinson's poems of the 50s, collected in *The Necklace* (1955) and *Seeing is Believing* (1960), have a different look. They sounded a note of ascetic anti-romanticism which at the time, in the wake of Dylan Thomas's influence, we took to be their central strength. Linguistic restraint, the ordering of confusion, the moderation of expectations—a literary regimen of chastening, corrective severity—were what these poems recommended and vigorously demonstrated. We received Constable's 'labour of observation/In face of meteorological fact', in 'A Meditation on John Constable', as part of a polemic against subjectivism. Submission of the eye to the objective world—'for what he saw/Discovered what he was'—and of the mind to a consciousness of natural limits, as the oxen, described in 'Oxen: Ploughing at Fiesole', proudly submit to the necessity of service, 'Content to remain content' (both acquiescent and contained): these were the imperatives we heeded. We noticed too that the poems disclosed not only an objectivist but an Augustan frame of mind, with a diction of civil Latinity and a verse movement that sometimes echoed the balances and antitheses of Augustan poetry. These qualities are undoubtedly there, and we felt their invigorative power, but the growing-points in Tomlinson's poetry were elsewhere. In the light of the later work we can see, what the oxen's proud gesture hints, that sane acknowledgement of necessity is only a pre-condition for more ambitious feats, and we pay more attention now to the conclusion of the Constable poem, which speaks of the humanization of the object: 'The artist lies/For the *improvement* of truth. Believe him'.

The improvement of truth is a Romantic prerogative and the inter-relations between man and nature is a Romantic theme. The skirmish against the neo-romantics of the forties and the comic portrait of the Symbolists' world in 'Antecedents' distracted us from the obvious. For one measure of Tomlinson's major stature is that he has, by way of Ruskin and Lawrence, opened up serious communication again with Wordsworth and Coleridge. A poet whose first influences were Blake and Yeats, energetic Romantics who favoured the clean hard outline, he combines an Augustan vigour of mind with, say, Hopkins's passionate interest in sense experience expressed in a muscular, kinaesthetic language. Not judicious restraint but a 'seething' excitement is the key quality ('seething' was Williams's word for the poems in *Seeing is Believing*). In a recent sequence, 'Movements' (*Written on Water*, 1972), which are themselves celebrations of the poetic art, he writes that 'man/In an exterior, tutelary spirit/Of his own inheritance, speaks/To celebrate'. He has compared the poem to a ceremony of initiation (*The Poem as Initiation*, 1967), and he has been drawn to describe ceremonies by the correspondence between their ritual and his poetic consecration of reality. He represents the dancers in 'The Matachines' as saying: 'whatever we/do we mean/as praise'. The Romantic word 'joy' does not appear, but we half expect it. Both in 'Oxen: Ploughing at Fiesole' and in the later 'Swimming Chenango Lake' (*The Way of a World*, 1969) we are very close to the religious paradox, 'Whose service is perfect freedom'. Of the lake he writes;

> Its coldness
> Holding him to itself, he grants the grasp,
> For to swim is also to take hold
> On water's meaning, to move in its embrace
> And to be, between grasp and grasping, free.
> He reaches in-and-through to that space
> The body is heir to —

a space that constitutes the boundaries of possibility but also releases self from its isolation. Tomlinson speaks a language which scarcely distinguishes between submission (recognition, acknowledgement) and freedom. A series of poems, 'Manscapes' (*The Way In*, 1974), occasioned by a visit to Stoke, the 'grey-black' environment of his youth, does not— and could not— 'explain' this poetic combination but provides an insight into the *personal* compulsion originally motivating his poems.

> It was a language of water, light and air
> I sought—to speak myself free of a world
> Whose stoic lethargy seemed the one reply
> To horizons and to streets that blocked them back
> In a monotone fume, a bloom of grey.

The disciplined submission of the eye to the natural world was the will's contrivance of a visual and moral liberation: release as much from the blocked views of a life without possibility to vistas of hope as from the violated nature of the industrial Midlands. The water that seeped up from underground to fill the 'marl-pits', which give the poem its title, 'In slow reclaimings, shimmers, balancings' was, like his poetry, 'a second nature', affording glimpses of, and the incentive to restore, a primal perfection— 'And words and water came of the same source'.

'Appearance' (*Written on Water*) may be read as Tomlinson's rewriting in the 70s, or a correction of our misreading, of a 50s poem: having the same preoccupations yet giving a little more prominence to the transformative power of the imagination, the mood celebratory rather than admonitory.

> Snow brings into view the far hills:
>   The winter sun feels for their surfaces:
> Of the little we know of them, full half
>   Is in the rushing out to greet them, the restraint
> (Unfelt till then) melted at the look
>   That gathers them in, to a meeting of expectations
> With appearances.

The delight in the object, as the Constable poem also said, is part of our knowledge of it. There is the snowscape (fact) and there is light: light, as always in Tomlinson's poetry, transfigures the scene and melts restraint of feeling. And light on the snow not only delivers the scene clearly to the eye but comes as 'a glance/Of fire, sizing our ignorance up,/As the image seizes on us'. The object is still primary—what we see discovers what we are—but unmistakably the reversal indicates a process not of self-denial but of self-expansion; seizing, sizing—as the consonance tells us, the one presumes the other: 'sizing us up', the view both measures our former ignorance and enlarges us to its size in our increase of knowledge. Whereas in 'Tramontana at Lerici' (the trumpet-call of *Seeing is Believing*) keenness of sensation was presented as a threat to the subjectivity of 'politicians and romantics' and the emphasis was on the chill impenetrability, the resistance to human apprehension, of the non-human world, here 'the cold/Hills' invite 'a reciprocation,/Ask words of us, answering images,/To their range, their heights'. 'Song is being', said Rilke; Tomlinson answers, in 'Melody' (*The Way In*), 'Song is the measure, rather,/Of being's spread and height', and being, we learn from 'Appearance', is not self but self and its circumference of space, or as much of it as the senses can recover from the world beyond self. Nature, as far as it will allow (there *are* boundaries, negotiable boundaries), is humanized by the self 'rushing out to greet' it, and self, given the freedom and scope of space, is naturalized; the poem celebrates a reciprocal relationship and affirms, as Wordsworth's poems do, the existence of a human-natural world, in which 'you wear/The vestment of space' ('Mistlines', *Written on Water*).

This is not, however, a still world but one seething with movement: time is its element as much as space. Flux, transience, the interdependence of creation and destruction are as central to the 'nature' poems—'evanescences of daily air'—as to the poems of human, social, and historical content. The order sought in his poems is not the received, sanctioned order of Augustan poetry but an order won by labour from confusion. The process is imaged in 'The Way of a World' first spatially as the supple resistance of boughs to the 'weightless anarchy/Of air' in high wind, and then as memory's comparable rescue of the whole scene from the flow of time, recovery not merely of the scene but of its 'worth', its meaning as an image of the will to find 'the shapes of change', definition and permanence in 'a world that must decay' ('Mistlines').

The muscular vigour of Tomlinson's verse enacts the workings of will. The quite literal muscular effort of the 'rower', in the poem of that title in *Written on Water*, is the counterpart of the poet's straining to impart definition to a 'nebulous' morning of veiled sunlight and to introduce a human sense of purpose into the 'drifting' scene of 'a slack tide'.

> And though the ripple
> Is beneath him now—the pull and beat
> Unfelt when further in—he cuts athwart it
> Making his way, to the liquid counterpulse
> Of blades that draw him outwards to complete
> The bay's half-circle with his own.

The rower's exertions, like the mind's, establish a relation-in-tension with the element in which they are applied, in opposition to and collaboration with the resistant non-human world. 'Athwart', rather than 'across'—suggesting deliberate counteraction and recalling its opposite, the 'thwarted possibility' visible in the 'meanness' of a blighted industrial landscape—is a characteristic preference. The aim is to complete the half-circle of the bay with the reverse half-circle of the boat's track, giving the natural world its human complement, plotting (in one sense) the space between shore, cliff and boat, and (in another sense) the otherwise eventless stretch of time, which had been—both space and time—until then 'a plotless tale'.

Memory and will, notably, in this poetry work to give form, purpose and value to life in space and time. In this, reason is their accomplice. Tomlinson's is increasingly, to an extraordinary degree, a poetry of colons: that is, a poetry which 'plots' its tales and spaces and insists on logical and analogical relations, on symmetries, equivalences, evolutions and consequences, on the connection of parts—but parts that are multiple and minutely and vividly particularized—to the whole: it gives us the reasoned variety of a single vision. In quoting the opening lines of 'Casarola' (*The Shaft*, 1978), however, I mean to illustrate more than this.

> Cliffs come sheering down into woodland here:
> The trees—they are chestnuts—spread to a further drop

> Where an arm of water rushes through unseen
>   Still lost in leaves: you can hear it
> Squandering its way towards the mill
>   A path crossing a hillslope and a bridge
> Leads to at last: the stones lie there
>   Idle beside it: they were cut from the cliff
> And the same stone rises in wall and roof
>   Not of the mill alone, but of shed on shed
> Whose mossed tiles like a city of the dead
>   Grow green in the wood.

The order in which the details of the scene are released to us unfolds their meaning: the discipline of the eye (and ear) is also the discipline of the mind. Uncropped, 'the chestnuts/Dropping, feed the roots they rose from', but the cliffs, dropping down to woodland and then again to the water below, no longer feed human purpose with the stone it needs. The eye is taken over by the energies of nature, is precipated sheer down the cliff and over the 'further drop', in imagination 'rushes' with the river and expectantly crosses hillslope and bridge, to arrive with a sense of anti-climax and failure, however, at its opposite, a scene of stillness and lassitude. The second 'drop' leading to 'lost' and the explicit 'squandering' of the water's power prepare us for this final disappointment. Then the eye 'rises' in re-enactment of the mill's and the sheds' erection that had once been the human counterbalance and answer to the falling power of nature. Now nature commands, its energies unchecked as unshared, its 'green' life making and signifying 'a city of the dead'. The details are patiently gathered in and the relations between them plotted, but the discipline of observation and reason brings a completeness and order that transform record into vision: making the world intelligible, they *release* meaning. And the meaning, here and everywhere, is more than the sum of the facts. Labour faithfully and a grace will be added. Here is 'a 'desolation/Of still-perfect masonry'—the present fact joined to the past achievement, holding an image of hope—and therefore 'There is a *beauty*/In this abandonment'. Complete truth is a marriage of fact and possibility, of what is and what is not but has been or might be; this in the human world parallels the visual 'meeting of expectations/With appearances'.

Tomlinson's poetry has always been a celebration of the possible; knowing this, we perhaps did not comprehend its full implications, however, until *The Way of a World* (1969), which included poems with titles like 'Eden' and 'Adam'. In the former he writes:

> I have seen Eden. It is a light of place
>   As much as the place itself; not a face
> Only, but the expression on that face: the gift
>   Of forms constellates cliff and stones.

'Lost in the meagre/Streets of our dispossession', there is no bridge back but 'the thread of patience, no way/But the will to wish back Eden'. Arden, he writes in a later poem, 'In Arden' (*The Shaft*), is where we live, a place in time that echoes with memories of eternity, 'voices/Of the place that rises through this place'. 'Before the Dance' (a Navajo dance), a poem about the quality of suspended time in the Indians' waiting for the dance to begin, captures the sense of the co-presence of time and eternity in a surprising formal invention. They refuse to measure time, he says, 'the moment/is expansible'; then later, repeating the phrase *sotto voce*,

> they wait, sitting
> (the moment)
> on the earth floor
> (is expansible).

The will to find the Eden image, notable in his graphics, is also every-where in the poems, even in the poems recalling the grimy, faded shadow-ings of civility in the Stoke of his boyhood, now that it is being destroyed and remade into 'mannerless high risers'. For he writes 'to rescue/What is no longer there'.

> I thought I knew this place, this face
>   A little worn, a little homely.
> But the look that shadows softened
>   And the light could grace, keeps flowing away from me
> In daily change; its features rendered down,
>   Collapse expressionless. . . .

This stanza from the title poem of *The Way In* even remembers the open-ing lines of 'Eden' quoted above. The form, the features, the expression on its face, its manners, constitute its homeliness, the human lineaments that dwelling imparts to a place; this is the edifice of civility, and the light of possibility in which it was built is the Eden light that 'could grace' it.

  'Seeing is believing' was his battle-cry in the 50s, and though more was intended by the phrase, and the poems so entitled had more to offer, than a bracing scepticism, the words, and sometimes the poems, smacked a little of doubting Thomas. Tomlinson has never ceased to see clearly but the word he found for his gift in 'Eden' is 'clairvoyant', a clear seeing that sees through from Arden to its 'rhyme' Eden. If seeing is now clair-voyance, believing is, rather, the placing of fact in the strong, transfigur-ative light of possibility. He can afford to speak, in 'Mushrooms' (*The Shaft*), with a certain insouciance now of the 'myth of clarities' (though the message itself, defiance of the literal, was proclaimed in 'A Meditation on John Constable'): 'For realer than a myth of clarities/Are the meanings that you read and are not there', the resemblances more real than the thing seen, since 'a resemblance, too,/Is real and all its likes and links stay true/To the weft of seeing'. This explains the role of 'seem' and 'as if' in Tomlinson's poetry. England, mapped by arterial major roads, he notes in 'Bridges' (*The Way In*), is 'lost to silence now', but the old men who habitually watch from the bridges 'seem not to hear the roar in Albion's veins,/As though the quiet, rebegotten as they lean, survived/Through them alone'. It is not unlike the role of seeming in Wordsworth's poetry: it allows the illusion of desire, the 'will to wish back Eden', to transform fact without disguising what 'Mushrooms' calls the 'sleights of eye' practised.

I must now qualify my remarks about the logical and analogical relations exemplified in 'Casarola'. For, though carefully spun, the web of meaning in that poem is a more delicate thing than it is in his earlier work in that verse form: details, seeming less marshalled, having a living casualness, their significance inconspicuously embedded in the poem. In this it is typical of many poems in the two most recent volumes, *The Way In* and *The Shaft*. A comparison between the poems in *The Way of a World* (1969) which have revolution as their subject and those in *The Shaft* (1978) would demonstrate this. 'Charlotte Corday', for instance, is a more calmly impersonal poem than 'Assassin'; its diagnosis of revolutionary idealism is no less trenchant for letting an enquiring wonderment influence the tone and feeling. Now and again a poem has the seemingly off-hand anecdotal quality of Edward Thomas. It is not a question of influence: I do not mean the two poems in *The Shaft*, 'Old Man's Beard' and '. . . Or Traveller's Joy', that openly refer to Thomas, but poems like 'Mushrooms' and its neighbour, 'Providence'; though they also have affinities with the well-bred casualness of Graves in the 60s or, in the case of 'Providence', with a poem of the forties, 'Language of the Seasons'. Many poems share with 'Mushrooms' a quality almost of insouciance, as of one who is not so much a signpost to as a dweller in the transformed world of his imagination.

This is what distinguishes 'Hill Walk' (*The Way In*), for example, from its predecessors. Tomlinson recalls a walk in an unfamiliar, Provençal countryside of 'unnameable foreign flowers' on a cold day of a 'reluctant April'—reluctant to admit Spring and reluctant to yield itself to the embrace of human imagination. Yet among the flowers,

> rosemary and thyme
> Assuaged the coldness of the air, their fragrance
> So intense, it seemed as if the thought
> Of that day's rarity had sharpened sense, as now
> It sharpens memory.

Though 'the thought/Of that day's rarity', by sharpening sense and memory, rescues it from a reluctant (later an 'inconstant') April—as also the walls he sees, 'half undone/By time', are 'patched against its sure effacement'—yet the day feels like a grace of time rather than something won from it by an action of the will, as it was in 'The Way of a World' and

'The Rower'. The Edenic implications are stronger. 'Time used us well that rhymed/With its own herbs', he continues—thyme with time, that is, and, as Arden rhymes with Eden, so rosemary with memory. It uses them well, too, in letting them reach the hill-top, which they 'crested idly', without effort, and letting their eyes measure the space covered and the time taken.

> All stretched to the first fold
> Of that unending landscape where we trace
>   Through circuits, drops and terraces
> The outworks, ruinous and overgrown,
>   Where space on space has labyrinthed past time:
> The unseizable citadel glimmering back at us,
>   We contemplated no assault, no easy victory.

Seeing the 'unending landscape' of space and time, they see that it is their home, that they are part of it. The citadel is where they have come from and where they will return: it is, as I understand it, the Eden source in which the end is also the beginning.

Tomlinson's 'will to wish back Eden' differs from that of the revolutionary idealists mentioned in 'Prometheus' (*The Way of a World*), for whom

> Each sense was to have been reborn
> Out of a storm of perfumes and light
> To a white world, an in-the-beginning,

only in the continence that knows it cannot *storm* the citadel. For him the possibility of Eden is an acknowledgement and assuagement of time and necessity, not the defeat of it. The relationship with time, like the language used, is a civil one—a relationship that calls on such words as 'truce', 'negotiation' and 'comity'. Not only are the human 'outworks', remnants of civilization, evidence of the Eden wish at work in society, but civility is a language of Eden, importing humanity even into a relationship that acknowledges the non-human.

Definition and flow:
Thom Gunn in the 1970s

THOM GUNN's *My Sad Captains,* first published in 1961, has two
sections quite distinct in character, the first consisting of poems in traditional metres, the second of apparently lighter pieces in syllabic verse.
Gunn has since renounced syllabics in favour of free verse, but his
publications still require the reader to accept that metrical poems are different in kind from poems in 'open' forms. D.H. Lawrence, in the Preface to the American edition of his *New Poems* (an essay whose influence
Gunn has acknowledged), arguing the case for such a distinction, wrote of
free verse as pre-eminently the medium of present-tense meditation, of
perception in the process of taking form. By contrast—so he argued—the
great stanzaic poems deal with ends and beginnings, past and future:

> It is in the realm of all that is perfect. It is of the nature of all that is
> complete and consummate. This completeness, this consum-
> mateness, the finality and the perfection are conveyed in exquisite
> form: the perfect symmetry, the rhythm which returns upon itself like
> a dance where the hands link and loosen and link for the supreme
> moment of the end. . . .But there is another kind of poetry: the poetry
> of that which is at hand: the immediate present. In the immediate
> present there is no perfection, no consummation, nothing finished.
> The strands are all flying, quivering, intermingling into the web, the
> waters are shaking the moon. There is no round consummate moon on
> the face of running water, nor on the face of the unfinished tide.

Though Gunn's poetry is hardly dance-like, it certainly used to be remarkable for rhythms returning upon themselves, for the finality of its
meditations; yet at the same time what did it celebrate but flux, risk, the
unpredictable future, the unfinished artefact? Although much of its
interest lay in the tension between form and content, one is hardly surprised to learn that Gunn has come increasingly to admire a poetry which
possesses the very qualities that move him in life. All that the poetry of
Whitman and Lawrence, Williams and Snyder must have lacked to so
skilled and deliberate an artificer was a sense of the necessary and inevitable artificiality of poetry, the supreme fiction.
  When Gunn finally discarded the somewhat arbitrary discipline of
syllabic verse in the mid-sixties, it was mainly to William Carlos Williams
that he turned for a model of free-verse prosody: the right choice, surely,

for few modern poets have combined Williams's level of craftsmanship with such apparent informality. Now, ten years later, in *Jack Straw's Castle* (1976), the relationship between Gunn's two modes is becoming clearer. In the metrical poems the rhythms are looser, the language more conversational, the structures based more on sequences of perception than on patterns of logical thought. The free verse gains in authenticity from Gunn's sense of how a poem is made and how its making must relate to what already exists in the world. A sense of the limits of both flux and artifice is built into the poetry. Lawrence was original in his insistence that the two kinds of prosody fulfil different functions and must therefore continue to co-exist. Metre will still be called upon to embody the products of concentrated thought, to give the semblance of immutable form to (relatively) immutable verities. For this it depends on an element of predictability in its movement. Free verse, however—if it is wholly distinct from metre, as Lawrence's is and Williams's—depends on the opposite, on our inability to predict the rhythmic outcome. Gunn, like Williams, plays on this, tantalizing the reader with weak line-endings and long sinuous sentences broken into short lines. This procedure emphasises the overall rhythm (as against the line-as-unit) and suggests the hesitancy of the human voice as it shapes its utterances. The poem seems to discover its meanings as it proceeds, as if it were a sequence of thought enacted before us, affected by the moment: we seem to acquire a new awareness of thought (and poem) as *process*. This method—exemplified by a poem as early as 'Touch', published in 1967—enables Gunn not only to describe the world, but at the same time to dramatize the ways in which we come to know it, in terms which point ultimately to his own beliefs about its nature.

But there is nothing especially new about such discoveries. On the contrary, they are based on ideas associated with the adolescence of the modern movement. Their importance for us lies in the fact that Gunn, as a poet once associated with quite different attitudes to the function of poetry, has rediscovered them for himself. When he wrote *My Sad Captains*, Gunn was virtually a disciple of that implacable anti-Modernist, Yvor Winters, whose continuing influence on him has been considerable. Yet Gunn today can write of Ezra Pound as 'probably the greatest poet we have had in this century'; and any poet who turns to Williams as a model must ultimately come to terms with a Poundian view of literature.

Winters, a classicist and neo-humanist in the Jonsonian mould, held that a good poem was a rational structure composed of connected propositions, to which form was the objective equivalent. As such, he rejected the irrationalist assumptions of Modernist poetics as firmly as the Right-wing politics associated with its founders. For politically Winters was the most redoubtable of liberals. He held that political and literary irrationalism make men the victims of their history and experience. Poetry was only of value if its end was understanding; the poem was not a kind of secondary organism that partakes of life, but a skilfully contrived artefact set apart from the flux it seeks to evaluate. But Winters's view of understanding itself often seems excessively restricted; he always considers it in terms of completed perceptions and achieved ideas. For Gunn, ideas and understanding are more closely entwined in the process of language. He has written of Gary Snyder that 'like most serious poets he is mainly concerned at finding himself on a barely known planet in an almost unknown universe, where he must attempt to create and discover meanings. Discovery of a meaning is always also the creation of it, and creation is an act of discovery.' Then, of one specific poem, 'it is. . . .a series of pictorial perceptions made by a man embedded in time, who advances into the sensory world opened by his waking'. This conception of poetry and the terms Gunn uses are largely dependent on Winters's example. What he adds is a greater respect for the force of sensuous and instinctual awareness.

Gunn would now probably agree with Donald Davie who, in a recent study of Pound, takes issue with Winters's view of the *Cantos* but finds his objections to them illuminating. Winters, he writes,

> conceiving of an idea as that which could be stated in the form of a proposition, recorded his experience of reading the *Cantos* by saying, 'we have no way of knowing whether we have had any ideas or not'. . . .if we take account of what he understood 'idea' to be, Winters' remark is one of the few valuably exact formulations that we have of what reading the *Cantos* amounts to, and feels like.

For Pound an idea was not a proposition but 'The *forma,* the immortal *concetto'* which Allen Upward had described in these words: 'The idea is not the appearance of a thing already there, but rather the imagination of a thing not yet there. It is not the look of a thing, it is a looking forward to a thing'.

Gunn rejects Wintersian 'propositions' in favour of something rather like Pound's *forma* in a poem called 'The Outdoor Concert'. The title is a play on words: the 'concert' is both a musical performance and an experience of unity. The poem describes a 'secret' at the heart of a shared experience, a kind of synthesis. The act of discovery is not a lonely quest but the participation of one man in a group.

> The secret
> is still the secret
>
> is not a proposition:
> it's in finding
> what connects the man
> with the music, with

> the listeners, with the fog
> in the top of the eucalyptus,
> with dust discovered on the lip.

A proposition will not embrace the multiplicity of experience—nor indeed will any formulation—but to perceive *connections* is also a form of understanding. The poem constructs a *web*—an organic image which, since the poem is in free verse, may remind us of Lawrence. In more mechanical terms we might call it a diagram. *Jack Straw's Castle* does in fact contain a poem called 'Diagrams', which is written in strict heroic couplets and, with fourteen lines, recalls that most elaborately artificial of forms, the sonnet. We can now perceive how Gunn's preoccupation with reason and volitional form has developed. He is now concerned with 'models' of thought—as Poundian an interest as it is Wintersian, for what are Pound's ideograms but models, the matrices on which ideas are formed?

The ideogram in Pound's theory, though related to rhythm, is primarily a matter of content, of images and ideas. It was of no interest to Winters. And I doubt that Winters's scrupulous distinctions between metre ('the arithmetical norm, the purely theoretic structure of the line') and rhythm ('controlled departure from that norm') would have appealed to Pound. But both conceptions are of relevance to Gunn (and to many more of us). His own conception of metre remains as mathematical as Winters's; metre is, he has written, 'an unbodied abstraction', then goes on, like Winters, to emphasize that the life of a poem depends on it. For Gunn and Winters, all structures, whether of language or society, are frameworks which sustain a life, though—of their very nature—quite separate from it.

When we read Pound, however, we experience an attempt to push the artefact as close to the given world as it will go. The rhythms of speech are attuned to those of nature. The very structure of the *Cantos* is fragmentary, as if they had been worn down by the wind and water whose acts of erosion they so insistently and delectably evoke. Yet no reader could ever pretend that the hand and mind of the artificer seemed absent from the enterprise, whatever its aspirations or shortcomings. Moreover, though the overall structure of the work may appear loose, the individual details are remarkable for their hardness and definition. It must have been tensions of this sort that first made Pound's poetry available to Gunn.

Of the book that preceded *Jack Straw's Castle* Gunn has written—in language that might have been used to register his admiration for Pound—that 'It could be seen as a debate between the passion for definition and the passion for flow. . . .' Yet that book, *Moly* (1971), seemed to mark a retreat from the open forms he had developed in *Touch* (1967). The passion for definition is most in evidence in the elegant form-

ality of the rhymed stanzas; that for flow in the varieties of energy they
contemplate. But 'the *sense* of movement', of energy, has changed. Gone
are the uniformed heroes for whom the will 'cannot submit/To nature,
though brought out of it.' In their place are the surfers of 'From the
Wave'. Though, like the tearaways of 'On the Move', they become what
they are through movement, they do so by adapting themselves to nature.
Their skill and balance enable them to act in concord with the waves—
and these are qualities which require a harmony between knowledge and
instinct, consciousness and action.

The debate to which Gunn referred is continued in the group of metrical
poems that make up the first section of *Jack Straw's Castle*. The free verse
poems in the other two sections approach similar problems from a
different angle; there definition is arrived at, not imposed. 'The Plunge'
tries in its language to enact the process of acquiring knowledge by total
immersion. A diver plunges into a pool and stays under till he can take no
more, till he reaches the limits of the self. This discovery of limits is a discovery of definition, of essential form. 'How much more can the
body/take?' he asks, driving himself to the point where process must stop
and formulation begin. For 'Thomas Bewick', immersion in the detail of
the natural world is like a return to the womb. The umbilical cord that
binds him to the rest of the material universe not yet cut, he is conscious
but not yet individual.

> Drinking from
> clear stream and resting
> on the rock he loses himself
> in detail,
> 　　　he reverts
> to an earlier self, not yet
> separate from what it sees,
>
> a selfless self as difficult
> to recover and hold as to
> capture the exact way
> a burly bluetit grips
> its branch (leaning forward)
> over this rock
> 　　　and in
> The History of British Birds.

Immersion in process reaches its limit in a new kind of permanence—the
book for which Bewick's name is remembered, capitalized and visually
set apart from the rest of the poem. The rhythm enacts the flow of
experience into record.

If such poems are necessarily composed in open form, how do they
differ from those written in traditional prosody? What Gunn has discovered through free verse has inevitably affected his standard metre,

sometimes to its detriment. His attempts at the conversational can be banal: 'More meteors than I've ever set eyes on' for example. Or rhythmically confusing: the line, 'It doesn't matter tomorrow. Sleep well. Heaven knows', is only theoretically a pentameter; it is impossible to *hear* five feet, iambic or otherwise. But just at the edge of clumsiness, there are some felicitous variations, as in a mimetic view of a watersnake: 'I see a little snake alert in its skin/Striped head and neck from water, unmoving, reared'. The precariousness of such failures and successes is part of the whole debate between flux and definition, the intrusion of 'natural' rhythms into the fixities of traditional prosody.

The debate is initiated by the first three poems in *Jack Straw's Castle*. One of these, 'Diagrams', explores the illusion of permanence and the containment of flux. A skyscraper is being built. In its unfinished state it resembles a mesa, as if it were not an artefact at all but a permanent feature of the landscape. To the European reader, both mesa and sky-scraper evoke the American landscape; this is important, for Gunn, though English by birth, is now deeply concerned with the United States as a political and geographical entity. Significantly, the men at work on the steel mesa are aboriginal Americans:

> On girders round them, Indians pad like cats,
> With wrenches in their pockets and hard hats.

Their agility expresses their closeness to the environment, mesa or sky-scraper. The human embodiment of American 'nature', they are engaged in creating the human contribution to that landscape. They are the pre-siding deities of *Jack Straw's Castle*, moving like animals among pro-visional human artefacts, yet equally at home in the given world. Gunn shows them poised between permanence and flux, rather as a Renaiss-ance poet might show man poised between earth and air:

> They wear their yellow boots like moccasins,
> Balanced where air ends and where steel begins,
> Sky men. . . .

Their boots—products of industrial society, used for work among that society's structures—are worn like the shoes they would wear on a real mesa. The building they are erecting, though intended as a fixed and stable thing, appears as it grows to absorb and transform the energies that surround it. It becomes a 'giant' that 'grunts and sways', rising into the air: 'And giving to the air is sign of strength.' As in 'From the Wave', to bend to the power of the elements is to derive strength from them. But the ordinary meaning of 'give' is also present: the building appears to seep energy into the air. The contrast with the solitary heroes to whom Gunn bade farewell in 'My Sad Captains' could not be greater:

> They were men
> who, I thought, lived only to

>renew the wasteful force they
>spent with each hot convulsion.

The consumption of their energy was magnificent but, ultimately, waste. For Gunn today, the transformation of energy is 'sign of strength', the adaptation of self to environment.

The diagrams of the title are cranes and exposed girders, but I take it that Gunn is also thinking of other structures that bear upon the poem's meaning—notably, the grid of its own metre. And most of these recent metrical poems are concerned with moments in which fluidity takes on permanent form. Such permanence is illusory but necessary. American permanence, in a political sense, is embodied in its constitution, which itself has its origin in revolutionary change. Gunn is not a political poet in the sense of being 'committed'—he is primarily concerned with identities and relations we think of as pre-political, with 'finding himself on a barely known planet in an almost unknown universe'. But as Camus (one of his most honoured heroes) discovered, freedom and choice do not exist in abstract purity; once a man is oppressed, he discovers his political nature whether he will or no. It was under Camus's influence, in *My Sad Captains,* that Gunn first tried to show how the individual's choices may operate in society. Like Camus, he was thinking of an extreme kind of society, though, unlike him, he had not lived in one. The political positions adopted are therefore limited in application, though quite clear: specifically anti-fascist, broadly anti-totalitarian. The rational individualism of 'Claus von Stauffenberg, 1944' might be called liberal. It is strange to recall that Gunn's early poems were often accused of fascism— especially in the light of his recent testimony that as an undergraduate (when he wrote *Fighting Terms*) he was a pacifist and a Fabian socialist. The violence of those poems is examined outside a social context and not proposed as a good. The dissolution of self in the group and the adoption of various 'uniforms' are choices made voluntarily by individuals. The heroic stance is precisely that: a stance, a posture by which a man defines his identity: it is frozen action, the fluid given the appearance of permanence. If Gunn seemed obsessed with Nazism—its history, postures and regalia—this has something to do with growing up in time of war and reaching manhood when the struggle was over. *Not* having fought in that war is the context a recent poem like 'The Corporal' requires. So, in *My Sad Captains* and *Touch,* Gunn criticizes his earlier stances in such a way as to acquit himself of this accusation. Since *Touch,* his politics have become decidedly American. It is possible to read the Arcadian world of *Moly* as a new version of the American dream—the New World as the second Eden. But such an Arcadia must become mere escapism in the years of the Vietnam war and Nixon's presidency, if actual political issues are not faced. *Jack Straw's Castle* is the only book of Gunn's which shows the need to deal with contemporary history. 'Nixon's era', with its corruption and rigidity, is regarded as a betrayal of the system of institutionalized change on which the United States was founded. Iron Landscapes', the one poem to deal directly with these issues, is brilliantly written, but flawed and problematic.

It is a meditation on an antiquated iron pier and a girdered ferry-building beside the Hudson River. Gunn's newly-acquired modernism is in evidence, not least in the rhythmic flexibility.

> A girdered ferry-building opposite,
> Displaying the name LACKAWANNA, seems to ride
>
> The turbulent brown-grey waters that intervene:
> Cool seething incompletion that I love.

In these lines, the iambic pentameter is the norm from which the rhythm departs. The first and fourth lines are regular. The other two depart from that pattern, much as the non-verbal facts they attempt to encompass elude verbal formulation. In the first of these, the capitalized name (does this too have Indian associations?) fits so awkwardly into the line that the hard physical intractability of the other artefact comes alive to us. (Gunn's admiration for similar rhythmic and verbal angularities in Thomas Hardy comes to mind: 'They present things with immediate authority.') Variation in the third line achieves a different effect: we feel the elusive fluidity of the perception by contrast with the formulaic precision of the regular line that follows. Regularity, of course, is appropriate to commentary, to formulations necessarily of the mind.

It is not just a matter of rhythm. Free verse enacts a different kind of thought and thinking. If we look at some of Gunn's best early poems—at 'Innocence' or 'The Annihilation of Nothing'—we are struck not only by the exactness of the metre (in contrast with the awkwardness of 'Iron Landscapes') but, more, by the perfection of the argument. *Too* perfect, you might think, too coherent to allow for the fluidities, the innate contradictions of the subject. Life is almost imprisoned by the subject, not enlarged. But in this poem we are able to follow the poet's train of thought as the different elements that compose the argument are brought together. It is not, as in the free verse, a poetry of process. The different elements have been prefabricated, as it were, into blocks. Our attention is drawn less to thought-as-process than to the way experience is shaped into form and formula, to become idea, concept, belief, opinion.

The poem begins with the 'bare black Z' of the pier and the poet beneath it, looking across the river to the ferry-building. The zigzags of the iron structures 'come and go' in the water, become fluid in the water's reflection of them. Separate perceptions are brought together, not by volition but by contingency. This provokes the central paradox, the conflict between Gunn's passions for definition and for flow. Then a third per-

ception comes into play. Glimpsed downstream, the Statue of Liberty
provokes reflections on the present state of the nation. Gunn has just declared his 'passion for definition', having earlier declared his love for its
opposite, 'Cool seething incompletion'.

> But I'm at peace with the iron landscape too,
> Hard because buildings must be hard to last
> —Block, cylinder, cube, built with their angles true,
> A dream of righteous permanence, from the past.
>
> In Nixon's era, decades after the ferry,
> The copper embodiment of the pieties
> Seems hard, but hard like a revolutionary
> With indignation, constant as she is.
>
> From here you can glimpse her downstream, her far charm,
> Liberty, tiny woman in the mist
> —You cannot see the torch—raising her arm
> Lorn, bold, as if saluting with her fist.

Thus from stability and flux, iron and water, the poem moves on to an
historical plane: the rigidity of reactionary government is now set against
the principle of change on which the Constitution is founded. First, the
identification of buildings with institutions is made; the dream from the
past is, among other things, the dream of the original revolutionaries
whose Utopia is embodied in another metal artefact, the statue. The difficulty is that they created their liberal revolution in the image of the old
order: they tried to institutionalize change. Today's revolutionaries
aspire to base new societies on change, but their weakness (implicit here
or not?) is their failure to recognize the human need for fixities. The poem
ends with an image of the old revolution (the statue) transformed into the
new (the clenched-fist salute), and 'Liberty' is neither permanent nor
fluctuating but *constant*, a principle existing in time with changing
manifestations, itself unchanging.

Inevitably writing of this sort raises questions. After all, these are
matters we argue vehemently about, yet the poem — though it appears to
take sides—is an unresolved embodiment of the issues. This is a case
where we *need* Wintersian propositions but are left with a web of gestures,
even of prejudices. For example, the poem depends on the assumption
(which I happen to share) that the Nixon era was a bad time; but this is
something we need to be persuaded of. A similar doubt infects the poem's
technique. Is Gunn being relaxed and flexible, or merely clumsy? Does
the rhyme 'ferry'/'revolutionary' work? Yet the rhythmical counter-
point in the last stanza is as beautiful and assured as anything in Gunn's
work. His gaucheries sometimes seem Hardyesque authentications of his
honesty; here he is most fluent where difficulties need to be raised, where
the thought should meet with most resistance from the verse. It is a con-

vincing conclusion to a line of thought but, finally, no more than a gesture—and it is a good many years now since Gunn first questioned the validity of 'the large gesture of solitary man'. In his earlier work, stance, pose and gesture were important as moments of stasis through which people established their identities, breaking temporarily free from 'movement'. Moreover, these stances, though they involved commitment to action, did not involve action in terms of the stance. The fetishistic dandy with the swastika-draped bed in 'The Beaters' is in no sense a Nazi. But in 'Iron Landscapes', the emotion compels us to identify with a pose which is intended to issue in specific actions with public implications and, however much one may sympathize with such a response to the Nixon era, one must ask what essential difference there is between the clenched fist and a Nazi salute. True, one is a gesture of resistance, the other of oppression. But both are salutes; both call for public violence; both deny the validity of rational discussion. Of course, it is not Gunn's purpose to declare a commitment or to invoke the detail of political argument. It is a fine poem, and not the least of its virtues is that it is able to provoke such questions and to show historical patterns growing from the matrices of feeling the landscape represents. It shows American society as necessarily based on the dialectic of permanence and change, the very dialectic which determines the creative tensions of Gunn's poetry.

We have reached a stalemate: one though, as it seems to me, that is at the root of modern poetry. 'Iron Landscapes' attempts a reconciliation between the fluidity of the modern (free verse and all that goes with it) and the monumental qualities of the classical (the metred stanza). Whatever one makes of the metric, it should be clear that the internal structure is Modernist, almost Poundian; for it is concerned not with ideas but with the raw material of thought. It is significant that the internal structure resolves itself in a gesture: which is precisely the weakness of much of Pound's poetry. But what Gunn brings to this new Modernism is respect for the classical as a living concern. Whatever we make of the clenched fist, there is no mistaking the fundamentally liberal position of 'Iron Landscapes', a position reinforced by, for example, his version of colonization in the sequence called 'The Geysers'. The Indian workers of 'Diagrams' belong to a race displaced and humbled by colonialism, yet— as 'The Geysers' shows—*all* human habitations are colonies. The perpetual challenge faced by the liberal is how to make such colonies humane, how to establish a fruitful harmony between man the artificer and man the creature. Gunn is a highly civilized artist — hence his continuing loyalty to the old forms. Despite his enthusiasm for the new, he does not welcome—as some writers whose names have been misleadingly linked with his appear to do — the collapse of our civilization. Rather he sees change and the capacity for change as *the* essential qualities of a living civilization, and so celebrates its continuity.

Note A longer version of this essay, with modifications, first appeared in
Poetry Nation Review V, 3, pp 51-7.

Ted Hughes

> Why has not England a great mythology? Our folklore has never advanced beyond daintiness and the greater melodies about our country-side have all issued through the pipes of Greece. Deep and true as the native imagination can be, it seems to have failed here. It has stopped with the witches and the fairies. It cannot vivify one fraction of a summer field, or give names to half a dozen stars. England still waits for the supreme moment of her literature—for the one poet who shall voice her. . .
>
> E. M. Forster

IN HIS DISCUSSION of Ted Hughes's poetry in *The Art of the Real* (1977), Eric Homberger's obloquy stops little short of a fearsome tirade, bent, one feels, on connecting Hughes to his 'elemental power circuit' and to a voltage to dispatch him netherward to the dark world of the gods. There, Homberger suggests, Hughes might find much to disabuse himself about the nature of his preoccupation with elemental and primal forces; and his shamanistic return, if Homberger could conceive of such an event, might be with a 'new word' repentant and exclusively for *this* world, preferably enunciating a suitable political creed:

> Socialism [writes Homberger] is one of the expressions of intense and reasonable desire to abate that 'elemental power circuit of the Universe' which regularly swept people into misery, sickness and death. That Hughes can so confidently dismiss it as a part of the hubris of an aggressive rationalism tells us something about the place that the sympathetic instinct occupies in his world-view. None—at least in theory.

Hughes, on the other hand, (in the *New Statesman*, 6 September 1963) would have no truck with such a provisional myth-kit of survival, regarding socialism as 'the great "cooperatives" of non-competitive mutual parasitism', simply another grand advance on the rationalist humanist position, more irrefutable evidence with which to swell his own Book of Revelations. Yet, if we can see our way through Homberger's incessant barrage, there is much to sympathize with in his argument. Take, for example, the well-anthologized 'Hawk Roosting'.

In an interview with Egbert Faas, Hughes has commented on this poem: 'That bird is accused of being a fascist. . . .the symbol of some horrible totalitarian genocidal dictator. Actually what I had in mind was that in

this hawk Nature is thinking. Simply Nature.' *(London Magazine,*
January 1971).Yet it takes little stretch of the imagination to fit the
political interpretation to the poem. Indeed, by the lack of any note of
ironic self-awareness, it seems almost to invite such an interpretation.
The assertive personal pronouns and aggressive verbs toned in an un-
swerving and laconic mode, make the poem read almost as a personal
declaration of Hughes' own position, unrepentantly aloof from the world,
except in the occasional mindless forays and kills. Nevertheless, we
should, I think, be duly cautious about falling too easily prey to the convenient option, most readily open to us now, of resurrecting the ghosts of
Marinetti and Mussolini in such poems of Hughes which seem to exalt
violence. If history should, at some future point, be diverted into a
tyranny of authoritarianism from either political extreme, I doubt very
much whether Hughes would have any colours to reveal.

  Still, it is a common, even fashionable image of Hughes to see him wad-
ing bloody-toothed-and-clawed through the detritus of a collapsed
civilization with a wry grin of satisfaction on his swarthy face. One
wonders whether Hughes, imagining the possibilities of such a folk-devil
myth, used it as a model for *Crow,* which some believe is his sharpest
blade for making the critics smart and take stock of their position. And if
Hughes has been more than once reviled by the critics, he has not been
timid in his replies.

  On the perennial question of 'violence' in his poetry, Hughes has remarked in the Faas interview, illustrating from Shakespeare's *Venus and
Adonis:* 'Venus. . . if one reads between the lines eventually murdered
Adonis. . . she murdered him because he rejected her. He was so
desensitized, stupefied and brutalized by his rational scepticism, he
didn't know what to make of her. He thought she was an ethical peril. He
was a sort of modern critic in the larval phase. . . .a modern English critic.
A typical modern Englishman.' One detects in this broadening to
include the 'typical' English character an allusive Nietzscheanism: 'The
man *who has become free*—and how much more the *mind* that has become
free — spurns the sort of contemptible well-being dreamed of by shop-
keepers, Christians, cows, women, Englishmen and other democrats.
The free man is a *warrior.* How is freedom measured in individuals as in
nations? By the resistance which has to be overcome, by the effort it costs
to stay *aloft.* ' *(Twilight of the Idols.)* But we should not align Hughes with
the theories of *Ubermensch* and the 'will to power', although there is evidence of a Dionysian pessimism in his work. If that is true, we can readily
see its antithesis, as perhaps Hughes does, personified in the typical
English critic, as a *poverty of life* (Nietzsche, *The Gay Science),* a notion of
art and knowledge as providing 'rest, peace, a smooth sea, delivery. . . .' a
sense of comfortable inertia and complacency.

  Though it is not within the scope of this essay to discuss the English critical tradition, it is a discussion worth bearing in mind when one considers Hughes's now notorious disclaimer in his Introduction to Keith Douglas's *Selected Poems* (1964), 'the terrible, suffocating, maternal octopus of ancient English poetic tradition', and the significance it has had in the development of his work. Yet, discernibly, many features of his disaffection with the English Liberal tradition emerge, paradoxically, out of the main concerns of that tradition. One only has to recall the attempts of the Modernists and pre-Modernists to reinvigorate language and form in order to restore some meaning to an otherwise complex and incomprehensible world, to discover many of Hughes's root preoccupations. Eliot, we remember, was there before him. Nevertheless, we can detect, even in Hughes's earliest work, an urgent attempt to restate these concerns.

Another well-anthologized poem is 'The Jaguar'. Formally, the poem appears well gauged and controlled to produce a maximum effect without threatening its overall cohesion. But one feels a progressive unease with the poem on each re-reading (a characteristic feeling with Hughes's poems), as if he had beckoned us over to the cage, then quite suddenly opened the door. For it is not a polite and ruminative diction that overwhelms us, but a solid phalanx of buffeting verbs and steel-heeled nouns in a jostling syntax, heftily thrown out in drummingly irregular three and four stressed lines. Like Lawrence, in *Sons and Lovers,* Hughes is concerned not to describe experience but to embody it wholly, in a tremendous exertion of will to expose '. . . .the very quivering tissue, the very protoplasm of life. . . .'. If one feels, at times, overwhelmed by Hughes's almost hedonistic relishing for the unharnessed elemental powers in all their 'conflagration and frenzy' and blood-bolted imagery, the reply we must expect from Hughes is that it is part evidence of the hubris of our liberal humanist outlook, our willingness to settle for a 'minimum practical energy and illumination.' It is a simple statement of faith—one to which we assent or dissent. No compromise is available to us.

Crow is no exception. In its burlesque of flamboyant rhetoric, precocious imagery and unpoeticalness, rather than providing a nostrum for our English malady it seems intent on worsening it—a strange physic indeed! But it is easy to treat *Crow* lightly and with the same ribald humour in which it is presented. Significantly, it is Hughes' first work to employ an elaborately conceived mythology, though how well it works in the end is debatable. In his essay 'Myth and History in Recent Poetry', in *British Poetry since 1960: a critical survey,* eds G. Lindop and M. Schmidt (1972), Terry Eagleton remarks on the Crow myth: 'Crow's triumph over the alienating casualties of history seems too cheaply bought: the inviolable security of myth has replaced, rather than confronted, the contingencies of history, as simple compensation.' But as a symbol, Crow's function is primarily to represent, not to confront, those contingencies. It is the mode of presentation to which we might finally take exception. Here is part of 'Crow's Account of the Battle'.

And when the smoke cleared it became clear
This had happened too often before
And was going to happen too often in the future
And happened too easily
Bones were too like lath and twigs
Blood was too like water
Cries were too like silence
The most terrible grimaces too like footprints in mud
And shooting somebody through the midriff
Was too like striking a match
Too like potting a snooker ball
Too like tearing up a bill
Blasting the whole world to bits
Was too like slamming a door. . .

It is a glaringly unsubtle piece, dependent for its effect on a frenetic accumulation of physical images and a bludgeoning rhetorical tone. Argument rather by way of assault than persuasion. A long way, one might think, from the careful artifice and nuance of Geoffrey Hill's poetry. But whereas Hill runs the risk of an aesthetic ingrownness, Hughes, conversely, ventures too far into the other extreme, threatening total self-annihilation. There is little in the way of a conscious formal boundary or inner discipline. Consequently, what is depicted, rather than approximating to the fulness of the experience, instead veers off into meaninglessness and caricature—precisely the effect Hughes is after. For it is a minor triumph of *Crow* that Hughes manages to strike, with such devastating accuracy, the one discordant note in the human rhythm to release that suppressed and perverted part of our imagination over which we like to think we have achieved complete control. Far from being an historical, transcendent view of the world, *Crow* represents, in its total vision, history as the embodiment and expression of an alienated modern consciousness, questing vainly for access to a reality where the certainty of one's identity is not for ever turning to illusion and nightmare. But the overriding argument in *Crow* asserts that the defective imagination prevents ultimately its discovery, rising spectrally into the very medium in which are invested the hopes of such a discovery-language.

Crow
Decided to try words.

He imagined some words for the job, a lovely pack—
Clear-eyed, resounding, well-trained,
With strong teeth.

You could not find a better bred lot.

He pointed out the hare and away went the words
Resounding.
Crow was Crow without fail, but what is a hare?
It converted itself to a bunker.
The words circling, protesting, resounding.

Crow turned the words into bombs—they blasted the bunker.
The bits of bunker flew up—a flock of starlings.

Crow turned the words into shot-guns, they shot down the
starlings.
The falling starlings turned into a cloudburst. . . .

'. . . if thought corrupts language, language can also corrupt thought'
wrote George Orwell in his essay *Politics and the English Language.*
Hughes reminds us (in the *Listener,* 20 July 1970) that in parts of the narrative Crow has an ambition to become a man, though in fact, he never
quite succeeds in this. The above poem, perhaps, is one instance of that
attempt. But what for Orwell becomes a speculative truth and a way to fix
and resolve the corruption, for Crow, half dressed in human consciousness, language becomes a horrifying chimera of violent metamorphoses, as the instinctive and rational parts of his consciousness are
thrown against each other.
  For Hughes, language is an intrinsic part of his vision, an organic
monitor to record the gradual disintegration of society and civilization.
With such a view of the world, it would seem best to remain silent but
ever alert, as Hughes suggests, for the 'new word'. But it is an obvious
fact that in *Crow* the 'new word' is not delivered up to us, or if it is, we are
deafened to its sound by the nuclear blast which comes in 'Notes for a
Little Play'. The bleakness of the vision and the lack of even a vestigial
hope for redemption makes *Crow* at times unbearable. The sense of
Hughes off-loading on to us the dead wood of our civilization makes even
the humour of *Crow* seem weighted against us. For in its obviously ironic
mode, it comes to represent for Hughes a personal refuge not from the
world, but from its insanity — an insanity we alone are left to suffer. It is
the unheuristic nature of the Crow myth, its inability to point towards a
more heartening condition, that eventually threatens the myth with complete isolation.
  What are we really to make of such poems as 'Glimpse', 'King of
Carrion', 'Two Eskimo Songs' and finally "Littleblood'? If they represent a new mythology to replace the Christian one they do so without full
awareness of the massive complexities — cultural, social and historical —
that should inform such a task. That *Crow* is pre-eminently a psycho-
mythological drama, should not automatically allow Hughes licence to
ignore those other complexities. Of course, one might argue Hughes's

direly pessimistic vision in a broader and more inclusive context by locat-
ing him in that nineteenth-century tradition of pessimism of which he
seems so much a part ('We living, are out of life' — Conrad). In the interview with Egbert Faas Hughes commented that with *Crow* he 'projected
too far into the future', and one can guess, as a consequence of this, that
the dynamic of his imagination discovered new and hitherto unexplored
areas into which he ventured perhaps too readily and impulsively. And
there is much past as well as future in the poem.

In *Cave Birds,* Hughes has attempted to provide his explorations with
a better sense of proportion and balance and has kept his eye firmly on his
subject. The concerns of *Cave Birds* parallel and extend those of *Crow*,
which is hardly surprising after the clear indication Hughes gave in the
Faas interview that he had in mind enlarging upon the Crow myth. But
unlike *Crow* the narrative of *Cave Birds* is clearer and better constructed.
The protagonist is a Socratic Everyman figure, who remains intractable
in his rational sceptical outlook. The narrative recounts his eventual psychic crisis and abduction by spectral birds into the underworld where he
is tried for the crime of his outlook. Condemned to death, he goes on to
experience a variety of bizarre ordeals and initiations, emerging finally in
the form of a falcon. The drama is, of course, enacted in the form of a
dream, in the incurably schizophrenic consciousness of the protagonist.
But a more significant reading of the text is suggested by Baskin's own
words that preface Keith Sagar's chapter on *Cave Birds* in *The Art of Ted
Hughes* (1978): '. . . . My owls of night and ignorance, genitaled and sex-
less, hulking, brooding, wailing and screeching, distorted into my vision
of aggressive predatory tyranny.' The notion here of a fusion of pure
instinctive aggression and perverse rationality seems to pervade *Cave
Birds:*

> When I said: 'Civilization,'
> He began to chop off his fingers and mourn.
> When I said: 'Sanity and again Sanity and above all Sanity,'
> He disembowelled himself with a cross-shape cut.
> I stopped trying to say anything.
> But then when he began to snore in his death-struggle
> The guilt came.
> And when they covered his face I went cold.

The imagery here works more effectively than that of *Crow*. Its anti-
phonal voice, compassionate, even generous, permits rather than prevents the canting protests of 'civilization'. It displays rather than censures
the self-inflicted suffering of our world, no longer with a tone of an
embattled rhetoric, but one peculiarly composed, even humble. Is it, at
last, Hughes admitting the possiblity of innocence in guilt? Hughes
seems close here to what he has discovered in the poetry of the European
poets, particularly that of Vasko Popa:

This helplessness in the circumstances has purged them of rhetoric. They cannot falsify their experience by any hopeful effort to change it. Their poetry is a strategy of making audible meanings without disturbing the silence, an art of homing in tentatively on vital scarcely perceptible signals, making no mistakes, but with no hope of finality, continuing to explore. Finally, with delicate manoeuvring, they precipitate out of a world of malicious negatives a happy positive. And they have created a small ironic space, a work of lyrical art, in which their humanity can respect itself. (*Vasko Popa, Selected Poems*, with Introduction by Ted Hughes, 1969)

Hughes comes close, but not always. Partly because, and for obvious reasons, his experience is historically different from theirs (he is not Milosz, after all), and partly, having something to do with that dissimilarity of experience, he falls short of their characteristic openness and simplicity, becoming at times involved with a dour and impenetrable abstractness.

One can admire the driving originality of Hughes's imagination and his reluctance to surrender the least meaning that might diffuse the energy of his perceptions. The compressed and highly charged metaphors seem to want to enthral rather than illuminate us with the awesome forms they invoke and upon which they gradually, almost tentatively, come to focus. The focus is kept teasingly blurred. Yet it is not a technical effect, part of the overall strategy of Hughes' art. It is more that Hughes himself is unable finally to adjust the lens to make those forms intelligible to us. In many ways, the density and unconnectedness of the metaphors explain his artistic predicament, acknowledging as he does the extraordinary fertile ground of his new imaginative experience but simultaneously discovering the inadequacy of language to give it direct and coherent expression. Consequently, in many poems we have a series of closed metaphors, each one suggesting a great occasion of insight, of imminent revelation, which is subsequently left in mid-air, as a new metaphor arrives, apparently nearer to the meaning of the experience under way:

> And suddenly you
> Have not a word to say for yourself.
>
> Only a little knife, a small incision,
> A snickety nick in the brain
> And you drop off like a polyp.
>
> Only a crumb of fungus,
> A pulp of mouldy tinder
> And you flare, fluttering, black-out like a firework.
>
> Who are you, in the nest among the bones?
> You are the shyest bird among birds.

'I am the last of my kind.'
                        ('Only a Little Sleep, a Little Slumber')

The tensions set up in the language, though often threatening obscurity, are not the result of an excited over-indulgence, a sort of perverse linguistic filibustering. Rather, they derive their impulse from a genuine anxiety with the world in which the human consciousness can make only futile appeals to commonsense and reason—futile, because such appeals habitually reveal themselves as ultimately calamitous for us. Such are the horrors of the world, we try to exclude them from our minds, but always at our peril for they return more threateningly, agitating like an involuntary twitch in the corner of the eye:

> While I strolled
> Where a leaf or two still tapped like bluetits
>
> I met thin, webby rain
> And thought: 'Ought I to turn back, or keep going?'
> Her heart stopped beating, that second.
>
> As I hung up my coat and went through into the kitchen
> And peeled a flake off the turkey's hulk,
>   and stood vacantly munching
> Her sister got the call from the hospital
> And gasped out the screech.
>
> And all the time
> I was scrubbing at my nails and staring through the window
> She was burning.
>
> Some, who had been close, walked away
> Because it was beyond help now. . . .
>   ('Something was Happening')

The title of this poem could well stand as the motto of *Cave Birds,* for many of the poems exhibit a peculiar and uncanny resistance to full explication. They seem to exist in those areas of uncharted experience where one feels they can only be fully comprehended in their emotional and psychological impact, as if to seize upon any one aspect of their composition would be only to reveal the other areas of experience on which any single aspect depends wholly for its meaning. One wonders whether Hughes, whilst writing these poems, had in mind Marlow's comments on our 'inability to interpret aright the signs which experience (a mysterious thing in itself) makes to our understanding and emotion. . . ' (Joseph Conrad, *Chance*). It is a difficult business indeed to come to any final decision as to whether or not Hughes himself has interpreted those signs aright. Once again, it is a simple note of faith, one which finds confirmation in our impressions or else does not.

Many of the same interpretative problems arise with *Gaudete*. It represents a further extension (though I hesitate to say refinement) of Hughes's previous mythopoeic ambitions, but with the difference that in *Gaudete* the mythology strives for an autonomy which before was only tentative. And finally it succeeds or fails on Hughes's terms only, as if we were placed in the wake of his mythologizing, obliged to gauge its aim and direction by an assortment of vaguely related events along the way. There is a narrative which is briefly summarized at the front of the book, but as one might suspect in such a lengthy work, it becomes considerably more complex and mystifying. This has to do with the lack of sufficient commentary on the action and pattern of events (it was originally conceived as a scenario for a film) and the problem of differentiating between the real and changeling Lumb. It has much to do with Hughes's own uncertainty about the nature of his mythology and how he might best develop it without baffling himself.

As a fiction, mythology is required to work within strictly defined limits and conventions, a fact Hughes acknowledged when he described Crow's folkloric origins in the Faas interview. But by attempting to use these conventions with mythological interests appropriate in modern context, Hughes seems to have taken a risk, trying to merge two very different cultural histories and world-views without fully considering the types of consciousness involved. Consequently (the schizoid mind of Lumb is an emblem of our perplexity) we are never given the opportunity of experiencing and therefore judging either the debilitating illusions of our own grim world or the spiritually 'reinvigorating' landscapes of Hughes's newly ennatured world. It is Hughes's belief that with the return of the Shaman — and we must presume Lumb is cast in this role — the effect on the audience will be cathartic, a profound refreshing of their deepest feelings. Is this the experience of *Gaudete*? Here is one initiation of our Shaman:

> Half a ton of guts
> Balloon out and drop on to Lumb.
> He fights in the roping hot mass.
> He pushes his head clear, trying to wipe his eyes clear.
> Curtains of live blood cascade from the open bull above him.
> Wallowing in the greasy pulps, he tries to crawl clear
> But men in bloody capes are flinging buckets of fresh blood over
> him.
>
> Many bulls swing up, on screeching pulleys.
> Intestines spill across blood-flooded concrete.
>
> ('Prologue')

Can we accept such verbal belchings as a serious offering of spiritual refreshment? One can appreciate Hughes's attempt to strip away the polite accessories of poetic language and restore its more vital mimetic

speech-rhythms to give a sharper resonance and directness of address,
but Hughes's voice keeps it on a too cramped and severe course. And
when it does gain release, it achieves such an ecstatic rhetorical pitch that
it seems close to bursting:

> . . . She moves robed invisibly with gorgeous richness.
> She knows she is burning plasma and infinitely tiny,
> That she and all these women are moving inside the body
>   of an incandescent creature of love,
> That they are brightening, and that the crisis is close,
> They are the cells in the glands of an inconceivably huge
>   and urgent love-animal. . .

Those heaped-up adjectives give us little sense of the apparently sublime
sensual delight which Felicity is meant to be experiencing. Their straining abstractness seems rather to admit the inadequacy of the language, a
falling short at the critical moment of spiritual orgasm. And all this
happens in a Women's Institute, of all places! The failure is, and I return
to an earlier point, that Hughes is unable to find a sufficiently plausible
setting in which to enact his mythological drama. To thrust modern-day
consciousness back into a pagan realm of mystery and magic in one
violent turn of the imagination, and once there, attempt its renewal by a
series of unnerving rituals, seems to require of us more than a suspension
of disbelief. It must be with some relief that we come to the Epilogue
where Lumb's poems are written out. And if they seem at all opaque in
their meaning their translucency of feeling is wonderful compensation:

> The lark sizzles in my ear
> Like a fuse—
> A prickling fever
> A flush of the swelling earth—
> When you touch his grains, who shall stay?
> Over the lark's crested tongue
> Under the lark's crested head
> A prophecy
> From the core of the blue peace
> From the sapphire's flaw
> From the sun's blinding dust.

'. . . out of a world of malicious negatives a happy positive'? Hughes
seems to have achieved in this section what he has been after for so long—
a quiet humility in awe of the majesty of the world, a renewed spirit happy
to go on searching, exploring.

ANDREW WATERMAN

The poetry of Geoffrey Hill

ALTHOUGH time finally sifts matters justly, meanwhile too many poets slog on turning the stuff out, and since only so many among all who 'want to write' have even that talent, their books receive tepid passes from reviewers for whom it is all much of a muchness, themselves prone to lapse from their crucial responsibility to be alert for the poets and poems of truly enduring value. In this inevitable context, it is reassuring that over the twenty years since *For the Unfallen*, 1959, and still imperfectly, the exceptional excellence of Geoffrey Hill's poetry has come to receive acknowledgement.

In his poem 'The Cave of Making', W. H. Auden observed

> After all, it's rather a privilege
>   amid the affluent traffic
> to serve this unpopular art which cannot be turned into
>   background noise for study
> or hung as a status trophy by rising executives,
>   cannot be 'done' like Venice
> or abridged like Tolstoy, but stubbornly still insists upon
>   being read or ignored. . . .

Truth particularly apt to Hill's poetry. No poetry, as Wordsworth put it, should 'level down/For the sake of being generally understood,' or wrongly conscious of audience court fashionable expectations and so perish with them; but Hill's is extraordinarily uncompromising, has a wholly self-preoccupied air; the reader may wander among its compelling splendours, but hardly feels invited or directly addressed. It is poetry intense with feeling, but not the accessible kinds arising directly from everyday experiences and relationships central in much of at least most poets' writing. The human content of Hill's poetry tends to be given elaborately remote frameworks: King Offa's Mercia and other recesses of history; religious concepts abstruse or arcane; the cryptic love of a fictive poet 'Sebastian Arrurruz'. Notes to Hill's latest collection *Tenebrae* declare 'Spanish and German poems have provided points of departure for several poems in this book'. While good poetry is owed attentive re-reading, how far need we follow Hill into his historical, religious and foreign-language sources? Personally, I know some history, have an alert agnostic's understanding of Christian concepts and ritual, and no adequacy in any foreign language. But good poetry stands self-sufficiently free of whatever its origins. 'Absalom and Achitophel', 'The Second

Coming', 'The Waste Land', would not exist without the constitutional controversy of Dryden's time, Yeats's idiosyncratic philosophy of gyres, and Eliot's reading in *From Ritual to Romance*, but the finished structures no longer depend upon the scaffolding necessary to get them up.

Altogether, the poet Hill insistently recalls is Eliot, whose own poetry magnificently passes what he defined as the 'test that genuine poetry can communicate before it is understood'. Hill's has comparable memorability: poems, lines, phrases, incise themselves on the imagination. Thus, the searing gnomic stanza from 'Dr Faustus' also made epigraph for *For the Unfallen:*

> A beast is slain, a beast thrives.
> Fat blood squeaks on the sand.
> A blinded god believes
> That he is not blind.

In *King Log,* Hill's 'Funeral Music' on the Wars of the Roses consummately realizes what his notes tell us he desiderated, 'a florid grim music broken by grunts and shrieks'; while ' "Domaine Public" ' has this image characteristically precise in its sensuous signification, about 'the Fathers':

> How they
> cultivate the corrupting flesh:
>
> toothsome contemplation: cleanly
>   maggots churning spleen
> to milk.

The Arrurruz poems conjure fluently graphic immediacies:

> Why do I have to relive, even now,
> Your mouth, and your hand running over me
> Deft as a lizard, like a sinew of water.

One can dip almost at random to find *Tenebrae* sustaining this ability to write poetry that stamps itself on the mind because definitively perfected:

> the stale head
> sauced in original blood; the little feast
> foaming with cries of rapture and despair.
>
> ('A Pre-Raphaelite Notebook')

Whenever poetry has such power, pervasive through Hill's, almost by imaginative sleight to make the reader feel he has known always lines just read, this arises not only from vivid precision of denotation and image, but also from the poet commanding the movement of his verse in a subtle distinctive music. Hill's frequent poem-titles with musical reference are as wittingly chosen as Eliot's 'Four Quartets'.

That his poetry *is* difficult has, inevitably yet surely shamefully, slowed and in some quarters apparently precluded its proper recognition. Hill is not mentioned in Donald Davie's *Thomas Hardy and British Poetry* and *The Poet in the Imaginary Museum,* in Ian Hamilton's *A Poetry Chronicle,* or in Jonathan Raban's *The Society of the Poem,* all generally perceptive on post-1950 poetry. Larkin's rise to due esteem was justly rapid, yet Larkin's own misrepresentation of Hill in his *Oxford Book of Twentieth-Century English Verse,* including only 'In Memory of Jane Fraser' about which Hill, when reprinting it amended as a 'penitential exercise' in *King Log* said 'I dislike the poem very much', seems as shabby as imperci-pient. But perhaps more characteristic through Hill's career has been the reaction typified by Kenneth Allott who introducing Hill in his *Penguin Book of Contemporary Verse* admitted 'I find the darkness of many of the poems so nearly total that I can see them to be poems only by a certain quality in their phrasing', understandable 'only in the sense that cats and dogs may be said to understand human conversations;' or by Alan Brownjohn reviewing *Mercian Hymns* for the *New Statesman* (6 August 1971) as the work of an 'implacably baffling talent', poetry that 'resists even several readings: yet the strange, ceremonial magnificence of it all is unmistakable'. Additional to the innate intricacy of Hill's poetic pro-cesses is his habit of frustrating most readers' expectations in the way defined by Gavin Ewart when, admiring *King Log,* he demurred 'yet contemporary life hardly exists in most of these poems, except by implication' (*London Magazine,* December 1968). Nor, though intensely aware of, and able poetically to realise, the power of the imagination significantly to mythicize untidy life, does Hill offer anything calculated so superficially to captivate as the instant cartoon-myth of Ted Hughes's *Crow* and other recent crass bestiaries, flinging the age an accelerated image of its own conventional grimace.

Yet, if very occasionally impenetrable, if sometimes as I think reading for example the striking 'Annunciations' in *King Log* excessive ellipsis grindingly short-circuits his lines as poetry, Hill's work everywhere con-vinces of its authenticity, and his difficulty need not be exaggerated. So much comes to mind as touchstones of a sensuous intellection healing that 'dissociation of sensibility' Eliot talked about, lucid enough even when at its highest pitch. Consider 'Te Lucis Ante Terminum' from *Tenebrae:*

> Centaury with your staunch bloom
> you there alder beech you fern,
> midsummer closeness my far home,
> fresh traces of lost origin.
>
> Silvery the black cherries hang
> the plum-tree oozes through each cleft
> and horse-flies siphon the green dung,

> glued to the sweetness of their graft:
>
> immortal transience, a 'kind
> of otherness', self-understood,
> BE FAITHFUL grows upon the mind
> as lichen glimmers on the wood.

Certainly done with consummate economy, through to the felicitous ·
final simile finding graphic sensuous imagery for its abstract concept, this
poem yields with subtle clarity its sense: that however passing life's
shows, the proper fulfilling response to recognizing this condition is an
accepting fidelity, organically experienced, to what one is, and what is
given, by which word I mean both 'predicated' and 'bestowed'. Yet,
'midsummer closeness my far home': man, burdened with self-
consciousness as animals and plants are not, must start spiritually remote
from the desired condition, however immediately its manifestations surround him.

Much of Hill's poetry is religious, but if less amenable to easy explication than, say, the later R. S. Thomas's religious poetry, this is precisely
because Hill gives complex spiritual experience and questioning resonant realization, where Thomas's poems spending most of their time
telling us what they are on about instead of getting on with being it, fall
towards the mere higher prattle of a metaphysically worried man.

Fifteen years ago, in a *London Magazine* (November 1964) article on
Hill's 'fiercely unaccommodating talent', Christopher Ricks per-
ceptively annotated early Hill's way of exploiting tensioned ambiguities
in particular words to bring alive a complexly ambivalent attitude mingling faith and doubt towards, for example, the pretensions represented by
the stained-glass saint in 'In Piam Memoriam':

> Created *purely* from glass the saint stands,
> *Exposing* his *gifted* quite empty hands
> Like a conjurer about to begin,
> A *righteous* man begging of *righteous* men.

My italics; and of course the conjurer simile too has divergent implications. Ricks also drew attention to Hill's potent revivification of cliché
and phrases gone dead in everyday usage. The poet is still doing these
things in *Tenebrae*, where a line like 'the clock discounts us with a telling
chime' ('The Eve of St. Mark') fuses both. I would also note here Ricks's
admirable detailed elucidation of 'Ovid in the Third Reich', Hill's eight
brilliant lines encapsulating in a complex statement of enormous scope
about the human condition, both what can be said for, and what must be
said against, those Germans who kept passively silent under Hitler.
While there is much more to Hill than can be accommodated within
Ricks's terrain of play on ambiguity and cliché, it is in Hill certainly poetically no trivial mannerism or flourish, but innate to his imaginative grasp

of life and centrally functional in articulating it. It enables, of course, as well as the extraordinary resonance whereby wordplay irradiatingly informs Hill's image of that saint to make it a vital focus for sinuous questionings, the exceptional economy with which he gets large things said. Consider just the play on 'cultivate' in the fragment from ' "Domaine Public" ' I quoted earlier. For Hill, as for Herbert or Marvell, ambiguity and paradox are not tricks of rhetoric or decoration, but necessary means of seizing and showing forth truths of life apprehended as the complex thing it is, so requiring correspondingly subtle use of language. Hill's 'difficulty' is demonstrably concomitant to unusual ambitiousness of both theme and method: few poets have begun a first collection with a shot at re-enacting the Creation like Hill's 'Genesis'. That he poetically chews as much as he bites off is not the least impressive thing about his poetry. One trusts it, however baffled occasionally, because it is never wantonly obscure or arbitrarily private, and its subtle compressions function crucially to give significant and illuminative imaginative realization to large matters.

Hill is impressively enough intensively himself to stand the comparison with Eliot. Both poets share historical awareness and perspective, and the poetic practice of bringing past and present into fruitful juxtaposition; though here, I shall argue, Hill's motives and effects generally differ from Eliot's. Hill also has an Eliotian predilection for poetic strategies calculated to achieve a seeming 'impersonality'. I am unimpressed by Eliot's argument in 'Tradition and the Individual Talent' of his 'impersonal theory of poetry', with its precisely meaningless postulation of complete separation between the artist's human and creating self, which reflects Eliot's polemical stance against the Georgian fag-end of Romanticism; in fact, Eliot's extraordinary poetic processes, whereby intensely subjective fragments of creative or actual experience and observation were slowly let aggregate and cohere within a dominant imaginative field, so that 'Prufrock', 'Gerontion', 'The Waste Land', achieve the paradox-form of Imagist epics, show him an extreme Romantic. But his espousal of 'impersonality' does express also a genuine temperamental bias, one Hill shares. Like 'The Waste Land', Hill's 'Funeral Music' and *Mercian Hymns* assume at least some air of being objective statements on the human condition delivered dispassionately from God's right hand. Or, like Eliot with Prufrock, Gerontion, Tiresias, Hill masks utterance with personae discrete from the authorial identity: King Offa, or in that oblique fiction 'The Songbook of Sebastian Arrurruz' what Hill's notes tell us is 'an apocryphal Spanish poet.' Thus much of Hill's poetry, like early Eliot, becomes essentially dramatic. In *Tenebrae,* 'The Pentecost Castle' sequence deploys seemingly various voices. Even where, in his early work, in a thread woven through *Mercian Hymns,* here and there in *Tenebrae* more intensely than ever, Hill modulates into a personal 'I', the reader as with Eliot's use of the pronoun in 'Ash Wednesday' or 'Four Quartets' feels its terms are sharply delimited by the poet, offer no admission-key to his personality or auto-biography. In Hill's 'Lachrimae' sonnets the 'I' is keenly insistent, yet never naked of artifice, and incorporates voices, consciousnesses, other than Hill's. One is Southwell's, the Elizabethan poet and Catholic martyr who provides the sequence's epigraph. But consider the apparently movingly direct and open final sestet of 'Lachrimae':

> So many nights the angel of my house
> has fed such urgent comfort through a dream,
> whispered 'your lord is coming, he is close'
>
> that I have drowsed half-faithful for a time
> bathed in pure tones of promise and remorse:
> 'tomorrow I shall wake and welcome him.'

This, Hill tells us, is 'free translation of a sonnet by Lope de Vega.' One does not doubt the feeling is validly Hill's, but so to find for such unusually simple emotion a guise that at once distances and con-firmingly sanctions it is a radical characteristic of Hill's poetic tempera-ment and strategy.

Again like Eliot, as well as masks of stance or personae Hill appropriates to his purposes and makes distinguishingly his own a range of poetic forms and manners, from the sonnet sequence, through verse with a Metaphysical ground-bass, to the prose-poems of *Mercian Hymns* and his recurrent Spanish derivations. C. H. Sisson has noted (*Agenda*, 13:3, 1975) Hill's 'singularly direct mind which, none the less, seems impelled to such indirect utterance.' Like Crashaw's, Sisson suggests, 'a mind in search of artifices to protect itself against its own passions.' No more than Eliot is Hill prone to offer personal experience with open straight-forwardness in the old-Romantic or new-Confessional I-fall-upon-the-thorns-of-life-I-bleed/My-mind's-not-right ways. His means are devious and oblique. His titles alone can be provocatively indirect: in *Tenebrae* the overall entitling of thirteen superb sonnets only loosely related and on the evidence of Hill's notes not homogeneous in con-ception, as 'An Apology for the Revival of Christian Architecture in England', seems less than inevitable. And yet, attentive reading shows any apparent 'impersonality' about Hill's poetry to be only his necessary guise or framework for a vision, a coherent array of attitudes and imagin-ative response, intensely subjective almost to idiosyncrasy.

If *For the Unfallen* was a first collection startling in the consummate finish of its writing and the amplitude of its aims, this sparing poet's next book, *King Log,* published nine years later in 1968, surpassed it in scope, penetration and mature poetic accomplishment. While in 'Ovid in the Third Reich' extreme compression superbly justifies itself, I would allow that occasionally elsewhere in *King Log* Hill's power-pack becomes a log-jam. In 'Annunciations', although such phrasing as 'the soul/Purples itself; each eye squats full and mild' stamps itself indelibly, and each line is in principle construable, the whole congestedly loses momentum. In 'The Stone Man', language like 'Words clawed my mind as though they had smelt/Revelation's flesh.... The sun bellows over its parched swarms,' seems overpumped, even ludicrous. Intensity of feeling is pervasive through *King Log*, and the repelled notation in 'Annunciations' of 'the steam of beasts,/The loathly neckings and the fat shook spawn', expresses a disgust for the flesh and its appetites recurrent in Hill, though coolly enough revolved through different perspectives, as my earlier quotation from ' "Domaine Public" ' and the 'horse-flies siphons the green dung' image in 'Te Lucis Ante Terminum' illustrate. But *King Log* frequently showed Hill in fluent relatively open style: in 'Cowan Bridge'; or 'Fantasia on "Horbury" ', that evoking a priest on a storm-threatened nineteenth-century West Riding day, his 'outworn pieties', how 'he will weaken, scribbling, at the end,/of unspeakable desolation. Really? Good Lord!' however concludes selfchasteningly:

> Consider him catspawed by an indolent poem,
> This place not of his choosing, this menace
>
> From concave stormlight a freak suggestion....
> These heads of nettles lopped into the dust....

Then there is the delicate perception, feeling subdued to tones appropriately crepuscular, of 'Old Poet with Distant Admirers':

> What I lost was not part of this,
> The dark-blistered foxgloves, wet berries
> Glinting from shadow, small ferns and stones,
>
> Seem fragments, in the observing mind,
> Of its ritual power. Old age
> Singles them out, as though by first-light,
>
> As though a still life, presenting some
> Portion of the soul's feast, went with me
> Everywhere, to be hung in strange rooms,
>
> Loneliness being what it is....

The eleven Arrurruz poems intensify sexual passion precisely by stripping it of circumstantial documentation, an effect similar to Eliot's with sexual disgust in the three Thames-daughter songs in 'The Waste Land', where the nature of his achievement appears clearly from comparing the finished poem's 'Trams and dusty trees' quatrain with the eleven-line equivalent in Eliot's earlier draft, full of background information about the girl and her family. If Hill follows a similar instinct to forfeit a documentary kind of intelligibility to bare finally more illuminating intensities, his results equally justify themselves. Thus, when in an unsympathetic review (*New Statesman*, 5 January 1979) of *Tenebrae* I have come across while writing this Craig Raine takes a sideswipe at the woman lamented in 'The Songbook of Sebastian Arrurruz' as 'shadowy', he seems wrong-headedly beside the point of Hill's psychologically subtle realizations of incandescent emotion. And within the sequence's cryptic framework and strategy, the writing is incisively fluent. The mistress-figure apart, one of the less-noticed poems, 'To His Wife', shows how the selectively sparing can intimate rich human substantiality:

> You ventured occasionally—
> As though this were another's house—
> Not intimate but an acquaintance
> Flaunting her modest claim; like one
> Idly commiserated by new-mated
> Lovers rampant in proper delight
> When all their guests are gone.

But it is the 'Funeral Music' sequence of eight unrhymed sonnets in *King Log* that marked a high point in Hill's poetic career. Here, the Wars of the Roses provide a gravitational field within which Hill can coherently cluster, explore, articulate, some of his huger themes and obsessions. The poems bear what Hill's notes term 'an oblique dedication' to three peers, variously representative of their time and encompassing humane and spiritual as well as ruthlessly worldly allegiances, all executed within the period. A central awareness in 'Funeral Music' is that medieval life was at once nasty brutish and short, and highly ritualized, ceremonious; fraught with spiritual aspirations liable to be broken with stark vividness on harsh and cruel actualities:

> The voice fragrant with mannered humility,
> With an equable contempt for this world,
> 'In honorem Trinitatis'. Crash. The head
> Struck down into a meaty conduit of blood.
> So these dispose themselves to receive each
> Pentecostal blow from axe or seraph,
> Spattering block-straw with mortal residue.

Everywhere, not through comment but by precise realization in the texture of his writing, Hill highlights the discrepancies, glaring in fifteenth-century life but by inference perennial, between the bloody and the formal, so that with two-way irony each becomes a criticism upon the other. His command of resonant ambiguity functions brilliantly to illumine the dichotomy: in 'dispose' in the passage just quoted; or 'scrape', hinting at 'bow and scrape', at the start of the second poem 'For whom do we scrape our tribute of pain. . . .' 'Funeral Music' alludes to the Battle of Towton in 1461, notorious for its carnage, and here Hill can particularly evoke the medieval mixture of ritual and butchery: 'fastidious trumpets shrilling into the ruck', the heraldic panoply and glitter of armies, resolves to 'reddish ice tinged the reeds'. The third poem achieves a pitch of suggestive definition quite exceptional in English battle-poetry:

> They bespoke doomsday and they meant it by
> God, their curved metal rimming the low ridge.
> But few appearances are like this. Once
> Every five hundred years a comet's
> Over-riding stillness might reveal men
> In such array, livid and featureless,
> With England crouched beastwise beneath it all.
> 'Oh, that old Northern business. . . .' A field
> After battle utters its own sound
> Which is like nothing on earth, but is earth,
> Blindly the questing snail, vulnerable
> Mole emerge, blindly we lie down, blindly
> Among carnage the most delicate souls
> Tup in their marriage-blood, gasping 'Jesus'.

A poetic style and tone Hill notes as 'ornate and heartless' is crucially instrumental to the total meaning of 'Funeral Music', implying, and through interrupting grunts and shrieks endorsing, a critique of its own limitations; and so effectively transcending these. Rarely is artifice so artfully significant; this is poetry of a formal magnificence that, in its own words, 'whines through the empyrean' aware, as that verb's connotations suggest, of its own ambivalence.

Beyond which, through the lives and times it articulates, 'Funeral Music' searingly meditates life's fundamental questions:

> Though I would scorn the mere instinct of faith,
> Expediency of assent, if I dared,
> What I dare not is a waste history. . . .

Is all human effort, the expense of blood and spirit, in these or any other wars, or other human enterprise, finally terrifyingly meaningless? Life subject purely to logic, rationality, is definingly evoked as a stasis of beautiful sterility, a haunting inhuman impossibility:

>   if intellect
> Itself were absolute law, sufficient grace,
> Our lives could be a myth of captivity
> Which we might enter: an unpeopled region
> Of ever new-fallen snow, a palace blazing
> With perpetual silence as with torches.

'Some parch for what they were'—yet neither does nostalgia, the yearning to start again pure, afford escape or exoneration. The figures Hill's poem meditates, whatever their temporal lives and desires, the meaning of their personal history or their time's, are now 'set apart in timeless colloquy' to 'bear witness' in the minds of those who contemplate them. Yet if for others they can thus remain, extracted from life's contingency, symbols to be given meaning as Hill's poetry has given it, still 'Funeral Music' closes insisting, in a strategy more powerfully enacting the poetic self-chastening of 'Fantasia on "Horbury" ', that that is no consolation or succour to their mortal lives:

> If it is without
> Consequence when we vaunt and suffer, or
> If it is not, all echoes are the same
> In such eternity. Then tell me, love,
> How that should comfort us—or anyone
> Dragged unnerved out of this worldly place
> Crying to the end 'I have not finished.'

The grave abstractness of those lines is beautifully weighted by that personalizing 'love', that final cry, the more concrete of the alternative meanings contained in 'half-unnerved' and 'worldly place'.

  Mercian Hymns, in 1971, surprised superficially by being a sequence of thirty prose-poems; thematically however it is consonant with 'Funeral Music': less intensively wrought, wider ranging, more sportive. It is no disadvantage to Hill's purposes that, Anglo-Saxon records belonging overwhelmingly to the later period of Wessex hegemony, and even archaeology having unearthed little, the powerful Mercian king Offa who controlled by conquest most of England and functioned as a European potentate, 'friend of Charlemagne', remains so sparsely documented, his testimony little more than his impressive money and the dyke he built against the Welsh:

> And it seemed, while we watched, he began to walk to-
>   wards us   he vanished
> he left behind coins, for his lodging, and traces of
>   red mud.

Thus hymn XXX. That the grandest worldly show is passing, is an awareness *Mercian Hymns* utters incisively as Shelley's 'Ozymandias'. Earth, the struggle to master it, and that all returns to it, is 'invested in mother earth' (IV), features crucially through the sequence, its details delicately observed; Offa *Rex Totius Anglorum Patriae* is as transient as a snail that 'sugared its new stone' (XIV). Yet also Offa is something perennial, the 'creature of legend' Hill's notes tell us might 'in this sequence be regarded as the presiding genius of the West Midlands, his dominion enduring from the middle of the eighth century until the middle of the twentieth (and possibly beyond).' The final hymn's 'traces of red mud' intimate more than the historical Offa's grandiose dyke; Hymn I, listing his worldly attributes, has him also 'overlord of the M5. . . contractor to the desirable new estates,' and gives clear guidance to Hill's framing strategy for the sequence, which is comprehensible enough. One should note though that if occasionally Hill collocates ancient and modern with the Eliotian motive of ironic contrast, as when suburban dwellings are named 'Ethandune', 'Catraeth', 'Maldon', 'Pengwern', generally his intention is the reverse, akin in its historical vision to that of David Jones in *In Parenthesis*: to suggest parallels, continuities. This allows him, through a book refreshingly humorous for Hill, to enjoy concocting anachronisms such as 'Merovingian car-dealers'; but the purpose is serious, and the vision coherent.

But the energies of *Mercian Hymns* flow not only along this axis between past and present, but concurrently along another vitally linking public and private worlds, those of temporal power and of a childhood evidently the poet's. Hill thus establishes a four-way system of metaphor of considerable resonance. And as with Joyce's equation of Leopold Bloom and Ulysses, the perspectives upon one another of past heroic modes and anti-heroic modern private life qualify the former, overtly present in Hill as not in *Ulysses*, as well as the latter, and finally inform and help understand both. Concerned with power and self-aggrandizement, Hill is interested not in their means and instruments, but the underlying subtle private impulses which will and energize them. Richly fruitful here is his use of childhood, which has its fantasies of power and command, whim, wanton cruelty, grievances, terrors, egotistic desires, but confined to expression objectively trivial. But if in adulthood such impulses obtain the means of power, there ensues inordinate enactment, most extremely exemplified in a Hitler, Stalin or Amin, perhaps bridled generally only insofar as given political systems check it. Hill clearly believes that power corrupts and absolute power corrupts absolutely; and Offa, whose early-medieval society desiderated military autocracy, becomes the type of a human phenomenon perennial if modulating its guises in the modern England of motorways, commerce and political democracy. Yet by implicating his own boyhood as a single child who 'fostered a strangeness; gave myself to unattainable toys' (VI) in his unsparing creation of this figure, Hill enables us to understand compassionately his common human nature. In Hymn VII we read: 'Coagulations of frogs: once, with branches and half-bricks, he battered a ditchful;' then,

> Ceolred was his friend and remained so, even after the day of the lost fighter: a biplane, already obsolete and irreplaceable, two inches of heavy snub silver. Ceolred let it spin through a hole in the classroom-floorboards, softly, into the rat-droppings and coins.

> After school he lured Ceolred, who was sniggering with fright, down

to the old quarries, and flayed him. Then, leaving Ceolred, he journeyed for hours, calm and alone, in his private derelict sandlorry named *Albion.*

The various dimensions richly connect here: particularly charged is the last sentence, where that sandlorry given England's name becomes receptacle for solitariness, fantasy, stasis, which comprehend child and king, past and present. Again, when in Hymn XIX Hill writes 'They haul a sodden log, hung with soft shields of fungus, and launch it upon the flames,' he is deploying metaphor to show that power is indeed child's play, transfiguring the latter into mimic enactment of Anglo-Saxon regal burial ritual.

Obviously Hill's strategy in *Mercian Hymns* allows enormous scope to his talent for verbal punning, refined and applied as felicitously as ever: the protagonist is a 'staggeringly-gifted child'; on his coins Offa appears 'cushioned on a legend', with a play on both 'cushioned' and the numismatic and larger meanings of 'legend'. Three of the hymns are about 'Offa's Coins': an arbitrary ruler's mark-making equivalent to the boy carving his name on desks. So, 'the masterful head emerges, kempt and jutting, out of England's well' (XIII), his name a 'best-selling brand, curt graffito. A laugh; a cough. . . .A specious gift. . . .The starting cry of a race. A name to conjure with.' (II). 'Hymns' implies, whatever else, celebration; yet Offa's legacy may be no more than—for the whole work's closing 'traces of red earth' bear another connotation—money and blood. Imagist epic seems an appropriate term for *Mercian Hymns,* where intensely worked and polished fragments cohere within a grand structure to intimate a vision of huge scope.

Tenebrae, the 1978 collection of Hill's subsequent work, shows some of his most purely beautiful writing in a return to traditional, rhymed forms, particularly the sonnet, by this poet always exceptionally intent on disciplining emotion. Much of the emotion in *Tenebrae* is religious, a desire trustingly to believe agonized by doubt; Hill's has always seemed perhaps a style learnt from a despair, and *Tenebrae* more than ever recalls Donne's observation, 'Grief brought to numbers cannot be so fierce,/For he tames it, that fetters it in verse.' But not only 'tames': also clarifyingly explores and articulates it as undisciplined utterance could not. And in any case, as 'Funeral Music' particularly, but his work pervasively, has shown, for Hill the tension between artifice of expression and immediacies of experience, which his poetic forms enact, is itself a central troubling theme in his engagement with the human condition. The nagging paradox is defined in the four-line poem closing both the title-sequence of *Tenebrae* and the book:

> Music survives, composing her own sphere,
> Angel of Tones, Medusa, Queen of the Air,
> and when we would accost her with real cries

> silver on silver thrills itself to ice.

Sharp as ever in *Tenebrae* is Hill's fearful awareness that in 'composing', conferring articulate order, whether in life or upon the materials of a poem, we abstract, petrify, real feelings, cries, within a realm inaccessible and unsuccouring to the actual contingent world we thus invade. The helpless gulf between the timeless yet literally unalive truth of our supreme imaginative constructs, and the timebound, transient anarchy of 'breathing human passion', has always registered at the heart of our poetic tradition, in such works as Keats's 'Ode on a Grecian Urn' and Yeats's Byzantium poems. And Hill knows, as they did, and extendedly in his own terms Wallace Stevens, that our composed structures, however they chill and in a sense deny life, are also its supreme enduring expression, are moreover necessary, forms sustaining and generative of values in a world perhaps otherwise void of meaning. Always recognizing and often enacting the conflict between imaginative order and life's fearsome anarchy, Hill by giving each grave weight tensions a polarity which enricheningly energizes his poetry.

These considerations are especially relevant to the seven 'Lachrimae' sonnets, which take their epigraph—'Passions I allow, and loves I approve, onely I would wish that men would alter their object and better their intent'—and more, from Robert Southwell the Elizabethan Catholic poet who despising all things worldly composed his life towards martyrdom and in suffering torture and death achieved the consummation he devoutly wished. As sonnet 5, 'Pavana Dolorosa', puts it:

> Self-wounding martyrdom, what joys you have,
> true-torn among this fictive consonance,
> music's creation of the moveless dance,
> the decreation to which all must move,. . . .

A 'self-seeking hunter of forms', the martyr makes his real agony the focal point of a contrived artifice in which even his torturers are his collaborators, material for his composition; within which design, as Hill's earlier 'Ovid in the Third Reich' had it, 'They, in their sphere,/Harmonize strangely with the divine/Love.' So, 'Pavana Dolorosa' insists,

> None can revoke your cry.
> Your silence is an ecstacy of sound
>
> and your nocturnals blaze upon the day.

To express his sense of a resonance irrefutable and formally perfect found paradoxically through extinction at the worldly level 'Pavana Dolorosa' uses music and dance as analogy, a dimension of metaphor framing the whole 'Lachrimae' sequence, subtitled 'Seven tears figured in seven passionate Pavans' in allusion to the music of Southwell's Catholic contemporary John Dowland. Of course the relation between the violent human content and the poetry's formal qualities and tones of elaborate stately melancholy enacts the paradox at the heart of Hill's pre-occupations: his skill at thus implicating form in theme is more intensive-ly managed than in Keats's Ode or even Yeats's two hammered-gold Byzantium poems.

In Hill's first sonnet, 'Lachrimae Verae', Christ is addressed as

> the castaway of drowned remorse,
> you are the world's atonement on the hill.
> This is your body twisted by our skill
> into a patience proper for redress.

More 'fictive consonance', as Christ's body is not only literally 'twisted' to the Cross, but distorted by human concepts into a beautiful emblem for suffering: the fury and the mire of in this case possibly superhuman veins translated into an aesthetically satisfying image for our consola-tion. As 'Funeral Music' insisted, we perhaps abuse the lives we thus use 'set apart in timeless colloquy' to 'bear witness'; although in 'Lachrimae' complex considerations arise because the suffering contemplated is martyrdom, perhaps self-abuse when human like Southwell's, claiming divine nature and purposes when Christ's. Or attributed with them, 'twisted by our skill'; for this is a poetry of doubt. And in any case, per-haps in composing its own sphere wearing again the unconsoling face of Medusa, and icily inviolable when accosted with our real cries. The 'Lachrimae' sonnets certainly insist upon an unsatisfactory gulf between the poet and the saviour whose 'body moves but moves to no avail':

> I cannot turn aside from what I do;
> you cannot turn away from what I am.
> You do not dwell in me nor I in you. . . .
>   ('Lachrimae Verae')

Indeed, Hill's tone modulates into hostility, given ironic edge by the wordplay, in 'Lachrimae Coactae':

> You are the crucified who crucifies,
> self-withdrawn even from your own device,
> your trim-plugged body, wreath of rakish thorn.

And 'Martyrium' too shows distaste for this 'Jesus-faced' figure:

> Clamorous love, its faint and baffled shout,
> its grief that would betray him to our fear,
> he suffers for our sake, or does not hear
>
> above the hiss of shadows on the wheat.

That incorporation of 'amorous' into 'clamorous' love, in the context of a sequence throughout preoccupied with passion in both its religious and secular senses and the conflict and interplay between them, is characteristically masterly, and the last quoted line shows the incisive sensuousness repeatedly vivifying this poetry of abstract concepts. Like 'Funeral Music', 'Lachrimae' profoundly articulates a question acknowledged, for the closing sonnet translating Lope de Vega from which I have already quoted is a real human cry for a peace that passes understanding, as incapable of resolution: how far can composition, artifice, form, all imaginative mediation of life whether by poet or martyr, redeem and reconcile life's brute fact; how far, in reducing life to essence, are they its illusory shadows merely? Yet if art cannot cancel horrible realities it confers significance upon them: he who composes is forging in the smithy of his soul the uncreated conscience of his human race. As for words, as Saul Bellow's Moses Herzog puts it to himself, 'What can thoughtful people and humanists do but struggle towards suitable words?. . . .I go after reality with language.' 'Lachrimae' exemplifies an art of language superbly self-reflexive, that questions critically what it is itself up to. The tensions between art as sublime significance and shadowy sublimation are done memorable justice; human passions, needs, fears, realize themselves through this poetry's smooth shapeliness like the glitter in shot silk.

That in 'Lachrimae' Hill's poetic manner adaptively assumes some characteristics of the Elizabethan Southwell about whom the preoccupations of the sequence gather, is of course an effect knowingly managed and part of the poetry's point; and given that it works, preempts Craig Raine's complaint (*New Statesman,* 5 January 1979) that 'the traditional diction makes for glum reading,' and his pejorative designation of Hill, a poet preoccupied with perennial man in temporal history, as 'archaeological'. The kind of languorous wordplay illustrated in some of my quotations from 'Lachrimae', typified by the close of 'Pavana Dolorosa',

> I founder in desire for things unfound.
> I stay amid the things that will not stay,

recurs in the book's title-sequence 'Tenebrae', where the second section is a tissue of it and the brief fourth has lines like 'Light of light, supreme delight;/Grace at our lips to our disgrace.' Distinct from the concentrated ambiguity within a single word or phrase by which Hill has always clarifyingly focused his understanding of life's paradoxes, this is less a 'metaphysical' than, consciously, a conventional Elizabethan kind of wordplay, a more decorative slow juggling of words to revolve their varieties of signification or merely achieve symmetries. Lines like Sidney's 'My heart was wounded with his wounded heart' or early Shakespeare's 'Light, seeking light, doth light of light beguile' would blend in harmoniously. Of course this, in collaboration with traditional verse forms, procures a fluency Hill occasionally forfeited in earlier books when compressing meaning as ruthlessly as those machines which crush scrapped cars to cubic inches. The euphuistic manner might lend itself to formulations superficially neat and reductive, but Hill employs it to purpose in specific poems, not self-indulgently; and if *Tenebrae* is throughout his most fluent collection, this is certainly not at the expense of the intensities which are this poet's hallmark, nor of that meticulously expressive articulation of syntax characterizing all his writing.

I do nevertheless find the 'Tenebrae' sequence a weak area in this collection, for overall it reads too much like Hill just letting his machinery tick over. And although in a way more enterprising, I cannot say that 'The Pentecost Castle' interests me greatly. Fluency, an exceptional openness of style for Hill, its short-lined stanzas certainly have. The notes to *Tenebrae* tell us that 'The Pentecost Castle' is 'particularly indebted' to Hill's reading of the *Penguin Book of Spanish Verse*, and browsing around that, with particular indebtedness in my case to the prose translations, I can see what Hill owes texturally, what has stimulated his poetry's tone, ballad musicality, temper, occasional piercing bitter-sweetness and glitter. These qualities acknowledged, there seems little more to say about 'The Pentecost Castle': although each section is tellingly charged with implication, I do not feel that as a whole the sequence shapes sufficiently into gathered articulation of the themes adumbrated in its epigraphs, from Simone Weil about love's egotism, and Yeats's 'It is terrible to desire and not possess, and terrible to possess and not desire.'

But generally *Tenebrae* sustains magnificently the development within continuity Hill's poetry has always achieved. Among several excellent individual poems are 'A Pre-Raphaelite Notebook', 'Te Lucis Ante Terminum' which I have already discussed, 'Ave Regina Coelorum' brilliantly starting 'There is a land called Lost/at peace inside our heads', and 'Terribilis Est Locus Iste', dedicated to 'Gauguin and the Pont-Aven School' and effecting dextrous verbal capture of

> marginal angels lightning-sketched in red
> chalk on the month's accounts, or marigolds
> in paint runnily embossed. . . .

Particularly, the thirteen sonnets, less intensively interrelated than those of 'Lachrimae', gathered under the devious title 'An Apology for the Revival of Christian Architecture in England', gravitating meditatively around Coleridge's hankering for 'the spiritual, Platonic old England,' mediate its personal, geographical and historical intimations in poetry as impressive as any Hill has written. The second sonnet, 'Damon's Lament for his Clorinda, Yorkshire 1654', exemplifies a lucidity, intensity and perfect pacing characterizing the sequence:

> The North Sea batters our shepherds' cottages
> from sixty miles. No sooner has the sun

> swung clear above earth's rim than it is gone.
> We live like gleaners of its vestiges
>
> knowing we flourish, though each year a child
> with the set face of a tomb-weeper is put down
> for ever and ever....

Anything but precious, Hill's fastidiousness of diction is as trenchant as it is elegant, as appears in his choice of verbs in this from the seventh sonnet 'Loss and Gain':

> brown stumps of headstones tamp into the ling
> the ruined and the ruinously strong.
> Platonic England grasps its tenantry
>
> where wild-eyed poppies raddle tawny farms
> and wild swans root in lily-clouded lakes.

But the final sonnet, 'The Herefordshire Carol', fittingly illustrates the kind of felicities abundant through this sequence, every sleight of phrase and cinematically sharp particular working within a poetry of packed lucidity to vitalize a delicate conception:

> So to celebrate that kingdom: it grows
> greener in winter, essence of the year;
> the apple-branches musty with green fur.
> In the viridian darkness of its yews
>
> it is an enclave of perpetual vows
> broken in time. Its truth shows disrepair,
> disfigured shrines, their stones of gossamer,
> Old Moore's astrology, all hallows,
>
> the squire's effigy bewigged with frost,
> and hobnails cracking puddles before dawn.
> In grange and cottage girls rise from their beds
>
> by candlelight and mend their ruined braids.
> Touched by the cry of the iconoclast,
> how the rose-window blossoms with the sun!

Hill's poetry here loses nothing in intensity for being more than usually at peace with the world. If an excitement of following it has been that its development from collection to collection is at once surprising and recognizably harmonious, in *Tenebrae,* his craftsmanship more adequate than ever to the intensity of his vision, and avoiding the occasional lockjaw hesitation of some of his earlier work, he has achieved his most eloquent poetry yet.

Generally, Hill's work, never condescending for the sake of yielding instant meaning, keeping aloof from superficialities of fashion and true to

its imaginative temper and purposes, has through decades of much
sloppy self-indulgent and makeshift writing, a certain literary chaos, con-
ferred intellectual and emotional dignity on poetry. That in our place and
time it exists, is an unqualified good for poetry and readers. Intricately
exploring and enacting through diverse ramifications the central human
tension between imaginative order and life's anarchy, employing a consummate technique commensurate with his ambitiousness, Hill like an
old-timer panning for gold sifts life and language, prospecting among
their silt for glinting richnesses. To borrow one of his own immaculately
apt images, his poetry 'grows upon the mind/as lichen glimmers on the
wood.'

BLAKE MORRISON

Speech and reticence: Seamus Heaney's 'North'

WHEN SEAMUS HEANEY's *North* was published in June 1975 it met with the kind of acclaim which, in Britain at least, we had ceased to believe poetry could receive. The book had barely come back from the printers before various funding bodies were rushing to cast their cheques at Heaney's feet. *North* was made the Poetry Book Society choice; it won the Duff Cooper Memorial Prize and the £1,500 W.H.Smith Memorial Prize; it was gushed over on television and radio. It also (and this does not automatically follow) sold remarkably well—over 6,000 copies in the first month: that is a figure which outdoes even Larkin's *The Whitsun Weddings* and Hughes's *Crow*. As a result of *North*'s success, Heaney is now firmly established as one of our most popular poets and (his genial presence helps here) is much in demand for public appearances: his audience at an early evening reading at the National Theatre in January 1977 was the biggest I have ever seen a poet command.

A sceptical observer might have suspected that there was rather more to the acclaim for *North* than appreciation of the book's literary merits. A glance through the reviews—for instance Martin Dodsworth's *Guardian* comment that *North* was 'testimony to the patience, persistence and power of the imagination under duress' makes it clear that much of the collection's pulling power can be explained by the fact that it had come out of, and had concerned itself with, Northern Ireland. For some years, in a new version of the old cry 'Where are the war poets?', critics had been calling for a poetry that would 'deal with' the Northern Ireland 'problem', and in the reviews of *North* there is an almost audible sigh of relief that at last a poetry of stature had emerged from the 'troubles'. At the same time it was noticeable that, with the exception of Conor Cruise O'Brien in the *Listener,* hardly anyone seemed interested in what it was that Heaney had to 'say' about Northern Ireland. Indeed the suggestion seemed to be that while it was good to have a poet like Heaney 'involve himself in' the Ulster troubles, his poetry was valuable insofar as it could not be seen to be making statements: poetry, after all, should not mean but be. The response to *North* was therefore a complex, but not a contradictory, nor indeed an unfamiliar one: good though it was to know that poetry was being made out of the stuff of the times, it did not pay to look too deeply into what that poetry was saying.

This response is unfortunate, for it obscures one of the central features of Heaney's development: namely, that it is through an increased public consciousness that he has transformed himself from a pleasing but peripheral figure into one of the best poets now writing in English. And yet it would have to be admitted that Heaney himself contributed to the 'apolitical' reception of his book. Having grown up in a community, the Catholic minority in Ulster, where to speak openly is a dangerous activity ('whatever you say, say nothing' as one of his poems has it), and belonging as he does to a modern poetic tradition which distrusts poetry that too explicitly 'states', Heaney is loth to wear the mantle of the political poet, and has discouraged us from searching his book for messages and meanings of a 'public' kind. 'My view and way with poetry' he has said, 'has never been to use it as a vehicle for making statements about situations. The poems have more come up like bodies out of the bog of my own imagination'. Similarly, in a Poetry Book Society Bulletin accompanying *North*, he remarked: 'During the last few years there has been considerable expectation that poets from Northern Ireland should "say" something about "the situation", but in the end they will only be worth listening to if they are saying something about and to themselves.' These views need to be taken in the context of other remarks Heaney has made about the exploration of his own identity being a means of exploring national identity, and about personal search being a kind of historical research; otherwise they promote too rigid a distinction between private and public. In this respect, the division of *North* into two parts, evidence though it is of the Yeatsian care that went into the organizing of the collection, may have been a miscalculation. The division was originally intended to create some kind of historical perspective on present-day events: 'North'—contemporary Northern Ireland as depicted in the looser poems of Part Two—was to be seen in terms of a larger 'North'— the two thousand years of Northern Europe explored in the tightly packed poems of Part One. The division is logical, but it does tend to create a false gap between past and present, private and public, and thus to make us miss the collection's unifying vision.

This is a pity because, notwithstanding Heaney's ability to give his poems several 'layers of meaning' (he rarely settles for anything so straightforward as one-level 'statement'), *North* is the first collection in which he has had something undeniably important to say—both about his country and about his place in it. To make this claim is not to disparage the early work but merely to get it in proportion. The main concern of his first collection, *Death of a Naturalist* (1966), was simply to re-create and celebrate his childhood world—a world of cows, barns, wells and tadpoles, of blackberrying, churning, fishing and digging. For Heaney, as for one of the main influences on him, Patrick Kavanagh, simply 'naming these things is the love-act and its pledge'. Accurate physical detail — as when he describes his father digging

> The coarse boot nestled on the lug, the shaft
> Against the inside knee was levered firmly.

—is a way of preserving that world. (Heaney has now largely moved away from explorations of childhood, but 'Sunlight', the first poem in *North* and a beautiful tribute to Mary Heaney —

> And here is love
> like a tinsmith's scoop
> sunk past its gleam
> in the meal-bin.

—shows that when he does return to it, the results can be even more impressive.) The potential danger in such subject matter—namely, a lapsing into cosy rusticity—was at this early stage of his development counteracted by the Hughes-like vision of a raw and often violent natural world: frogs are described 'poised like mud grenades, their blunt heads farting'; water goes over a fall 'like villains dropped screaming to justice'; and a trout is compared successively to 'a fat gun-barrel', a torpedo, a tracer-bullet and a ramrod. Indeed so menacing was the imagery that it was sometimes a problem to assess how far Heaney dissociated himself from the violence he detected: often brutal and sensitive responses were allowed to co-exist in the same text. In 'The Early Purges', for instance, two viewpoints—that of a child and that of an adult—are played off against each other. Where the child sees kittens drowning, Dan Taggart sees only the elimination of 'scraggy wee shits'. The language of the poem embodies the contrasting feelings: 'frail', 'soft', 'bobbed', 'sadly'—this is the child's view; 'soused', 'slung', 'snout', 'pump'—this is Dan Taggart's. The balance is disturbed, however, in the last two stanzas where a third voice—that of the child grown up—intervenes to settle the matter in Dan Taggart's favour:

> Still, living displaces false sentiments
> And now, when shrill pups are prodded to drown
> I just shrug, 'Bloody pups'. It makes sense;
>
> 'Prevention of cruelty' talk cuts ice in town
> Where they consider death unnatural,
> But on well-run farms pests have to be kept down.

There is something deliberately tight-lipped and square-shouldered about the end of 'The Early Purges', a sense that Heaney is not only suppressing his own sensitivities, but rather relishes the idea of shocking town-dwelling pet-lovers and members of the RSPCA. (If this is so then he might have been gratified to read in the *Daily Telegraph* of 20 July 1976 that when the poem was set as an 'O'-level text, it 'brought protests from parents on grounds of both content and the poem's earthy language. The poem "Early Purges" was described by Mr Eldon Griffiths, Conservative MP for Bury St Edmunds, as "sick", Written by Sean Heany (sic)... it begins "I was six when I first saw kittens drown", and goes on to describe their death in language not encouraged in most homes.' From the point of view of Heaney's later development, what is interesting about the poem is that an initially sympathetic and pitying response succumbs to a shrug of resignation, an acceptance of killing as part of an inevitable pattern. This double response — sympathy and resignation — is dramatized more fully in *North*, where the victims are not animal but human, and where Heaney weighs civilized outrage against the laws of the tribe.

There was, however, little promise of the work to come in Heaney's second collection *Door Into the Dark* (1969). As its opening lines half-concede—'Must you know it again?/Dull pounding through hay,/The uneasy whinny'—this reworks the ground of the first collection almost to the point of self-caricature. A parody in the *Review* in 1970 indicates the role in which Heaney was now in danger of being cast: it described him as a 'longhorn Cow, a big, heavy and ungainly stock once widely distributed in England and Ireland'. At any other time, Heaney might have remained untroubled by this for there is a long tradition of Irish writers being taken up by English publishers, and of those publishers wanting them to play the role of straw-chewing rustic and/or word-spinning Celt: as Patrick Kavanagh, who resisted the pressure, put it, 'the English love "Irishmen" and are always on the lookout for them', or—much earlier—in the words of Bernard Shaw: 'the Englishman instinctively flatters the fault that makes the Irishman harmless and amusing to him'. In 1969 Heaney's seeming willingness to go along with this was beginning to look a bit questionable: with rioting in Londonderry, the calling in of British troops, the disarming of Protestant vigilante groups, and the formation of the provisional wing of the IRA, it was not really a time for 'country matters'. In Seamus Deane, to whom one of the poems in *North* is dedicated, Heaney had a friend who understood and resented the implications of the Irish caricaturing which *Death of a Naturalist* and *Door into the Dark* encouraged: Deane has argued that 'a reputation for linguistic extravagance is dangerous especially when given to small nations by a bigger one which dominates them. By means of it Celts can stay quaint and stay put.' (Similarly one might argue that the familiar caricature of 'mad'—ie, lovably eccentric—Irishmen is convenient to the English because it so readily becomes in times of crisis a caricature of 'mad'—ie, insanely dangerous—Irishmen).

In the troubled climate of the late 60s and early 70s Heaney began to change tack; his collection *Wintering Out* (1972), though in many ways less enjoyable than the first two, was a necessary break with former habits. Simply the physical appearance of the words on the page—what John Wilson Foster in his excellent introductory essay on Heaney (*Critical Quarterly*, Spring 1974) calls 'spare and vertical shapes,

. . . .serious attempts to sink shafts narrowly and deep'—gives evidence of a new profundity and self-discipline; and it was here that the verse forms of *North*, the two-stress lines and dense quatrains, began to evolve. There is the first of Heaney's 'Bog' poems, 'The Tollund Man', and there is above all a passionate interest in the political implications of language. Several poems are an ardent saying aloud of old words or place names ('Anahoorish', 'Toome', 'Broagh'); others like 'The Backward Look' and 'Traditions' assess what has been lost by the replacement of Gaelic or Irish with the English language. In Heaney's characteristic compacting of word, territory and sex, English is seen as a male language, a language of invasion, a language of consonants; Irish is seen as a female language, a language of vowels, a language subjected to rape and conquest:

> Our guttural muse
> was bulled long ago
> by the alliterative tradition,
> her uvula grows
>
> vestigial, forgotten. . .

By the time of *North*, Heaney's mastery of this kind of multi-layering effect is complete. His preoccupation with the peat bogs of Northern Europe (it is worth mentioning that he did not visit Denmark, where some of the preserved bodies can be seen, until October 1973, and that most of his material is therefore drawn from P. V. Glob's accounts and photographs in *The Bog People*) not only gives him a subject matter, but an analogy for the poem: like the bog, it must have several 'preserving' layers. Heaney now strives to produce images which are simultaneously linguistic, historical, geographical and sexual. 'Ocean's Love to Ireland', for example (the title is an echo of Ralegh's poem to Queen Elizabeth, 'The Ocean's Love to Cynthia'), is a poem about possession which works on these various levels:

> Speaking broad Devonshire,
> Ralegh has backed the maid to a tree
> As Ireland is backed to England
>
> And drives inland
> Till all her strands are breathless:
> 'Sweesir, Swatter! Sweesir, Swatter!'. . . .

There are, first of all, the historical allusions: to Ralegh's part in the Elizabethan colonization of Ireland; to the small Spanish-Catholic defence force routed at Smerwick in 1580; and to John Aubrey's description of the young Ralegh's amorous adventures: 'He loved a wench well: and one time getting one of the mayds of honor up against a tree in a wood ('twas his first lady) who seemed at first boarding to be something fearful of her honour, and modest, she cryed. . . .Sweet Sir Walter! Sweet Sir Walter!

Sir Walter! At last as the danger and the pleasure at the same time grew
higher, she cryed in the extasey Swisser Swatter Swisser Swatter. . . .' On
another level the poem describes a linguistic and literary conquest,
Ralegh's 'broad Devonshire' overcoming the 'Irish' of the ruined maid,
and 'iambic drums/Of English' beating through the woods that once har-
boured Gaelic poets. Again, 'Ireland backed to England' is how, geographically and politically, Heaney sees the Ireland-England relationship; in another poem from *North*, 'Act of Union', England and
Ireland are pictured as a man and woman lying together, England the 'tall
kingdom, imperially male' lying 'over the shoulder' of Ireland. And in
both these poems there is also the use of sexual metaphor to describe
invasion: Ralegh's 'superb crest' (boat-prow, penis, heraldic emblem)
'drives inland'; the ruined maid is exploited for temporary pleasure, but
all the while Ralegh's real loyalties lie at home with Queen Elizabeth.

'Ocean's Love to Ireland' expresses a resentment of English colonization which might be taken to denote a marked degree of Republicanism
on Heaney's part, a conviction that the contemporary troubles can be explained in terms of the centuries-old domination of Ulster by an
'imperialist power'. If we look further we can find other poems where
Heaney's prejudices or loyalties as an Irish Catholic reveal themselves:
there's a hostile caricature of a parading Orangeman drummer 'lodging
thunder/Grossly there between his chin and his knees'; there's the description of the 'obstinate fifth column' sprouted by the Act of Union, the
Ulster Protestants with their 'parasitical/And ignorant little fists'; and
however lightly worn there is the fear of Protestant and British army
harassment which comes over in poems like 'The Ministry of Fear' and
'A Constable Calls'. We know, too, from Karl Miller, for whose *Listener*
Heaney wrote several front-line Belfast reports in the early 70s, that 'at
the time of the Civil Rights marches Seamus Heaney wrote a polemical
ballad entitled "Craig's Dragoons", in the Irish folk-song tradition. . . .
(which) seems to have circulated anonymously, as *samizdat*';
the poem is reprinted in the *Review*, nos 27-8.

Heaney's Catholic resentment of Protestant colonization is, however,
tempered not only by his feelings of indebtedness towards English language and literature ('Ulster was British, but with no rights on/The
English Lyric' as one poem puts it), but also by the knowledge that
Ireland was subject to conquest long before the Tudors. The several
poems about Viking invasions in *North* enlarge the book's historical per-
spective, and oppose traditional Irish nostalgia for a pre-colonial
Emerald Isle. Heaney may be more sympathetic towards the
Vikings—they are the 'fabulous raiders'—but they are still invaders,
'haggers/and hagglers, gombeen-men,/hoarders of grudges and gain'.
Further historical enlargement comes from Heaney's descriptions of the
Bog People, the victims of an Iron Age culture which, in order to survive

each winter, sacrificed some of its people to a mother goddess. Heaney's nearly necrophiliac fascination with the terrible beauty of the peat-preserved bodies can have the effect of obscuring the analogy he intends. But that analogy is crucial to what he has to say about Northern Ireland and he has explained it (*Listener,* 7 December 1972) as follows:

> you have a society in the Iron Age where there was ritual blood-letting. You have a society where girls' heads were shaved for adultery, you have a religion centring on the territory, on a goddess of the ground and of the land, and associated with sacrifice. Now in many ways the fury of Irish Republicanism is associated with a religion like this, with a female goddess. . . . It seems to me that there are satisfactory imaginative parallels between this religion and time and our own time.

This analogy between ancient and modern, between the Iron Age and the IRA, can be seen operating in Heaney's poem 'Punishment', which describes a girl who has been hanged, and her body then thrown in the bog, as punishment for committing adultery. Heaney's details are partly sensuous, drawing attention to the girl's attractiveness (her nipples are 'amber beads', her features 'beautiful'), and they are partly preparatory for the intended analogy: the girl has a 'tar-black' face and a 'shaved head', and so do the 'betraying sisters' of present-day Ulster, the girls who have been tarred and feathered by the IRA (punished, that is, either for 'informing' or for going out with British soldiers). Heaney's own stance is noticeably ambivalent: he pities the victims of punishment, but his pity is offset and finally outweighed by his understanding of the motives for judicial revenge:

> I who have stood dumb
> when your betraying sisters,
> cauled in tar,
> wept by the railings,
> who would connive
> in civilized outrage
> yet understand the exact
> and tribal, intimate revenge.

The word 'connive' is crucial here, for it suggests that Heaney's 'civilized outrage'—the kind of response he describes in a poem from Part Two of *North:* 'Oh, it's disgraceful, surely, I agree,/Where's it going to end? 'It's getting worse.' — is forced and artificial in comparison with his intuitive understanding of the laws and needs of the tribe. We are back again in the world of 'The Early Purges'. Pity for a 'frail', drowned victim is finally overruled by the adult voice of necessity, and a shrug of resignation takes its place.

It would be going too far to suggest that 'Punishment' in particular and

the Bog poems generally offer a defence of Republicanism; but they are a
form of 'explanation'. Indeed the whole procedure of *North* is such as to
give sectarian killing in Ulster a historical respectability which it is not
usually given in day-to-day journalism. In 'Kinship' Heaney asks (and
the word 'report' is carefully chosen):

> report us fairly,
> how we slaughter
> for the common good

> and shave the heads
> of the notorious,
> how the goddess swallows
> our love and terror.

That phrase 'slaughter for the common good' is reminiscent of, and might
be said to be as controversial as, Auden's line in 'Spain' about 'the necessary murder', a line that Orwell objected to on the grounds that it 'could
only be written by a person to whom murder is at most a word,. . . . is only
possible if you are the kind of person who is always somewhere else when
the trigger is pulled.' The difference is that, although so far as I can see
Heaney intends no obvious irony in the phrase, he cannot bring himself to
share Auden's ameliorism: slaughter may be *intended* for 'the common
good' but (and the later Auden would have agreed) does not achieve it.
Heaney understands tribal impulse only too well, but, however much he
might want to, he cannot see any hope of a 'solution' in Ulster. His
allusions to former cultures amount to a sort of historical determinism: he
sees that ritual murder is no short-term expedient, but has always been
and always will be a part of Northern European experience. Describing
'bangs' of gunfire in Belfast he writes

> It's tempting here to rhyme on 'labour pangs'
> And diagnose a rebirth in our plight

> But that would be to ignore other symptoms.

Even more decisive than this is the 'framing effect' which Heaney
achieves by having the two Antaeus poems begin and end Part One of
North: the placing suggests that dispossession is the inevitable lot of the
Irish. In the first poem the native Antaeus, whose survival depends on
staying in touch with the earth, maintains his position of security; but in
the second poem, Hercules, colonial invader, hero of light and
technology, 'his mind big with golden apples, his future hung with
trophies', dispossesses Antaeus by lifting him into the air and thereby
banishing him to 'a dream of loss and origins', Heaney's sympathies may
be with the Catholic minority in Northern Ireland, but his historic sense
prevents him from developing any hope for their success, or indeed any
hope of solution generally.

There are those who would argue that the tone of resignation and
stoicism in *North* is in some way comforting, and that contemporary
events in Ulster become more bearable, perhaps seem smaller in significance, when placed in the context of two thousand years' Northern European experience. Yet Heaney himself derives no such consolation; his
collection is often deeply pessimistic, and an air of guilt and defeat
surrounds its last poem, 'Exposure', where, isolated in Wicklow
(Southern, rural, away from the troubles), he looks back on his failure to
uplift his tribe. We have seen him in previous poems under pressure to
'try to touch the people', and part of him had wanted to be politically
inspiring. He imagines himself as

> . . . .a hero
> On some muddy compound,
> His gift like a slingstone
> Whirled for the desperate.

But Heaney cares also for the 'diamond absolutes' of his art, and the poem
implies that it may have been necessary for him to have 'escaped from the
massacre' in order to continue to write. The very last lines of *North* are
typically ambivalent: has Heaney, by leaving 'the important places' of
Ulster, 'missed/The once-in-a-lifetime portent,/The comet's pulsing
rose'? Or is it those who stay there who have missed it while he,
'grown long-haired/And thoughtful', withdrawn in his art, has earned the
chance to see it. The syntactical ambiguities of the ending (who does that
'who' refer to? why is it 'have missed' and not 'has missed') make it difficult to tell, as if Heaney, in this important meditation on the conflicting
demands of art and social concern, is still uncertain of what he feels. One
should not, however, be deceived by the reticence. Heaney's willingness
throughout *North* to expose a private world of divided feelings enables
him to come through with something strong and coherent to say about
one of the decade's most pressing political problems, and to write fine
poetry.

Three 'neo-moderns':
Ian Hamilton Finlay, Edwin Morgan,
Christopher Middleton

A distinction of neo-modernisms

IN A WELL-KNOWN ESSAY ('Modernisms'),[1] first published in 1966, Frank Kermode made a characteristically bang-up-to-date, wide-ranging, and probing examination of contemporary usage of the term 'modernism'. Professor Kermode argued that fundamental distinctions must be made between the artistic quest for order and the artistic making of an order. The neo-moderns had moved away from the former and in this they differed from most artists of the past, including many of their 'palaeo-modernist' immediate ancestors. Neo-modern rejection of order could be traced back to those would-be nihilists, the Dadaists, and to such precursors of Dadaism as Guillaume Apollinaire:

> There seems to be much agreement that the new rejection of order and the past is not quite the same thing as older rejections of one's elders and their assumptions. It is also agreed that this neo-modernist anti-traditionalism and anti-formalism, though anticipated by Apollinaire, begins with Dada. Whether for the reason that its programme was literally impossible, or because their nihilism lacked ruthlessness, it is undoubtedly true, as Harold Rosenberg has observed, that Dada had many of the characteristics of a new art movement, and that its devotees treated it as such, so in some measure defeating its theoretical anti-art programme.[2]

Few of the 'palaeo-modernists' were able to be so loftily detached from the provocative and destructive activities of Dadaism and Surrealism as Professor Kermode managed to be in this passage and, indeed, throughout the essay. In his brilliant autobiography *Blasting and Bombardiering* (1937), Percy Wyndham Lewis gave his version of what had happened to modern art before and after World War I:

> A few arts were born in the happy lull before the world-storm. In 1914 a ferment of the artistic intelligence occurred in the west of Europe. And it looked to many people as if a great historic 'school' was in process of formation. Expressionism, Post-impressionism, Vorticism, Cubism, Futurism were some of the characteristic nicknames bestowed upon these manifestations, where they found their intensest expression, in the pictorial field. In every case the structural and

philosophic rudiments of life were sought out. On all hands a return to first principles was witnessed....These arts were not entirely mis-named 'new' arts. They were art especially intended to be the delight of this *particular* world. Indeed, they were the heralds of great social changes. Then off came the lid—the day was lost, for art, at Sarajevo. World-politics stepped in, and a war was started which has not ended yet: 'a war to end war'. But it merely ended art. It did not end war.

Before the 'Great War' of 1914-18 was over it altered the face of our civilization. It left the European nations impoverished, shell-shocked, discouraged and unsettled. By the time President Wilson had drawn up his famous Fourteen Points the *will to play* had been extinguished to all intents and purposes forever in our cowed and bankrupt democ-racies.[3]

For Lewis, Dadaism (and all it was to lead to), far from being a new art movement, was the principal betrayer of the Modern Movement in paint-ing and literature. A growing public for new art which had come from the *will to play* had been turned off art altogether by the antics of the Dadaists and Surrealists.[4]

It may be argued that Lewis, deeply pessimistic and writing just before another great war, was in no position to see how the methods and even some of the attitudes of Dada/Surrealism would eventually influence the producers of such a variety of activities as, for example, Abstract Ex-pressionism, the New York school of poets, Pop Art, the Liverpool poets, and concrete/phonic poetry. But Lewis did know the achievements and aspirations of pre-war art, and it is in this context, I believe, that his crit-icism must be judged.

The Arts Council's exhibition 'Paintings from Paris' (1978-9) must have brought home to its visitors the marvellous variety, the energy, the hope-ful vitality, and the humanity of the School of Paris. The binding genius of that school of painters and poets was Guillaume Apollinaire. But though it is true that Apollinaire—who wrote *L'Antitradition Futuriste* and scandalized Paris with his pornographic writings—'anticipated' some Dada attitudes, it would be an error to regard him simply as a pre-cursor of Dadaism. Apollinaire's brand of provocation was a necessary leavening within his naturally good-humoured and hopeful personality. In the same way, the School of Paris 'contained' Apollinaire's brand of anti-traditionalism and anti-formalism, as it also contained the taunting spirits of Rimbaud and Jarry. The exuberance and good-nature of Apollinaire and of most of the art movements which he championed more than counterbalanced any tendency towards the destructive. Dadaism, too, had devotees (Schwitters and Arp, for example) who were never really anti-art, but in the period between 1916 and 1922 their creativity was completely overshadowed by the manifestations of nihilistic and irrational hysteria. As Wyndham Lewis argued, by the mid-1920s the

vision and the will to play which had permeated successive art movements from Expressionism to Futurism had disappeared entirely, and
apparently for ever. The post-war was totally different in spirit from the
pre-war, whose representative poet could write:

> Nous ne sommes pas vos ennemis
> Nous voulons vous donner de vastes et d'étranges domaines
> Où le mystère en fleurs s'offre à qui veut le cueillir
> Il y a là des feux nouveaux des couleurs jamais vues
> Milles phantasmes impondérables
> Auxquels il faut donner de la réalité[5]
>
> > (Apollinaire, from 'La Jolie Rousse')

Ian Hamilton Finlay

In the early 1960s Ian Hamilton Finlay decided to abandon traditional
syntax and structures in his poetry. By the end of the decade he had discovered new creative directions and a distinctive poetic language. Like
Augusto de Campos of the Brazilian Noigandres group and Eugen
Gomringer in Germany, Finlay had developed his individual poetic language by finding kinship with pioneers of experimental modernism from
whom there is an unbroken tradition of exploration into new possibilities
of shaping expression. Occasionally he has used the labels 'Fauve' and
'Suprematist' to characterize some of his work in the new manner; among
modernists to whom he has since paid tribute, directly or indirectly, are
Seurat, Picasso, Juan Gris, Malevich, Kandinsky, Schwitters, and, inevitably, Apollinaire (as well as Donald McGill and Victor Silvester!).
  Finlay's poetry is at once 'minimalist' and expansive. Words, letters,
and even numbers are explored as objects or signs which may be re-
organized in typographical space so that we may see new scope in them as
poetic language. Not all his experiments have come off with equal
success, of course, but when they have worked Finlay has produced compressed expressions of unusual power and beauty, as well as wit and
humour. His minimalist modes produced critical misunderstanding and
abuse from the beginning; his work has been dismissed as naive and
'twee' by the more hostile British critics. Because his poems are often
worked out in unconventional materials, including slate, metal, wood,
glass, embroidery, and concrete, some literary critics have committed a
'category' fallacy by banishing his work to distant plastic or visual realms.
His close collaboration with various artists/craftsmen who have realized
his conceptions in the materials of their own media has also been a cause
of critical confusion or uncertainty. 'Reading' a poem by Finlay, even the
most minimal and apparently simple, requires critical openness, along
with some willingness to make the effort to break through traditional

barriers of media and method.

It is true, too, that Finlay has employed some methods akin to those used by the Dadaists and by the more irresponsible neo-modernists. His work of the late 1960s and early 1970s contains 'found' elements, for example. Newspaper headlines, names given by trawlermen to their boats, and— most provocatively, perhaps — fishing-boat port registration letters and numbers were basic material for many of Finlay's poems during this phase. The newspaper *Fishing News* provided three magical found headlines which were incorporated into card-poems:

> From 'The Illuminations of *Fishing News*'
> 'OCEAN STARLIGHT TOWED OFF ROCKS'

> From 'The Metamorphoses of *Fishing News*'
> 'SHETLAND BOATS TURN TO SCALLOPS'

> From 'ΤΑ ΜΥΘΙΚΑ of *Fishing News*'
> 'ZEPHYR JOINS AVOCH FLEET'

The names chosen by trawlermen for their fishing-boats are not chosen at random, of course; Finlay has recognized that given the restriction of two or three words a fisherman naturally and skilfully chooses something of significance. Names for the sea and sky, the names of girls, desires of all kinds—these are poetic stuff in themselves and they become rich material for a kind of collage poetry in Finlay's work. Two boat names placed together[6], for example, can be full of meanings; tender love and the hard-headed commercial realities of the fishermen's trade are completely inter-locked here:

> BE IN TIME
> FRUITFUL VINE

Another set of names can become a fisherman's love lyric:

> Green Waters
> Blue Spray
> Grayfish
>
> Anna T
> Karen B
> Netta Croan
>
> Constant Star
> Daystar
> Starwood
>
> Starlit Waters
> Moonlit Waters
> Drift

Three boats—envisaged as '3 Blue Lemons' (in a tidal bowl, Peterhead)—are at once a sort of still life by Juan Gris and a message about natural beauty:

    ANCHOR OF HOPE
    DAISY
    GOOD DESIGN

'Sea Poppy 1' is a flower-shaped 'arrangement' of boat letters and numbers, the meaning of which becomes clearer when we appreciate that letter groups evoke ports of origin, so that, for instance, AH stands for Arbroath, UL for Ullapool, and BCK for Buckie.

Most of these early works were created by Finlay's own Wild Hawthorn Press (including the magazine *Poor Old Tired Horse*), though Stuart Mills's Tarasque Press (and his magazine *Tarasque)* and the Cambridge experimental-modernist magazine *Form* were active on behalf of Finlay's talent. In his constant exploration of the relationship between shapes and textures in letters and natural things, Finlay's poetry attained quite original lyrical and evocative intensity.

Many of Finlay's works—particularly those created in more durable materials—were created for his garden at Stonypath, a farm on the Pentland Hills. Here Finlay has created a landscape which is at once a home for his poems and a display gallery to demonstrate the possibilities of his art.[7] These earlier poems made lyrical connections between land, sea and sky. They also proposed the possibility of order—an order which man can shape for himself and also the order which Finlay believes lies in and beneath the world of things. His values are Christian, classical and conservative. Despite his methods he is a traditionalist who believes in such unfashionable concepts as craftsmanship and beauty. His uncompromising integrity as man and artist has cost him much trouble in the sloppier circles of contemporary art.

In the Stonypath garden there are sundials and other objects in stone or wood which bear brief inscriptions. The effect is like that of passing through one of the great formal gardens of Italy, brought down to a much more human and domestic scale. At least, this was the case until Finlay accepted the challenge to his medium by embarking on the exploration of the epic. Some of his earlier inscriptions had, as I have already suggested, a depth of lyrical expression which suggested classical models. An inscription on a marble 'cloud-form':

THE CLOUD'S ANCHOR
SWALLOW

is a rich complexity of meanings. Clouds are *not* marble, and cannot be held in stone (or art). The swallow—which is anchor-shaped in flight—dives from the boat-like cloud into the blue sky/sea. But the bird cannot anchor the insubstantial cloud-boat, and we are left with a poignant sense of man's and the artist's struggle to hold time.

Finlay's work of the mid- and late-1970s has been a development of several strands of the earlier work extended from lyrical into epic dimensions. Great heroic battles of World War II, the weapons of both world wars, the uniforms, flags and military insignia have all become disturbing yet appropriate features of this new poetry. Some of Finlay's epic poems were shown at the Arts Council Exhibition in London's Serpentine Gallery during the autumn of 1977. There, the rooms were organized to show different aspects of the new development of his art. For example, the first room was a 'neo-classical' interior where the visitor was invited to contemplate many sculpted and inscribed objects. Renaissance-style emblems had been employed anew in order to celebrate and mourn the heroism of the warfare of our age. This was disturbing in at least two ways. Can modern warfare be commemorated as classical and Renaissance battles could be? And can the minimalist techniques of the epigram and emblem bear the burden of such commemoration? Many of Finlay's critics failed to distinguish these questions from each other, and important critical issues were fudged. The weapons of mass-destruction—fighting-planes, aircraft-carriers, tanks, artillery—were linked by Finlay to their classical counterparts, so that he, at least, was asking the questions, posing the problems for himself.

In another room of the Exhibition was a large tableau in which the
visitor was asked to ponder the decisive Battle of Midway in terms of several related emblems. Doomed Japanese and American aircraft-carriers
had been transformed into beehives, their aircraft into bees, and the
Battle into a burning garden apiary, the fire fuelled by the honey/petrol.
The provocative artificiality of this construction caused strong critical
abuse at the time, much of it unconsidered and insolent. What was required, as usual, was a little critical modesty along with a modicum of
faith—or, at least, willing suspension of disbelief—in the artist's
integrity. Only after the visitor has discovered for himself (as, perhaps, he
should have known already) how decisive the Midway Battle was in
World War II, and also how heroically (in the best classical sense) it was
fought, would it have been possible for him to pass judgement on the
appropriateness of Finlay's realization.

Edwin Morgan

Like Finlay, Edwin Morgan is a Scottish poet who has achieved original
and interesting results by employing experimental methods which dis-
locate conventional poetic vocabulary and syntax—though by comparison with Finlay Morgan shows little interest in typographical experiment. At a technical level, however, Morgan is also rooted firmly in
traditional modes of writing. His poetry ranges, therefore, from original
work in English and Scots (including translation from several European
languages) to linguistic games of chance, many of which are certainly
more anarchically neo-modernist than anything by Finlay.
Wi the haill voice (1972), translations of twenty-five poems by Mayakovsky, is his most consistently successful volume to date. It demon-

BATTLE OF MIDWAY FOVRTH JVNE 1942

HIC PERIERVNT
AKAGI·KAGA·SORYV
HIRYV·YORKTOWN
ÆQVORIS·ALVI·MEL·SV-
VM·FLAMMIFERVM·EA
CONSVMPSIT·VNACVM
EXAMINIBVS·OPTIMIS

strates Morgan's ability to manipulate the natural rude vigour of Scots in order to capture the toughness and energy of the Russian writer, as in this extract from the title-poem:

> I'm no͠a dab͠at fleechin͠wi douce words;
>
> wee͠curly-haslockt lassies' earickies
> gae-na rid here͠fae hauf-obscenities.
> My pages are fechters͠I pit on parade,
> my lines are front-lines,͠I vizzy them lang and hard.
>
> Leid-solid͠staunds this verse. . . .

Morgan's rich, though sometimes over-scholarly, linguistic resources do not always work out so well as they do in his Mayakovsky translations. *From Glasgow to Saturn* (1973) was deservedly a Poetry Book Society

Choice. As the title indicates, the poems of this collection include both
local, sometimes most moving, social commentary and space-age science-
fiction narratives and episodes. There are traditional English and Scots
poems, including an effective sequence of ten 'Glasgow sonnets', and
'Stobhill', a set of five strongly ironic but ultimately compassionate
monologues revealing a dramatic gift which Morgan has developed only
rarely. His exploration of effects which can be achieved through gradual
shifts of sound and meaning produces several delightful poems for
performance, including a sci-fi black comedy 'The First Men on
Mercury' and the sequence 'Interferences'. But some of Morgan's
experiments fail to ignite, it seems to me, because he sets up games with
rules which are too mechanical and limited in potential linguistic out-
comes ever to achieve those effects of surprise and wonder for which he
aims. The 'Computer' poems in *From Glasgow to Saturn* fail to recapture
the humour of Morgan's earlier 'The Computer's first Christmas card'.
On the other hand, 'The Loch Ness Monster's Song' — a dada-style
phonic poem — does come over well in performance by the poet,
especially with the addition of special effects provided by the BBC's
Radiophonic Workshop:

> Ssnnnwhuf ff fll?
> Hnwhuffl hhnnwfl hnfl hfl?
> Gdroblboblhobngbl gbl gl g g g g glbgl
> Drublhaflablhaflubhafgabhaflhafl fl fl—
>
> gm grawwwww grf grawf awfgm graw gm.
> Hovoplodok-doplodovok-plovodokot-doplodokosh?
> Splgraw fok fok splgrafhatchgabrlgabrl fok splfok!
> Zgra kra gka fok!
> Grof grawff gahf?
> Gombl mbl bl—
> blm plm,
> blm plm,
> blm plm,
> blp.

The same criticism may be levelled at most of the experimental poems in
The New Divan (1977). There is something tedious and predictably dull
about poems such as 'Space Sonnet & Polyfilla', 'Lévi-Strauss at the Lie-
detector', and 'Wittgenstein on Egdon Heath'. To quote Edwin Morgan
himself, from a poem in *From Glasgow to Saturn:*

> —Although a poem is
> undoubtedly a 'game'
> it is not a game.
>
>   ('Not Playing the Game')

The fact is that these particular experiments *are* mere games, duller by far than ludo. It is in the translations that Edwin Morgan is at his 'neo-modernist' best.

Rites of Passage (1976) is a selection from Morgan's translations of many European poets, including Voznesensky, Pasternak, Quasimodo, Montale, Leopardi, Lorca, Martynov, Michaux, Brecht and Enzensberger. The volume includes experimental poems by Gomringer, Edgard Braga, Haroldo de Campos, and Nanni Balestrini. As a translator Morgan prefers to work directly ('poet-to-poet') from original texts. The result, by Poundian standards, may be less adventurous poetry in English, but Morgan creates scholarly and convincing versions of his poets. Some of the neo-modern translations remind the reader of Morgan's own experimental work at its most successful, especially Haroldo de Campos's 'Transient Servitude', a blend of formalist game with strong humanitarian sentiment (as in Morgan's 'Starryveldt'). Even this poem, however, seems artificial and abstract in comparison with the poems by, for example, Pasternak, Lorca, and Enzensberger. Probably the most enterprising experiment in *Rites of Passage* is Morgan's Scots version of Lady Macbeth's first speeches in Shakespeare's play. The second section of her interrupted soliloquy is spine-chilling:

> Cwa sichtless cailleachs o the warks of daith,
> transtreind my sex, drive into ilka sinnow
> carl-cruelty allutterly, mak thrang my bluid,
> sneck up aa yetts whaur peety micht walk furth,
> that nae saft chappin o wemen's nature shak
> my fey and fiendly thocht, nor slaw my steps
> fae thocht to fack! Cwa to thir breists o mine
> you murder-fidgin spreits, and turn their milk
> to venim and to verjuice, fae your sheddows
> waukrife ower erd's evil! Cwa starnless nicht,
> rowed i the smeek and reek of daurkest hell,
> that my ain eident knife gang blindly in,
> and heaven keekna through the skuggy thack
> to cry 'Haud back!'
>
> (from 'The Hell's-Handsel o Leddy Macbeth')

Christopher Middleton

In the poetry and poetic prose of Christopher Middleton distinctions between art and non-art, and between art as 'game' and game (in Edwin Morgan's terms), are frequently blurred. Middleton's 'neo-modernism' is founded on wide and deep knowledge of the extremer modes of Western modernism,[8] and his sympathetic assimilation of many radical theories, styles and techniques makes him potentially the most dazzlingly

versatile of contemporary English poets. Unfortunately, the more serious
impulses of the 'will to play' in Middleton the artist are often thwarted by
a recurring nihilistic unconcern, beyond despair even, from which he has
wished to be delivered:

> Also go to me,
> who am answerable,
> but walk a street through ruin
> without so much
> as the faint torchlight
> of dejection.

('Holy Cow')

Middleton's voyages around this central limbo take him through many
realms of media and mood. His best collection to date, *The Lonely Suppers
of W.V. Balloon* (1975), reprints 'The Fossil Fish' (1970) and *Briefcase
History* (1972). The fifteen 'micropoems' of 'The Fossil Fish' show the
range of his capacity for subtle language play, both sensitive and amusing.
One poem makes telling use of semantic dislocation:

> village quote idiot unquote
> look a walking often takes
> long at you
>
> stops & slow hows
> he comes through
>
>   screwy? clutched in
> his one scrotum hand the other
> crumpled hugs a fingering book

Another delicately fuses together sensual images and cold geometry:

> shorts white
>   at the sharp angle of
> trim bronze legs
>   to a melon balanced
> in one palm she subtends her
>   equilateral nose
>   deepening the hidden
> rose of that sphere
>   between cone & cone

Yet another is a mock-pastoral invocation (and a sure-fire recipe for
sexual success):

> to please a nymph
>   sip at her spring
> so her true voice told
>   first a far cry

> now sharper breaths
>> moisten this rosy moss
> & soon for sure
>> she will be coming

The whole sequence is brilliantly successful play, the serious 'game' of art.

Throughout *The Lonely Suppers of W. V. Balloon* (as the title-poem's found title suggests) we are made aware of the constant voyaging through many countries and times, even into pre-history. There are a few 'experimental' poems, including an attractive kaleidoscopic lyric ('A Cart with Apples') and a cut-up montage ('Chanel Always Now'), but the more moving poems in the collection seem to spring directly from the author's vulnerable self; these include 'Third Generation', 'Tall Grass', 'Nine Biplanes' (recommended as one of the most successful surrealist-style poems ever written by an English poet), and the deeply-felt 'Autobiography' which ends:

> Miles I limped past blackening heaps of snow
> Biafra bodies police pressure Britain Third Street

> As head touches pillow eyelid trap a vision
> My uncertainty is the soul of the weapons system

> They say my daughters they say my son
> At my age you'll not find any air to breathe

It is interesting that these poems are also the simplest in form and diction. When, in other poems, a similar simplicity is achieved (in 'Holocaust', 'The Pogroms in Sebastopol', and 'Old Woman at the County Dump' for example), it is almost always with a similar gain in direct emotional impact.

Pataxanadu and Other Prose (1977) is a collection of short pieces which take their inspiration from several European and American minimalist/modernist sources, including Dadaist nihilism at its blankest, Surrealist black-humour at its most irrational, and Franz Kafka in his bleakest masochistic moods. The title-work, 'Pataxanadu', is uneven in quality because the persona here seems nearly all the time to be walking 'a street through ruin/without so much/as the faint torch-light/of dejection'. This is not to deny that there is a good deal of zany humour in five of the pieces which borrow a technique of vocabulary substitution from Raymond Queneau. These pieces, originating in Malory, Melville, Urquhart, Charles Doughty and Swift, share the theme of journeying. Middleton's treatment makes them wild journeys into bizarre linguistic regions, as in his transformation of Swift:

> I had not germinated far when I mechanized one of these crawlers
> fugato in my water, and colouring up to me dippily. The uberous

monopode, when he secreted me, distended several ways every favour
of his virtue, and stood as at an obligato he have never secreted before;
then, applauding more naughtily, liberated his forehead, whether out
of curaçao or miscarriage, I could not tease.

The theme of journeys continues throughout the twenty-one pieces of the
sequence. Middleton's inventiveness is both fascinating and exasperat-
ing. He can move suddenly and with apparent artistic lack of concern
from sensitive evocation ('The Spaniards Arrive in Shanghai') and
superb political satire ('The Great Duck') to the most outrageous bad
taste ('Getting Grandmother to Market' and 'Adelaide's Dream'). The
minimal prose and poems of *Pataxanadu* are a self-conscious display of
enormous talent and vitality. Like all Middleton's poems and
imaginative prose-pieces, *Pataxanadu* shows different versions — the
creative and the destructive — of post-Modernism at work in the same
artist. Christopher Middleton's achievements in the creative mode make
him, for me, the most stimulating and provocative of English writers
since World War II. New explorations into experimental and formalist
modes, an inventive and amusing wit, and a genuine sense of art and
game have to be balanced against the anti-art and bitter cynicism of post
Dada. Only the former of these versions of the neo-modern seems to me
to be in the tradition of fully humane and creative Modernism.

References

1   Frank Kermode, 'Modernisms: Cyril Connolly and Others',
     Encounter XXVI, 3, March 1966, pp 53-8; 'Modernisms Again:
     Objects, Jokes and Art', *Encounter* XXVI, 4, April 1966, pp 65-74.
2   Kermode, p 66.
3   Wyndham Lewis, *Blasting and Bombardiering: An Autobiography
     (1914-1926)*, Eyre & Spottiswoode, London, 1937. New edition,
     Calder & Boyars, London, 1967, pp 257 and 259.
4   See, especially, *Wyndham Lewis the Artist: (from 'Blast' to Burling-
     ton House)*, Laidlow & Laidlow, London, 1939, pp 47-8.
5   Guillaume   Apollinaire,   'La   jolie   rousse',   *Calligrammes*,
     Gallimard, Paris, 1966, p 184.
6   Ian Hamilton Finlay, '2, FROM THE YARD OF THOMAS
     SUMMERS & CO. FRASERBURGH, SCOTLAND (FR.64 &
     FR.195)', Wild Hawthorn Press, 1968.
7   See Ian Hamilton Finlay and Dave Paterson, *Selected Ponds*, West
     Coast Poetry Review, Nevada, USA, 1975.
8   See Christopher Middleton, *Bolshevism in Art and Other Expository
     Writings*, Carcanet, Manchester, 1978.

DEBORAH MITCHELL

Modes of realism:
Roy Fisher and Elaine Feinstein

READERS of Fisher's *Collected Poems* might be forgiven for believing him to be a poet concerned with realism, albeit a realism used for his own ends. More recently, however, he has developed other aspects of his work and the industrial landscape whose presence was so overpowering in his earlier poems has now been assimilated. The sort of detail that we associate with his realism he now calls mere 'mouth-talk' which is made by a 'mouth of artifice' and, as he sardonically states it,

> (happy the world so made
> as to be
> blessed by the modes of art)

He has come then to believe that in the enumeration of 'realistic' detail there is as much exercise of subjective choice as in other kinds of artistic artifice. This is not of course an original idea; but it is one which he has arrived at in a peculiarly personal way.

The imagination which gave us such evocative detail in *City* was obsessed with the significance of physical reality. There was in *City*, as there still is in his more recent work, an intensity of perception and an insistence on the surface and detail of sensation which I initially connected with his defensiveness towards physical love—which he rejects for 'fear of being able to feel only vertically like a blind wall, or thickly, like the tyres of a bus'. The intensity would seem to be a direct result of sublimation. But he himself is equivocal:

> Lovers turn to me faces of innocence where I would expect wariness. They have disappeared for entire hours into the lit holes of life, instead of lying stunned on its surface as I, and so many, do for so long; or instead of raising their heads cautiously and scenting the manifold airs that blow through the streets.

Equally, we might see this intensity as a rationalization of the discomfort felt at living in an industrial landscape—a way of making this second-hand world interesting, and therefore bearable, to look at. He himself is not sure of his position *vis-à-vis* the physical, hence the ambivalence of such poems as 'Toyland' or 'As He Came Near Death'; he knows only that he wishes to perceive fully.

So he has set about formulating a grammar of sensory experience. The objections to lovers or environment, we find, are tangential to the real issues. It is the nature of human perception which denies us knowledge, however 'wary' we are to 'scent the manifold airs'. He longs 'to walk along two adjacent sides of a building at once, as of right', and instructs his reader:

> Watch the intelligence as it swallows appearances. Half the left side, a set of tones, a dimension or two. Never the whole thing at once. But we shouldn't need to comfort ourselves with thoughts like this.

Fisher's reaction to this problem is not that of the philosopher or the moralist—who might attempt to construct a solid reality from the fragments. He maintains his adherence to 'realism' only in this one sense—by remaining true to his perception as he experiences it.

To be true to his perception he must show 'clarity and confusion' simultaneously. The structure and syntax of his poems has altered correspondingly; he has moved away from the poem which proposes a simple relation between phenomena and which progresses in a line towards a conclusion. If the poem must be a 'line' then it must also defy attempts to begin it or end it at certain points: 'I could say/the poem has always/already started', he says of a poem whose chosen subject was his walking from one end of a beach to the other. His method now is much more often to cover a 'field' than to make a progressive exposition. About his collection *Matrix* he says:

> The poems are to do with getting about in the mind, and I tackle that in any way I can. I have to get from one cluster of ideas to another without a scaffolding of logic or narrative, but I want to make the transition within the terms of what I call poetry. I take it that the way a poem moves is the index of where the feeling in it lies: often, I think, my poems set up movements towards overt feelings from beginnings in neutral or enigmatic scenes.

Another correlative of his increasing interest in modes of perception is the change in his use of symbolic language. In his earlier work the symbolic value of the poem's images was brought about gradually as the poem progressed. 'The Poplars' for instance opens with a factual description; the image of the poplars then develops when he refers to the trees as 'lacunae of possibility' and finally he makes them a point of contrast for his state of mind: 'I think I am afraid of becoming/A cemetery of performance.' There is in this poem, as in another of his rightly praised early poems, 'The Hospital in Winter', a simple metaphorical relation between external phenomena and state of mind. Many of the poems in *The Thing About Joe Sullivan*, and also in *Matrix*, however, develop the techniques that he was using only in the prose passages of *City*, that is, of fluctuating between the various levels of meaning that lie between the factual and the symbolic. 'Handsworth Liberties', for example, begins:

Open—
and away

in all directions:
room at last for the sky
and a horizon;

in which the first two lines are unresolvably ambiguous and the image levels deliberately confused. Indeed the outward references of these and other poems are diffused almost to the point of abstraction; pronouns, for example, which would normally refer back to a previous subject do not or, if they do, represent an image or idea so undefined as to be almost unidentifiable. The syntactic manipulation—particularly repetition of syntactic patterns at points of transition—that he used in the prose of *City* he is also now using in his free verse with great virtuosity. This can sometimes be a self-conscious technique: section 13 of 'Handsworth Liberties' opens:

Shines coldly away
down into distance
and fades
on the next rise to the mist.

and section 6: 'Tranquillity a manner;/peace a quality'. Here he is perhaps too deliberately displacing parts of speech to confuse our normal perceptual categories. But he is also adept at using syntax to balance prose and verse rhythms. Here is the beginning of section 8 of 'Handsworth Liberties':

At the end of the familiar,
throwing away the end
of the first energy, regardless;
nothing for getting home with—

if there's more
it rises from under the first
step into the strange
and under the next and goes on
lifting up all the way;

The deliberate confusion of the reader is also counteracted by the constant attempt to register actual perception accurately; there are some poems, such as 'The Trace' and 'The Thing About Joe Sullivan', which are devoted solely to this. But, whether originally the cause or result of his beliefs, Fisher's emphasis on sensory detail has left him chronically uncertain of meaning: 'This is where the game gets Dirty./It plays the illusion/of insecurity,' And while he is exploring ways in which the meaning of language can be broken down to imitate the movements of the mind, he seems at the same time to have lost the impetus 'towards overt feeling' which gave his earlier work coherence and a wider frame of reference. Even the feeling that produced sarcasm has been pushed to one side; his satire is now largely (and entertainingly) concentrated in light verse.

He himself says that his poems are 'propositions or explorations rather than reactions to personal experience'; I feel that when he moves too far away from 'personal' experience into the area of perceptual problems even the symbolic value of his language may be lost in a diction too far removed from actuality to provide a frame of reference. In rejecting realism he sometimes forfeits reality as well.

Elaine Feinstein's poems *are* 'reactions to personal experience' and, for the most part, experiences close to her own daily life. Because she writes of personal events and the emotional ties of family and friends, her work gives the impression of being a diary—accessible to all types of reader. But she is in no sense the compulsive annotator of domestic life that we associate with the title of 'woman poet': her poems are saved from banality by the evident care which has gone into the selection of a particular event. It is not so much that the event in itself has greater significance than others similar to it, but simply that the poem gathers together accretions of detail from these other events, giving it a richness of metaphor unusual in this kind of poetry. At the same time she is able to prevent the poem from carrying off its subject by a watchful and conscientious fidelity to the particularity of experience. Though she does often write of sorrow she would, I think, agree with these lines of Fisher's:

> Because it could do it well
> the poem wants to glorify suffering.
> I mistrust it.

> I mistrust the poem in its hour of success,
> a thing capable of being
> tempted by ethics into the wonderful.

The domestic and the commonplace act as a brake on the temptation 'into the wonderful'. Her reality is not, as it is for Fisher, a problem of perception; she trusts in the actuality of her experience which pulls her back from fantasy and delusion. She fears lack of control in the mind and in the natural world, where forsythias can be a 'deranged yellow' and trees 'hiss'; the lack of control becomes menacing and may manifest itself as 'unkillable presences' in

> music of notes pitched too high even for

> dogs or prisoners, or the sick, as if there
> were messengers asleep in the grass like pollen
> waiting to rise up in sudden flower

This circumspection is both a virtue and a limitation, a modesty which demands the tact and integrity which we find in painfully equivocal poems such as 'Marriage', but which, when it inhibits imagination, can also narrow down the scope of her material. There has been an obvious effort to cut out the mannerisms and 'fanciful' imagery which occur in her earlier poems and to concentrate on the 'commonplace'. She is, I think, consciously risking prosaicism for the gain in pertinence and commitment to her subject matter.

Her long poem, 'The Celebrants', though not altogether successful as a unified sequence, does attempt to stretch the range of her material and to set problems which she normally treats more intimately within a larger time-scale. In it she contemplates the effects of the 'black drama/of the magician' that divides mind from body in its search for arcane knowledge through the centuries. The poets' 'boldest praise was always for/the holy stamina of body and spirit as one'. And it is this 'synthetic' approach to experience which creates the background to her poetic outlook; fear is to be subdued by sanity. She would like the mind and body to act as an entity and also to act within the larger 'body' of Nature. (Thus the metaphor 'the weather in the blood' and the general dominance of seasonal imagery in her work are more particular than the set of stock responses they first appear to be.) She works too close to the particular experience, however, to adhere to a philosophical 'scheme' and her visions and epiphanies are modest in scale; they are not so much transformations of reality as an admission of it. It is possible for 'our brackish waters' to be 'sweetened by a strange tree' but more often her happinesses are cautiously qualified; she is always aware how easily she 'could/feel caught again in lost hope like/a frog in a child's hand'.

Because she tries to recreate the mental fluctuations in reactions to experience she has developed great versatility in her approach to form. We feel in much of her work that the poem and the experience are not separate phenomena. 'Waiting' is one such poem:

> The house is sick. When I come down
> at night to the broken kitchen, the open wall, and find
> a grey-haired and courteous old
> cat asleep in a design of gypsum on the ground:
> I sense between iron girders and old
> gas pipes how many more ill-lit creatures of a damp
> garden are waiting. Under the provisional blossom
> of a plum tree they threaten a long siege
> whispering: they shall eat sorrow

which is the flesh of the rat, the
dead limb in the locked room.
And I can hardly remember the dream of sunlight and
hot sweet wall-flowers that led us to break through
to the almost forgotten lord of the dark outside
whose spectres are part of his word, and whose promise of
home always demands the willingness to move on: who
forces me to acknowledge his ancient sign.

The descriptive narrative which opens the poem sets the scene in a manner which reminds us that Feinstein is also a novelist, but she soon progresses from this to the noting of a semi-conscious reaction to the scene and probes towards recognizing an 'objective correlative'. The image surfaces; at this point the tone changes to the morbid and morally categorical language of biblical prophecy—a reflection of the age-old super-ego. Wistful drawn-out lines recall her wish for happiness and security, that fallible utopia which always exacts recognition of reality. The poem thus follows the process of its own making and each stage of its development is realized in the form: in line-length, rhythm, diction and syntax. Many of her poems formulate their own distinct patterns in this way—each appropriating a form particular to its subject matter. One feels that she must have been influenced by her translating of Tsvetayeva and other Soviet poets, whose attitude to traditional form is so much more innovatory than the British, as well as by her love of the American moderns. Her more conventionally constructed poems, such as 'The Sources' or 'Watersmeet', have the conclusiveness that we demand of 'art' but lack the spontaneity and immediacy that we connect with the main bulk of her work.

The danger of such 'transcriptions' of mental reactions is that, like experience, they tend to have no defined beginning or end. Unlike Fisher she does not discuss the problem within the poem itself but she often manages to get round it by opening *in medias res,* as in 'The Medium' which begins 'My answer would have to be music. . . .', or by closing with a technical *tour de force,* such as in the relative clauses of the final lines of 'Waiting', or as in one of the pieces from 'Ten Poems from a City Calendar' which ends 'to: discontinuity' — the space between the words making us so forcibly recognize their meaning that it compensates for the deliberately inconclusive nature of the subject. It is a pity that some poems are marred by indistinct punctuation and occasional unedited ambiguities when in every other way this technical inventiveness is her greatest asset. It is her fidelity to the actual processes of experience and her ability to recreate them that we must value in her work, whatever the flaws.

Mature students:
Peter Scupham and Andrew Waterman

BOTH Peter Scupham and Andrew Waterman came to poetry relatively late. Scupham says he had written scarcely a poem before the age of thirty; while Waterman was literally a mature student, going to university 'late after a bedsitter life with a variety of jobs'—as the blurb on his first collection puts it. Scupham's first book, *The Snowing Globe*, appeared in 1972 when he was thirty-nine; Waterman's, *Living Room*, in 1974 when he was thirty-four. Both writers stand apart from the literary fashions and cliques of the 1970s, if indeed there are any; and both, in different ways, seem anxious to make up for lost time; Scupham's fourth collection and Waterman's third are due to appear in 1980.

Peter Scupham's three volumes and the poems which will comprise his fourth represent one of the decade's most substantial poetic achievements. His thematic range may seem narrow—many of his poems are about the contents of his Hertfordshire home (his study in particular) or are celebrations of nearby places and near relatives—but it is explored with minute care and in intimate detail. His is a kind of poetry, like that of Edward Thomas or indeed of R. S. Thomas, which seeks patiently and quietly to evoke the historical and spiritual resonances of places and things; there is a hint of each of the Thomases in Scupham's poem 'Minsden', of which this is the opening stanza:

> The chapel bears this press of trees,
> Leading old windows, topping out
> Some roof above the fallen roof,
> Bustling their heavy green about
> The shrouded flint. A pallid breeze
> Picks at the twigs and faded stuff,
> Fussing the tangled floor: dust blurs
> Lost village and lost villagers.

In this poem, which appears in *The Hinterland* (1977), and in some of his more recent pieces, Scupham's concern with history is allied to an elegant lucidity of language and structure. Elsewhere, antiquarian interests have sometimes brought with them some awkwardly antiquarian language, at best used purposefully and effectively but liable all the same to give a curious wrench to otherwise plain diction. A line like 'Roads nod and shimmer at their scumbled edges' ('Dry Grass') seems exactly right,

despite the possible obscurity of 'scumbled'; whereas in 'Dull boots
unlaced, they cark at meddling children' ('As the Rain Falls') the archaic
word, despite the delight in language which it evidences, gets
momentarily in the reader's way.

An earlier poem, 'Address Unknown', illustrates at once Scupham's delight in language, his domestic subject-matter, and his antiquarian perspective:

> My house is clipped lightly to an old hillside,
> Held against cloud and shine by the wills of others,
> Tacked up with sticky grit and threads of power.
>
> Its teeth are set on edge by a guitar trembling;
> Each thought unpeels a slim skin from the paintwork.
> House, I have stuffed you with such lovely nonsense:
>
> All these sweet things: Clare's Poems, Roman glassware,
> A peacock's feather, a handful of weird children,
> A second-hand cat with one pad missing, missing.

Many of the other poems in *The Snowing Globe* are also stuffed 'with such
lovely nonsense': a frog 'Falls through water like a chipped pebble' ('At
Home'); hours 'Detonate. . . .like mad bird scarers' ('Good Morning');
and 'The rambling bee, obtuse and hairy,/Unzips with his dull purr/The
studious air' ('Early Summer'). Yet the delight in observing and cataloguing things is also a defence against despair, a strategy for survival, so that
these superficially light and jaunty poems always manage to imply more
sombre resonances. Scupham admits as much in a poem called 'Lessons
in Survival' where, amid a catalogue of inconsequential objects, he
advises:

> Survival is mostly a matter of oversight.
> Be an old pencil stub, a brass curtain ring.
> Don't keep your lid screwed on too tight.

In Scupham's second collection, *Prehistories* (1975), the finest effects
come, as before, from the juxtaposition of familiar detail and startling
image, but something of the earlier jauntiness has gone and the scope has
become wider, historically and geographically. The sense in which the
past, vital and consoling as it is, can also be menacingly powerful, is
splendidly caught in the last two stanzas of 'Public Footpath To':

> Though a church tower makes her slight invitation,
> Horizons alter as the bruised air thickens.
> Let the past keep her right of way, while you
>
> Are sensible, treading familiar ground again,
> Of labouring barns, one self-sufficient tractor
> Dragging the sullen landscape down to earth.

The whole poem evokes a vivid sense of the potency of landscape. Indeed, throughout the collection, the recurrent theme is that of mortal man over-powered, inevitably, by forces of history, geology, geography: 'All tenancies, save one, are held on lease' ('West Country'); 'Willow and osier take possession now/In a field of stones, dug out for victory' ('Hauxton'); 'Ghosts are a poet's working capital./They hold their hands out from the further shore' ('Prehistories'). Those last two lines are from the three-poem title sequence which connects, sparsely and surely, the poet with a vaster past than that contained in his earlier work.

Scupham's major achievement so far is the title sequence of *The Hinterland,* consisting of fifteen interlinked sonnets. It is not (or it does not contain) his best poem, but it is his major achievement, and it is worth insisting upon the distinction, if only for the benefit of reviewers such as Colin Falck, who in his account of *The Hinterland (New Review,* 4:38, May 1977) is astonishingly dismissive of 'technical virtuosity' and who, discussing this sonnet sequence, seems to align himself with 'Readers who suspect that this may be the kind of foolery that gets poetry a bad name'. Such reviewers would have us believe that Scupham's second crime, apart from actually daring to enjoy his native language, is to enjoy the craftsmanship of making poems in interesting forms. 'The Hinterland'—a sequence whose enmeshed themes include two world wars, the hot summer of 1975, and Dutch Elm Disease—consists of fourteen sonnets in which the last line of one becomes the first line of the next, and a fifteenth sonnet comprising the fourteen repeated lines. It is an ambitious structure, but hardly one which should excite a critic's scandalized bafflement. In fact, Scupham wisely allows himself some flexibility with rhyme and achieves unity instead through repeated images and carefully-placed echoing lines, such as 'The conversations of a house withdraw' in Sonnet 1 and 'The conversations of a house unfold' in Sonnet 14. Occasionally the diction seems strained, but even the 'synthetic' fifteenth sonnet is lucid and effective and would no doubt have been read as a characteristic Scupham poem if it had been published on its own:

> The summer opens where the days draw in,
> Leaves pressing home their small advantages;
> The rim of summer, when great wars begin.
> But there's a no-man's land where skull-talk goes,
> A hinterland to breed new summers in.
> The unfleshed dead, refusing to lie down—
> What inch of sunlight gilds their vanishings,
> Those penitential litanies of stone?
> A silence runs beneath these silences,
> And there our conversations must be held,
> Where blood and stone proclaim their unities

> And all the shadows cross on one high field.
>   Behind the parched leaves glistening in the lane,
>   Diminished thunders, breaking in new rain.

'If poetry is concerned with knowledge,' Scupham wrote in his Introduction to his first pamphlet collection, *The Small Containers* (1972), 'Auden is surely right when he calls it a game as well.' He has been from the start a formalist, both a game-player and a role-player, and above all a craftsman. His craftsmanlike approach to the making of poems is complemented and extended in his work as co-founder, printer and publisher of the Mandeville Press, which produces hand-set, hand-sewn pamphlets and anthologies as well as 'Mandeville Dragoncards'. Mandeville's first pamphlet, in 1974, was *Last Fruit* by Andrew Waterman.

The development of Waterman's poetic reputation has been even more rapid than that of Scupham's. He is, however, a very different sort of poet: a social observer, an accurate chronicler of urban decay, always on the periphery yet sufficiently close to events to catch, when necessary, the exact demotic note demanded by his subjects. This is a Larkinesque range—the similarities of theme and sometimes of detail are striking—but, where Larkin's tightly-controlled versification imposes a characteristic tone of his own, Waterman's more open (or simply more slack) verse can lead to the wrong kind of transparency, neutrality. An interesting early example of Waterman's strengths and limitations is the poem 'The New Young', thematically close to Larkin's 'High Windows', in *Living Room*. The poem begins promisingly:

> Again now spring's green burn,
> and the new young pushing through the streets,
> one harsh pullulation,
>
> new radio-music scorching the public grass,
> a flicker of sap along branches
> to ignite white blossom, tier on tier,
>
> massed chestnut chandeliers, a virgin flare
> shrivelling we who've lived to fall and blemish—
> dead-veined hands adrift on paper.

The opening movement of the poem is suitably urgent, the uncolloquial 'pullulation' (almost a Scupham trick) asserting the poet's distance from his subject; the 'radio-music' picks up the force of 'harsh' before developing the heat/light metaphor from 'burn' which, appropriately, leads to the 'chestnut chandeliers', representing the young and contrasted with those 'who've lived to fall and blemish': all this is deftly done, with sufficient panache for the reader to overlook the unsure punctuation and the awkward syntax of line 8. But in the next stanza things go decidedly wrong:

> Sweep us away who were young, it is time for the young.
> Across the park a haze
> of dust. They are demolishing buildings.

That first line is both vacuous and grammatically limp; 'a haze/of dust' is close to cliché, though the line-break is presumably meant to suggest a heat-haze before we are pulled up by 'of dust'; the ambiguity of 'They'—grammatically the young but actually quite separate workmen—is no doubt intended to link 'the young' with the idea of destruction in general, but the formal looseness blunts this point and makes it look more like a matter of careless syntax. After this, the poem recovers a good deal of poise.

Sometimes Waterman's precise observation is matched by more precise verse, as in the following poem which in an obvious way counterbalances the one I have just discussed:

> The old, cast up on lawns in wicker chairs
> sit waiting for the sun to drop,
> humped shoulders towards a screen of trees,
> hands fiddling with crochet or book.
>
> What should I say to them?
> That I have been far out in passion, rain,
> and come back streaked with light? They turn
> patiently features rubbed, effaced,
>
> or scored deep by more tides than they remember,
> tokens of enough weather; not
> really distracted from the branches charring
> where gold sinks at the garden's end.
>
> Outgrowths of themselves, they hobble in
> seeming out of habit merely propped
> on shapes long warped from, once
> tall in hailstorms, distant lanes' white heat.

That is the whole of 'The Old, Cast Up On Lawns' from *From the Other Country* (1977). Characteristically, Waterman refuses to let his rhythm settle down; and the condensed conclusion is characteristic too. There are echoes of two evident influences on Waterman's work: Larkin (there is something of 'The Old Fools' in the questioning method as well as in the subject) and Frost, whose 'Acquainted with the Night' is misquoted in the second stanza. But the sustained development of the image and the shrewd observation of the social context are very much Waterman's own.

Both 'The New Young' and 'The Old, Cast Up On Lawns' exemplify Waterman's generalizing habit: his is the stance of an outsider (compounded by the fact that he now lives in Ulster) whose externalized subjects are often, as here, 'they'; the sharpness of individuality is lost, but a clarity of context is gained. Yet there is a wistfulness in Waterman's detachment: after deflating suburban pretentiousness in 'Gardens', he concludes, 'Yet now, if I found myself settling for one,/I'd set about digging'; and when in 'Suburban Eden' he recalls his childhood—'As beyond the railings, the Addiscombe train slides past. . . '—one feels that Waterman's is indeed a view from 'beyond the railings', framed and excluded. He is well aware of the narrow line between detachment and exclusion, as the conclusion of a poem about his bedsitter days, 'Peanuts in Troy', demonstrates:

> Those were the days: all I owned going into one suitcase,
> everything possible, everything serving my turn;
> when being a loner flukily squared
> with what's less put up with, being alone,
> in the darkness, at one with the slow
> breathing of suburbs like lyrics expanding in stanzas.

Waterman's strengths, like Scupham's, are close to and occasionally indistinguishable from his weaknesses. The ease with which he handles vernacular language and colloquial diction gives authority to his extended pieces of social observation: the generally very successful 'Railway Poems' in *Living Room,* for instance, or 'North Derry Nocturne' in *From the Other Country,* or 'The Tasserty File' in the forthcoming collection, *Over the Wall.* 'The Tasserty File' carries an epigraph from Robert Frost—'All the fun's in how you say a thing'—which is fair warning: the sequence is a picaresque fiction centred upon the game-fixated Boppo, a jaunty outsider who creates havoc in academia (a favourite Waterman target: see 'A New Babel' in *From the Other Country)* and everywhere else. The inventive energy is remarkable and the humour lurches crazily from literary allusion to slapstick: as an entertainment 'The Tasserty File' is an unqualified success. The versification seems arbitrary, however, and one section is in fact in prose, emphasizing one's sense that Waterman's is, perhaps increasingly, a novelist's eye and manner.

I find I feel uneasy about Waterman's poems, rather as I feel uneasy about Ian McEwan's stories or Martin Amis's novels: there is a sense of everything going slightly too fast, everything acutely and wittily observed but somehow unpondered; a sense also of clarity shading into callousness, of detachment unsupported by a moral position. Perhaps all three of these writers—different as they are—would reply that this is the way we live now. Scupham's poems, like Wordsworth's, are to do with emotion recollected in tranquillity; Waterman's are to do with emotion recollected on the bus. Each of these processes has its value, but the former is the one more traditionally associated with the poet. This means, no doubt, that Scupham's poetry is the more easily placed, that its qualities and pleasures are the more easily recognized, and that Waterman's is the more awkward, rough-edged talent. Yet a talent it unmistakably is: both Waterman's *Over the Wall* and Scupham's *Summer Palaces* will be among the most important new books of poetry in 1980, and one of the virtues of English poetry now is that it contains two such independent and energetic writers, each of them making sense of a world.

Immersions

In the Distance, by Dick Davis, does not force itself on your attention. When I first read it, I thought: Well, that's nice. But I read it again, and then again, as things from it returned to my mind and I went back to confirm them. I began to realize that these poems will probably still be with me in ten years' time, and there are not many recent books of poetry I can say that about.

Dick Davis's discourse is quiet but insistent. It helps that he means what he says, that he is not too polite. He has a bold mind and imagination.

Here is a short example of the kind of poem that you almost pass over on a first reading. It is called 'Narcissus' Grove':

> A place for the evasive, self-lockt stare,
> The useless beauty that the world disowns;
>
> Water sedulous over the grey stones—
> The pines' sweet resin scents the sleeping air.

That seems simple enough. But then you read it again, and the statement becomes less clear-cut, less of a statement perhaps. You pause at the cool daring of the metrical substitutions in the third line, the almost but not necessarily human suggestions of 'sedulous' and 'sleeping', the increasing ambiguity of the second pair of lines in relation to the first. The scene contained in it is complete in itself, adequate, reminding you a bit of Whitman's animals, 'placid and self-contained'; but the more you think about it the more perplexing is the connection, and lack of connection, between words like 'evasive' and 'sedulous'. And that's what the poem is about; it isn't merely a muddle. In his four lines Davis has presented a mystery, and by presenting has not solved but intensified it. Both 'experience' and 'statement' are here, but not in exact relation: the experience does not simply illustrate the statement nor does the statement explain the experience. Each goes beyond the other, vexingly, wonderfully, as they do in our lives.

Davis's other poems explore similar or different patterns made between experience and meaning. But when I say patterns I do not mean to imply that he withdraws, that they are *merely* patterns. On the contrary, his typical image for the giving of self to experience is of immersion. In the brilliant early poem that starts the book, 'The Diver', a man sinks from the known day to the bottom of the sea and, confronting the treasure-wreck, 'hesitates, then/Wreathes his body in.' It is an action of total involvement. Similarly the art historian, when he seems to others at his most pedantic, immersed in the minutiae of his study, 'is desolate with love'. Only by such a complete giving of oneself to experience, for its own sake not for its meaning, can meaning be properly pursued.

And there is the constant use of images to do with sleep and dreams, being the types of self-immersion. Moreover in dreams we find incident loaded with meaning that is not quite revealed. Some of the poems about waking states carry dream-like feeling too. In one of the most striking poems of the book, 'Scavenging after a Battle', the scavenger is left with 'colour cupped in his hand' just as his own figure is cupped by the surrounding landscape. Every image contributes to a cold, fresh strangeness. The scene is presented physically and cleanly, but an unstated significance hovers around the edges.

Unexplained significance is the characteristic not only of dreams but of myths. Thus Actaeon, lost anachronistically among 'eucalyptus trails', sees Diana as if she were a hallucination, but feels the bite of her dogs *through* the dream'. The Virgin Mary is oppressed by the very folds of her clothes. And 'Jesus on the Water', infinite, realizing 'that no specific/Can contain my stare', observes how

> . . . my feet tread water
> Only, as a stare
>
> That blurs particulars
> In tears.

The interinvolvement of abstraction and particulars is both the subject and the method of these lines.

In some of the poems experience awaits meaning and it does not come— 'Desire' and 'North-west Passage' are two of the harshest poems in the book. In another, 'Childhood', experience waits, and the waiting, the tentativeness, the expectancy, are the subject. Here is the whole poem:

> Imperceptible, at sunrise, the slight
> Breeze stirs the dreaming boy, till silently
> He edges free from sleep and takes the kite,
> Huge on his shoulders like an angel's wings,
> To climb the hill beyond the drowsing city.
> Released, the first ungainly waverings
>
> Are guided out, above the still valley,
> Constrained to one smooth flow, diminishing
> Until the pacing boy can hardly see
> The dark dot shift against the constant blue:
> He squats and stares: in his hand the taut string
> Tugs, strains—as if there were still more to do.

I don't need to refer again to immersion or dream. It is as if the boy is led on by his own sense of luck, trusting in the intermittent but renewed pull.

That pull is like the verse-movement which leads us similarly to the last line where, as in the best of Davis's poems, it doesn't quite work out exactly, it isn't pat. 'As if there were still more to do'—a slight resemblance to E. A. Robinson here is forgotten in the gentle urgency of the feeling. For Robinson the line would signify possibilities neglected—but here it looks forward, mysteriously, beyond the end of the poem. It is the wind that powers the poem, that stirs, guides, constrains, tugs, and in the end suggests that there is still more to do. And the wind's imperative is something compelling and recognized but insubstantial and unformulable (Ezra Pound:

> 'This wind is held in gauze curtains. . . '
> No wind is the king's. . . ')

Experience is unformulable, and human beings have an uncontrollable urge to formulate. The paradox is old but basic, and it occurs throughout the book, both in the poet and in his subject matter. Poem adds to poem, the book is a marvellous accumulation, complex, complete.

It is a first book, but a very mature one. The style is firm, totally without pretension, but all art. The majority of poems are metrical: at a time when most American poets consider metre obsolete and most English poets who use it do so as if it *were* obsolete, it is wonderful to find a poet (English) whose poetry lives through its metre. His handling of it is masterful, and you are never aware of effort. And the language is exact but relentless, like the perceptions. On the basis of this book, I would say that Davis is one of the best poets around.

Young poets in the 1970s

> Not for me
> ... writing in a storm of creation,
>   or even
> ripping it up with mad Mike H
> and the children of Albion
> at pop-etry gigs in university halls!....
>
> I'm plainly
> for the poet keeping his cool in the city,
> being steady in the isolation
> of his mortgaged box,
> a monk without privilege or position,
> solitary in his cell,
> above the yelping and the traffic snarl.
>
> Wes Magee, 'Maybe I'd do well in Tibet'

I

'THE TYPICAL YOUNG POET of the 1970s...' I was tempted to begin — but there is, of course, no such person. There are only young poets (plural), and in their work can be found many different styles and concerns. To say 'typical' is to presume that there exists some kind of common experience or area of agreement; whereas most people's impressions of the 70s would, I imagine, be of bewildering diversity or (in the current jargon) of 'pluralism'. Standing out from the decade are the strong individual collections by already established names—Hughes's *Crow,* Hill's *Mercian Hymns,* Heaney's *North,* Larkin's *High Windows.* It is hard to see which are the important collections of the young; harder still to detect in them a dominant pattern.

But if the 70s were to lack any 'typical' new development, this would be an unlikely departure from the history of British poetry over the last fifty years. For each of the decades from the 30s onwards we have been presented with a clear picture of some 'typical young poet': he is a member of MacSpaunday in the 30s; a neo-Romantic in the 40s; a Movement poet in the 50s; a minimalist or perhaps a Child of Albion in the 60s. It is true that these are 'little more than labels' and that the real work of the literary critic must be done without them. But for the literary historian, and especially for one engaged in the writing of 'instant' history, such identikits are indispensable: without them it would not be possible to keep track of cultural change.

It is not my intention to impose any single 'image' here; in the latter parts of this essay I speak of three loose groupings or tendencies. But reading through the work of young poets in the 70s—which I take to mean poets born later than 1940 whose first collections were published this decade—I have built up a rough picture. Our 'typical young poet' is likely to come from a professional middle-class background, or if it is working-class we are less likely to hear about this than we would have been in the 60s. He—or she: but if I fail to add this qualification from here on that is because 'he' is still more likely to be the case—attended grammar school and then went on to university, probably Oxford or Cambridge. He will almost certainly have read English Literature, and there is a good chance that he will now be teaching it at a higher education level. His politics are on the whole quietly conservative, and where they intrude into the poetry at all it is as a kind of nostalgic liberal humanism. Our poet belongs to the tradition of the poet as *clericus,* and is out of sympathy with 60s Romantic notions of the poet as risk-taker, 'mad genius' or bard. He has a surprisingly strong respect for 'traditional' forms, even strict metre and rhyme. His attitude to Modernism is less partisan than was that of most of his twentieth-century predecessors: having read Pound and Eliot at a fairly early stage of his development, he does not feel the pressure to react extremely, whether in idolatry or repudiation, as seems to have been felt by his forerunners.

This last point, and I make it the last because to press any further, into 'life-style' and so on, is not going to be profitable, seems to be the most important. If first-hand accounts are to be believed, many modern poets' response to the art began as an adolescent infatuation with nineteenth-century Romantic poetry; one grew out of it later, usually with the help of Leavis, but one's first love was for Shelley or Keats. Nowadays it has become common for Modernism to exert this kind of appeal: so efficiently (if not always thoroughly) have the Modernists been assimilated, so capable is even the most indifferent of English teachers in putting Modernist work across, that most young people today will have read in their teens poetry which until comparatively recently would have been considered 'modern' and difficult, and which would have been read at school only by the inquisitive and pioneering few. I mention my own experience, at a Northern grammar school, in the 60s, only because I think it is indicative of the way things have moved. I was far from being a precocious student, and my due-to-retire English teacher was no great innovator. But I was introduced to Eliot's *Prufrock, The Waste Land* and *The Cocktail Party,* Joyce's *Dubliners, Portrait of the Artist* and *Ulysses,* Lawrence's *Sons and Lovers* and *Lady Chatterley's Lover,* Hardy's *Poems of 1912-13,* Sean O'Casey's *The Silver Tassie,* Wilfred Owen's *Collected Poems,* Beckett's *Waiting for Godot* and *Endgame,* plus bits of Yeats,

Sassoon, Rosenberg, Graves, Auden, Spender and Dylan Thomas.

I think that this sort of early exposure to British Modernism is common nowadays, and that it has had serious consequences. From the 30s to the 60s Modernism was the great parental shadow under which poets laboured to find their own voice. It was impossible for the serious practitioner not to undergo some violent Oedipal struggle with his Modernist fathers. Now, for a younger generation of poets, Modernism has become a grandparent—something safely old and remote. In adolescent years there might be some touchingly close relationship with it; in maturity interests shift elsewhere. In some respects this temperate, take-it-or-leave-it spirit is no bad thing. But the cost has been a loss of real engagement. It is as if some of the great Modernist issues had become dead issues, matters for the textbook. We speak now of 'The Lessons of Modernism', where previously nobody would have thought that they were in the classroom. And though Gabriel Josipovici in his book of that title pleads for the relevance of Modernism to our own concerns, it might reasonably be argued that once Modernism has become something so clearly understood as to be a 'lesson', it no longer has anything of urgency to say.

The fathers of the 70s generation of poets have not been the Modernists, but the dominant figures in British poetry since 1945. Few young poets today could be accused of writing like Eliot; but many—because these two are still close to us, still not properly assimilated and relegated (that is the pattern)—do sound distinctly like Philip Larkin and Ted Hughes. Larkin in particular has been a popular candidate for imitation, parody, tribute, deliberate or involuntary borrowing. There have even been poems about the difficulty of escaping from his fatherly or kind uncle's grasp. Take, for example, 'Valedictory', a poem by Simon Curtis (b. 1943). As the head of a Comparative Literary Studies department, Curtis might be expected to see Larkin as a reprehensible little-Englander; and he does certainly feel Larkin's 'ironically defeatist' vision to be a dead end. But Larkin's influence is not so easily thrown off. 'Valedictory' is Curtis's attempt to work Larkin out of his system, a moderately English version of Plath's 'Daddy':

> The gate's latch clicks behind me. I must go.
> Out from your suburb's impasse, into the night,
> From a beguiling round of fellowship, I know,
> But the need is imperious, and time forthright.

But to be conscious of the problem, as Curtis is, does not always make it easier to solve. Despite all the bold words about the need to abandon the parental verse-home, not many bags have been packed. Even those who have managed to escape the suburbs of Larkinland have tended to come back with the same message: that what counts in poetry is 'craft' and 'rational intelligence'. The best English poetry has always demanded something more than these qualities, but it has been one of the dominant myths of the decade that they are what our poetry is most badly in need of, and that a poetic apprenticeship under Larkin, Yvor Winters or Edward Thomas can be nothing but beneficial, so dominated is our culture by wild-man babblers like Michael Horovitz. Thus even Donald Davie, who is the last person you would expect to fall back on this argument, cheers himself up with the thought that a disappointing anthology of young British poets does at least contain work that is 'patient' and 'scrupulous', and that this is in itself an achievement 'when it is hard to believe that the midnight lamp burned for even five minutes over the artless lucubrations that we find extolled as the best poetry of our time'. The truth is sadder: there are few wild-man babblers; there are a large number of young poets who are competent, restrained, craftsmanlike—and dull.

This is especially sad since the 70s have been, in terms of opportunity for having one's work published, a surprisingly fertile period. There has been the usual talk of economic hardship, of profit-conscious publishing houses reluctant to back the young, of little magazines forced to close; and certainly the generous spirit of the 60s has disappeared. But the record is less bleak than all this would suggest. Two important new poetry-publishers, Anvil and Carcanet, have recently celebrated their tenth anniversaries: both they and a number of smaller presses (among them the Peterloo Poets) have been generous in their attention to the unknown and untried. Of the more established houses, Oxford University Press, Secker and Chatto have fair-sized lists, and there have also been several 'sampler schemes' designed as a testing-ground for new talent: Faber's *Poetry Introduction* series, Chatto's *Treble Poets*, Gollancz's *A Poetry Quintet*, Carcanet's *Ten English Poets*. Two big new anthologies have supplemented the long-running PEN *New Poems:* they are the Arts Council's *New Poetry* and Dannie Abse's *Poetry Dimension*. BBC Radio regularly broadcasts the *Poetry Now* programmes, and local networks have similar spots. There has been a growing number of poetry competitions—with the Cheltenham Festival awards, the BBC-*Sunday Times* contest, and the Poetry Society's 'Most Expensive Poem Ever Written' the most prestigious. Each year the respected and well-worth-having Gregory Awards are given to half-a-dozen poets under thirty. Little magazines like *Outposts* and *New Poetry* are specially aimed at the young, and in the middle of the 70s both *Stand* and *Agenda* had special issues on new British poets. There have been many other 'encouragements'—those mentioned are only the more obvious outlets. Self-pity and rejection slips might sometimes tell us otherwise; so might the theorists of cultural decline. But this has not been a difficult decade for young poets. The opportunities have been there for the taking.

They are, though, opportunities at a cost. At the beginning of the 70s Larkin was quoted as saying that 'poetry is like knitting', and that kind of view of poetry—as a useful art to be worked at in the comfort of one's home—has dominated the decade. At a time when the young have been ecology-conscious and reverential towards 'old things', it seems fashionable rather than dowdy to think of poetry as a 'craft'. You can judge how potent this analogy has become from the number of poems that have been written about ancestor-craftsmen: Seamus Heaney's early work helped popularize such poems, and nowadays the workshop noises — the planing of carpenters, the clanking of blacksmiths, the chiselling of stonemasons—are creating an almighty din. This trend is worrying not so much because of the sentimentality of the poems themselves (few of the poets have Geoffrey Hill's awareness that 'it is one thing to celebrate the "quick forge", another to cradle a face hare-lipped by the searing wire'), but because of the implied view of poetry. In itself, of course, 'craft' is far from being an invidious quality; quite the contrary. An ability to work out a single metaphor, to master given forms, to rhyme and reason—these are not to be sneered at. But as a criterion for encouraging the young, craft *can* be invidious, for it means that the simple job well done will always be exalted over the difficult one half-botched—not exactly a spur to ambition, radicalism and originality. No doubt those in the key positions (the selection panels, the grants-administrators, the men from the Arts Council) do try to remain receptive to all kinds of work; many of them, after all, are poets themselves. But it is easy to see why, when faced with having to make difficult decisions, they should fall back on safe-playing criteria.

It is not surprising, then, that some groups of poets should have felt alienated by the literary 'establishment', for there are certain modes which do not go down well in the important circles. One vociferous set of opponents has been of those associated with and promoted by Eric Mottram, who as a deposed editor of *Poetry Review* knows to his cost the 'establishment line'. Mottram's critiques can be found in various small press publications, one notable example being a 1975 article for *Poetry Student* in which he attacks what he calls the contemporary 'Horatian' theory of 'poetry as a rapidly consumable entertainment article on a par with cigarettes, newspapers and booze, a source of quick minimal kicks which do not interfere with the stability of class divisions and rigid labour/leisure proportions... The wreath is given to the hack who pleases the audience through recognitions of what it knows and likes rather than through an exploration of unconventional procedures'. Mottram's is a valuable dissenting voice, but one so inured by opposition that it repeatedly slips into absurdity: 'To use Jeff Nuttall as a classroom text would crumble the system.' Moreover, there is little sign yet of an important new poet emerging from under his wing: alongside Mottram's polemical theorizing—poetry as revolution and poetry as research—the poems themselves look wan. A more feasible alternative may come from the work and teaching of J. H. Prynne, who in Cambridge at any rate has a considerable reputation; but again there is no clear sign of what his following amounts to.

Another disaffected group are the feminists, whose opposition to a purportedly 'male-dominated' literary culture has led numerous women poets to retreat into small workshop groups. Anyone who has read the astonishing and hard-to-get-hold-of poem in which Robin Morgan accuses 'the entire British and American literary and critical establish-ment' of 'the murder of Sylvia Plath' will know how overheated feminist feelings can become; and though there need be no opposition between the two, a good many feminist poets are undoubtedly more interested in furthering the Women's Movement than in the distillation of their art. This is nevertheless a significant 70s development and, paradoxically, it helps explain the apparent paucity of new women poets: women who might in the past have published with the larger houses and magazines have begun to prefer the readership of the committed few. To readers who have struggled with the menstrual obsessions of Penelope Shuttle, the fire-and-brimstone of Abigail Mozley, and the banality that per-vades so much of the Women's Literature Collective's *Seven Women,* this will not come as bad news; better, they would say, to stick with the 'mainstream' work of such poets as Val Warner, Carol Rumens, Joan Downar and Connie Bensley. The truth is that we still cannot assess what has been done: Trevor Kneale's *Contemporary Women Poets* is the only serious anthology-attempt that there has been so far, and it was not a success.

Mention of only one or two of these movements and alternatives is enough to indicate how limited in usefulness is any assumption of a 'typical young poet'. We need as well as a tentative overall picture some specific reference to different tendencies and groupings. In what follows I try to take account of three such tendencies. They are not, as I have already made clear, the only ones. Nor do they allow me to take account of poets such as Andrew Waterman, John Mole, Peter Reading, Kit Wright, Jeremy Hooker and Jeffrey Wainwright. But many of the new names *are* here, among them the three I most value—Andrew Motion, Tom Paulin and Craig Raine.

II

At the beginning of the 1970s the minimalist poetry associated with Ian Hamilton's *Review* was in the ascendancy. There had been other collec-tive ventures in the 60s, including those represented in *A Group Anthology* and *Children of Albion,* but minimalism was the poetry that seemed historically 'right', offering a method whereby 'ordinariness' could be retained in poetry yet need not be treated with 1950s-like ration-alism. By withholding 'explanatory' information and 'prose links', poets like Hamilton, David Harsent, Colin Falck and Hugo Williams were able to charge quotidian reality with mystery or dread. It was a simple poetic method but an effective one, and when Hamilton's *The Visit* appeared in 1971 the pattern for the decade must have seemed set.

In the event, though, *The Visit* was an end rather than a beginning. Hamilton was to write little more in the 70s, and when the *Review* folded in 1972 an already faltering poetic movement came to an end. Hardly any new young poets in the 70s have interested themselves in the possibilities which Hamilton's poetry opened up: only Tony Flynn (b 1951), with his tiny pamphlet *Separations*, is an obvious descendant. If there is a *Review* tendency continuing at all, it is in the work of James Fenton (b 1949), who has published comic verse epistles like those of John Fuller and Clive James (the 'other' *Review* tradition). But Fenton's real loyalties go back to Auden, as can be seen from his precocious debut *Terminal Moraine* (1972) and the more recent (and preferable) *A Vacant Possession* (1978). He also shares a new generation's impatience with the 60s 'extremist' theory of A. Alvarez: one of his best pieces, published in the last issue of the *Review* in 1972, is a satire at Alvarez's expense:

> He tells you, in the sombrest notes,
> If poets want to get their oats
> The first step is to slit their throats.
>   The way to divide
> The sheep of poetry from the goats
>   Is suicide.

With the passing of the *Review,* English poetry was temporarily bereft of coteries. But alongside Fenton's poem in the final pages of the *Review*'s last issue can be found a full page advertisement for a small press called Carcanet founded just three years previously. It was from this press, by the middle of the decade a much expanded one, that something approaching a new 1970s 'movement' or 'consensus' first emerged, and it came in the form of an anthology, *Ten English Poets,* published in 1976. Among the poets represented in the anthology were Clive Wilmer (b 1945), Robert Wells (b 1947), Michael Vince (b 1947), Neil Powell (b 1948) and Grevel Lindop (b 1948), and all were said to 'seek through articulate forms and disciplines a truth to experience that accurately and fully engages our common concerns'. This—the blurb—sounded so vague as to admit almost anything, but Michael Schmidt's introduction was clear about what was to be excluded, unleashing an invective against 'unspeakable epic poets, tearful lyricists, rhetoricians of a political kidney, adolescent angst peddlers, geriatric lovers, spineless satirists, sinless confessional writers, pasticheurs of modernism'. Any suggestion that *Ten English Poets* might represent a 'school' or 'generation' was, in the usual 'English' way, fended off; but the biographical notes told another story. All the poets except Alistair Elliot had been born in the years 1945-51;

eight of them had studied at either Oxford or Cambridge; eight were teaching; most were based in the provinces; the homogeneity was striking. Later the suggestion was put about (it had its origins in Donald Davie's review of the anthology) that the volume represented a 'Wintersian conspiracy', an admiration for the work of Yvor Winters having developed at King's College, Cambridge in the late 60s, where Wells, Wilmer and Vince (along with Dick Davis, who was not in the anthology) had been undergraduates. Questionable though this seemed, it gave the poets a distinctive identity: they could be seen to share Winters's respect for 'reason', his reservations about Modernism, his preference for 'traditional' forms.

The reception of the anthology had its bizarre moments, not the least of which was Clive Wilmer's claim—in an attempt to squash the notion of a Wintersian conspiracy—that his colleague Robert Wells had been 'significantly influenced by no poet later than the eighteenth century'. This only confirmed some of the suspicions which were being felt about the anthology. At least one reviewer labelled the anthology 'Georgian', but so chastely Augustan was the language of some of the poems that many readers must have felt they were stepping back even further, into the 'lost garden' of the pre-industrial era. There were old-style exclamations ('Inopportune desire!'), capitalized personifications ('Truth', 'Time', 'Youth'), metre-conscious inversions ('fat grow the grapes', 'as climb the pickers'), and syntactical constructions that looked back to Cowper and Goldsmith—'This is my youth in love's default/To loiter on the verge of day'.

It was Clive Wilmer who explained that the archaism of *Ten English Poets* was something more than the result of inexperience in Eng Lit-sated young poets. Defending the anthology he spoke of the brutalization of contemporary language and of 'the holiness that archaism confers': his backward look had been a deliberate policy 'to reawaken in the reader some sense of the human loyalties latent in words'. This policy can be seen in Wilmer's first collection *The Dwelling-Place* (1977), which dramatizes in poem after poem a struggle between the forces of light (past civilization) and darkness (impending anarchy). Bright fragments of order, reason and art are shored up against the 'encroaching forest' of ruin and despair. Wilmer's outlook is best summed up in the epitaph for his goldsmith:

> To stay anxiety I engrave this gold,
> Shaping an amulet whose edges hold
> A little space of order: where I find,
> Suffused with light, a dwelling for the mind.

Many of Wilmer's poems are organized, like this one, into rhyming quatrains, and the tight discipline highlights rather than conceals a sense of deep personal disturbance. As Donald Davie once put it, 'the stain spreads furthest when the floor's not cracked', and Wilmer's carefully constructed dwelling-place is indeed a sensitive register of unease. Still, it is hard to feel much enthusiasm for a poet whose texts so consistently disown the 'malignant times' ('Terror stalks this land where once King Arthur/Ruled with virtue steeped in vision'), and whose sole source of comfort is the past. Time and again Wilmer identifies with historical figures themselves on the defensive: with his grandfather-blacksmith ('My own time's loss I feel in his lost youth'); with monks raising a citadel-abbey; with the late-Augustan rector-poet who was 'guardian of the Word'; with James Rivers—'scorning promiscuous rhetoric,/With chaste formality he spoke'. Wilmer himself appears as a questing knight-poet, 'strik[ing] chivalric postures' and undertaking to save the damsel-nation from distress. *The Dwelling-Place* is one of the most unified and well-organized collections to appear in the decade; but it is reactionary in the strict sense that it idealizes earlier forms of society which possess qualities (chastity, decorum, valour) which the present is felt to lack.

Robert Wells's collection *The Winter's Task* (1977) has its resemblances to Wilmer's (the tight forms, the archaisms, the allegorical modes) and is in some ways a similar retreat. But the concern is with landscape rather than with history (Wells has spent time working as a forester) and the feeling is purer: for all the woodchopping subject matter, there is little sense of a political axe being ground. Wells may not have that crisp receptivity to the natural world which one finds in that other poet-forester Snyder, but a number of his short poems do become strange and haunting. Good examples are 'At Midday', 'Breakfast', 'After Hay-making' and (below) 'The First Thing':

> This walking alone
> Is before either loneliness
> Or company. It is the first thing—
>
> And to set prints in the dust
> That the dry cold at night
> Will leave unstirred.

At times Wells's nouveau-minimalist poems look merely unfinished (beginnings that should not have been left as endings) but it is with this mode that he promises most. Both Wells and Dick Davis, whose *In the Distance* (1975) has much the same terseness, are more capable of resonance than most of their confederates. It is resonance which I miss from Michael Vince, whose *The Orchard Well* (1978) seems otherwise to come from the same school.

Two other collections to have followed from *Ten English Poets* are Grevel Lindop's *Fools' Paradise* and Neil Powell's *At the Edge* (both 1977). Lindop's is accessible and enjoyable: a typically 'less deceived' post 1945 poet, never allowing himself to overreact or be misled, he makes poems out of the most mundane of materials — a brewery delivery, a fruit machine, valentine cards, a dictionary — often playing with some central image (an apple with its 'star' at the core). But when he comes to tackle complex or emotional subjects he seems inhibited by this determinedly rationalist mode; perhaps his interest in the poetry of John Ashbery will provide him with an exit. Neil Powell also seems to be caught between an innate English scepticism and an awareness of more expansive American possibilities:

> Something in the weather or something
> in the light—it hardly matters which—
> enforces its own pressure. And yet,
> I once had the Transatlantic Dream,
> Black Mountainous and vast: the old need
> for a larger canvas, much more paint,
> a geography and not a view.

If there is an echo of the ideas of Donald Davie here, this is no accident: Davie is to Powell what Gunn is to Wilmer, the shaping spirit. Parts of *At the Edge* are derivative and misjudged (that 'I once had', for example, sounds grandiose in a little known poet not yet thirty), but Powell's strengths show through in the title-piece, with its 'vocabulary which does what it has to do/with ungraceful exactness', and in poems like 'The Way Back', 'In the Distance' and 'January'.

Other notable Carcanet debuts have come from Paul Mills, David Day, Roger Garfitt and Val Warner (the vivacious lady among the careful clerks). But in my view the real find has been Andrew Motion (b 1952), who combines the best qualities of the departing 60s generation and the arriving 70s one. From the *Review* school he has learnt the value of 'withholding': his first collection, *The Pleasure Steamers* (1978), is insubstantiality raised to a fine art. Its 'Anniversaries' sequence has several Hamiltonian qualities: a hospital setting, snatches of conversation, intense feeling for an unnamed 'you':

> I had imagined it all—
> your ward, your shaved head,
> your crisp scab struck there
> like an ornament,
>
> but not your stillness.
> Day after day I saw
> my father leaning forward
> to enter it, whispering
>
> 'If you can hear me now,
> squeeze my hand'. . .

But Motion also has a typically 1970s interest in the possibilities of a closely controlled syntax. In his case it has come through study of the work of Edward Thomas and through an affinity with Larkin. From them he has learnt the power of negatives (un-s and not-s and never-s) to create feelings of nostalgia, sadness and loss. He has, too, their sense of a negative ending: when he ends one poem with the image of 'a blurred riddle of scars/we could not decipher then,/and cannot heal now' he echoes the irrevocability of Larkin's 'Love Songs in Age': 'It had not done so then, and could not now'. And as the natural heir to Thomas and Larkin, he has a deep feeling for English land- and sea-scapes.

It is, of course, a twilight world—'a visible loneliness', vacant and post-imperial. Motion's favourite verbs are 'fade', 'slip', 'disappear'; his favourite nouns 'ghost', 'dust', 'mist', 'shadow', 'silence', 'stillness'; his favourite adjectives 'derelict', 'suspended', 'faint', 'lost'. Whatever he sees or touches is dissolved before him, and all his landscapes are (to use Colin Falck's memorable words about Larkin) 'bathed in the same general wistfulness'. Clearly this has its disadvantages. One begins to wonder whether Motion's slipping and shifting is not just evasiveness; it was this that led one critic to describe his work as 'a sort of spectral card-game where, in great decorum and an atmosphere of elegant hush, one negative sits and waits to be trumped by the next'. At times Motion seems to want not to have it both ways, so that in his poem on Belfast he can speak of 'the promise of conclusion/fading fast towards [him]': try working that one out. One wishes, too, for a more clearly visualized countryside than the vaguely perceived 'England' (he uses the word often and always with a slight lump in the throat) that he travels through. But his mistakes are those of a potentially very important lyric poet. *The Pleasure Steamers* has a rare integrity.

III

It is often said that much of the really promising new poetry in the 70s has come not from England but from Northern Ireland. The discovery of Ulster talent began in the late 60s, with Seamus Heaney, Michael Longley, James Simmons and Derek Mahon establishing their reputations. As the province's political troubles continued into the 70s, so did the search for new names, and nearly half of the contributors to the huge and indiscriminate Blackstaff Press anthology *The Wearing of the Black* (1974) were poets in their teens or twenties. Certainly there was an element of publishers 'cashing in' on the troubles, and of good poetry being confused with 'relevance' and eye-witness accounts; certainly, too, as Andrew Waterman has argued, Ulster writers have at times been chauvinistically complacent about the richness of their culture. But still the record is impressive. Not only have a considerable number of poets made their debuts—among them Hugh Maxton, William Peskett, Gerald Dawe, Eavan Boland, Paul Wilkins and Ciaran Carson—but at least three

have already paved the way towards impressive individual achievements: they are Tom Paulin (b 1949), Frank Ormsby (b 1947) and Paul
Muldoon (b 1951).

None of these poets has written about the troubles in such depth or with
such directness as have Heaney or Simmons. For this there are various
reasons. Paulin has spent much of his adult life in England; Ormsby
prefers the 'neutrality' of a low-key, domestic subject-matter; Muldoon
has defended the position of art for art's sake. Yet all three, however suspicious of the pressure put on them to be 'concerned', have reflected some
aspect of 'the situation' in their work. They are not in any sense a group
but, coming from the same generation and province, they can be looked at
together.

Tom Paulin stands out from many lesser poets because of his capacity to
see Ulster in terms of a fundamental moral problem: what is a just state
and how is it to be achieved? Can justice include mercy or must it always
be harshly retributive? These questions, and an argument between
pragmatism and idealism, can be found recurring throughout his first
collection *A State of Justice* (1977). There is no fatuous liberal 'con-
demnation' of violence in Ulster—Paulin shows how it grows out of a
'city built on mud and wrath' and from a history of 'nightlandings on the
Antrim coast' — but neither does the full horror of what is happening
'under the eyes' get missed:

>   streetlamps
> Light up in the glowering, crowded evenings.
> Time-switches, ripped from them, are clamped
> To sticks of sweet, sweating explosive. . . .
>
> Or, in a private house, a Judge
> Shot in the hallway before his daughter
> By a boy who shut his eyes as his hand tightened.

In other poets the description might look gratuitous, but in Paulin terror-
ism is placed within a larger moral framework, one that might equally
well have him looking at slum clearance in Nottingham. This, indeed, is
the subject of his poem 'A New Society', which understands the impulse
to preserve the old ('There were gas lamps, corner shops that smelt of
wrapped bread'), but is also attracted by images of the finally constructed
Just State of the future. Paulin's literary heritage (Auden, Larkin, Dunn)
shows up clearly here as he imagines a society

> Where taps gush water into stainless sinks
> And there's a smell of fresh paint in sunlit kitchens.
>
> Where rats are destroyed and crawlies discouraged,
> Where the Law is glimpsed on occasional traffic duties
> And the streets are friendly with surprise recognitions.

> Where, besides these, there's a visible water
>
> That lets the sun dazzle on Bank Holidays, and where kids
> Can paddle safely. There should be some grass, too,
> And the chance of an unremarkable privacy,
> A vegetable silence there for the taking.

It may be that, rather like Thom Gunn's first collection, Paulin's *A State of Justice* will not wear particularly well: there are occasional uncertainties of tone and an over-deliberate 'shockingness' (not the expletives so much as the curt refusals of feeling: 'My heart is stone. I will not budge'). But Paulin is a diverse talent, at times aggressive and opinionated, at others lyrical and meditative. One can expect to find in the 80s some development both of his imaginative participation in Asceticism and of his interest in narrative (these come together in the excellent 'In a Northern Landscape').

Frank Ormsby's *A Store of Candles* (1977) is a more straightforward first collection than Paulin's, but less wide-ranging. Ormsby's feeling for the practical, workaday world; his steady confrontation of childhood, marriage, work, family relationships; his even temperament; his earnest but far from humourless tone of voice—these make it a likeable if undistinguished first collection. They also ensure that in the few poems where Ormsby does turn his attention to public events, he does so obliquely and without hysteria. One poem sees outbreaks of violence in terms of the periodic 'floods' which visit Belfast—an analogy nicely clinched in the images of 'sandbagged doors' and 'furnished pavements'; another approaches Protestant-Catholic divisions by way of an old movie feud between 'sheepmen' and 'cattlemen', each side seeking 'excuses to resent the different'; and 'Spot the Ball', probably the best of Ormsby's poems because of its location of the chilling within the everyday, connects the popular newspaper competition with increasingly indiscriminate bombings: 'We are selective/No longer, the full hundred crosses/Filling the sky.'

Paul Muldoon has also been marketed as a bold new talent from the North, though on the troubles he has been provocatively taciturn; there is a strong element of self-accusation (but also ultimately of self-congratulation) in his 'Lunch with Pancho Villa':

> 'Look, son. Just look around you.
> People are getting themselves killed
> Left, right and centre
> While you do what? Write rondeaux?
> There's more to living in this country
> Than stars and horses, pigs and trees,
> Not that you'd guess it from your poems.
> Do you never listen to the news?

You want to get down to something true,
Something a little nearer home.'

'Stars and horses, pigs and trees' are very much the world depicted in
New Weather (1973) and *Mules* (1977), collections notable for their vivid
observations of the natural world, and for their acquaintance with prim-
itive superstition and legend. Muldoon's weakness is a tendency to push
metaphor into portentousness: this happens in 'Mules' itself, where the
striking images of 'the star burned in our mare's brow' and 'after-
birth/Trailed like some fine, silk parachute' are subsumed in a pre-
tentious earth-air dialogue; and it happens in 'Hedgehog', where the
image of hedgehog prickles as a 'crown of thorns' becomes an excuse for
sub-Lawrentian sermonizing. Muldoon is at times too swanky and
foppish, but there is no doubt about his imaginative powers.

IV

An important development in the decade has come at its very end—in the
poetry of Craig Raine and Christopher Reid which began to appear from
about 1977 onwards. Already, despite its limited size, a new 'school' is
being talked of, with Raine as headmaster and Reid his star pupil (Raine
did in fact tutor Reid at Oxford). Peter Porter dubbed these two 'the
Metaphor Men', a title which aptly summarizes their chief characteristic: an interest in coining bold comparisons. James Fenton put his finger
on another of their qualities when he called them 'Martians': they write
like visitors to the planet because, in his words, they 'insist on presenting
the familiar at its most strange'. This label was taken from Raine's poem
'A Martian Sends a Postcard Home', in which there are a series of riddles
about familiar objects—books, cars, watches and so on. The riddles *look*
difficult, but are to be solved less by heavy brainwork than through a
capacity to keep one's eyes and ears alert. Here, for instance, is Raine's
telephone:

> In homes, a haunted apparatus sleeps,
> that snores when you pick it up.
>
> If the ghost cries, they carry it
> to their lips and soothe it to sleep
>
> with sounds. And yet, they wake it up
> deliberately, by tickling with a finger

Raine's poetry begins with 'daily things. Objects/In the museum of
ordinart' because that is part of his programme: to show the wealth of fun
and interest to be found in surroundings which we normally take for
granted. It is this which has him focusing attention on something so
seemingly 'unpoetic' as room lighting—switches look 'like flat-
faced/barn-owls and light ripens/the electric pear'. But he knows also
about the great outdoors, where a rose stem is 'shark-infested', lizards are

'perched pagodas with tiny triangle tiles', a horse's 'puffy mouth is like a boxing glove' and (Raine is not afraid to mix metaphors) cows carry a 'soft chandelier of stalactites'. He is attentive, too, to human postures and actions: a gardener standing 'tired as a teapot' or a window-cleaner who

> listens to the squeak of puppies,
> litters he is paid to drown and strangle.
>
> All day he sees himself in the glass darkly
> and waves goodbye, goodbye, goodbye.
>
> All day he wrings his hands, crying buckets.

Christopher Reid also treats ordinary subjects with great imaginative zest, making poetry out of what is essentially a misreading of signs. As I write, his first book, *Arcadia*, has yet to appear, so it is difficult to give many examples; but there is, for one, his series of 'Haiku Adapted for Home Use': 'A twirly dragonfly/attacks a tin:/it is trying to break in', 'A clipper rounds the cape./Something drops overboard—/of a crescent shape'. He is perhaps more painterly than Raine, enjoying Rousseau's stripes and colours, and he is more experimental in the use of forms: where Raine sticks largely to couplets, Reid takes on all kinds of verse. It is what these two poets share, however, that is most important. Taking their bearings from Elizabeth Bishop, that neglected genius of the casual and metaphoric (you only have to glance at poems like 'The Bight', 'Seascape', 'A Map' and 'A Cold Spring' to see the influence she has had), Raine and Reid have opened up the area of metaphor at a time when, in the post-Movement legacy of plain speech, it had become virtually redundant. And along with this, into a poetic climate renowned for its grey light and level tone, they have brought a sense of warmth, colour, play, even Dandyism.

This is a significant enough development in itself, as some of the reviews of Raine's first collection *The Onion, Memory* (1978) have conceded. But there is also in some quarters a strong resistance to Raine's work, and two serious charges have been brought against it. One is that his poems are contrived and over-ingenious, too bent on demonstrating their author's cleverness, not sufficiently 'engaged'. Here it is useful to recall George Oppen's Objectivist critique of Imagism: the strength of Imagism, he said (and it is Raine's strength), is 'its demand that one actually look'; but he also wanted the image to be 'a test of sincerity as against. . . "The sun rose like a red-faced farmer leaning over a fence", which last is a "picture" intended for the delectation of the reader who may be imagined to admire the quaintness and ingenuity of the poet, but can scarcely have been part of the poet's attempt to find himself in the world'. Raine's poetry does sometimes fall down in this way: its concentration is not, in Elizabeth Bishop's phrase, 'self-absorbed' but rather self-advertising. This happens most in the middle sections of *The Onion, Memory*, where too many effects pile up and the ornamentation becomes (in Raine's own phrase) 'an elaborate architectural periphrasis/to avoid calling a spade/a spade'. He is, I think, aware of the problem: it is the difference between some of the eager-to-impress early poems and a later, unassumingly lyrical one like 'Memory':

> It is being blind in sunlight,
> with one shy hand on Cotswold stone,
> waiting for names to speak themselves. . . .

> Or else breath stumbles, and
> a river is the grey silk dress,
> because a mallard pulls a puckering strand.

This poem goes some way towards answering the other important charge against Raine: that he lacks feeling. When John Carey called him 'unerringly rebarbative' he seems to have had in mind Raine's lack of tact when dealing with emotive subjects. Though metaphor can often be humane, making us see value where we would normally miss it, there are occasions when it seems indecent or trivializing to compare something to something else (the 'thing in itself' should be enough), and Raine's refusal to stop where the lines are usually drawn (funerals, love affairs) can cause feelings of repugnance. Again this is a problem he will have to come to terms with: he is still discovering the limitations of the style he has made for himself. But it should not be supposed that to compare bodies in a mortuary to 'cheeses' is in some way 'heartless'; the detail of the woman's wrongly parted hair in that poem is a good example of the link between careful attention and caring. A more important question to my mind is whether or not the metaphoric mode, which has so far worked best in short poems, is compatible with long, narrative or sequential poems. Raine *has* written one sequence, 'Anno Domini': in it the New Testament myth is allowed to overlap with childhood memories and quotidian fragments, so that sacred and secular merge (those who hold that his poems 'don't add up to much' are missing this essential message: that the secular *is* sacred). But the problem of the long metaphoric poem has still not been properly solved. Whether it will be, what Raine will make of his talent, which other young poets will fulfil their early promise, where British poetry will go next—these are matters for the 1980s.

English and American in 'Briggflatts'

ANGLO-AMERICAN poetry... if we need such a category at all, and whatever we might mean by it, Basil Bunting's poetry seems to belong there. His sensibility is profoundly English — not British but *English*, and Northumbrian English at that; and yet his techniques, his acknowledged masters and peers in the present century, are all of them American. This makes him a difficult poet. For the American reader he is difficult because the voice that speaks in his poems (and in his case 'voice' must be understood very literally), no less than the range of his allusions, especially topographical ones (and in *Briggflatts* topography is crucial), utter insistently an alien, a non-American, experience and attitude. For the English reader he is difficult because, line by line and page by page, his words come at us according to a system of juxtapositions and disjunctions which, because we can find no precedent for it among English poets, strikes us as not systematic at all but random and arbitrary. But plainly, on this showing, the English reader is better placed than the American: whereas one hardly knows where to tell an American reader to start in order to come to terms with Bunting, the English reader has only to acquaint himself with the body of arguments and assumptions about poetry that Bunting in his youth worked out in alliance with certain American contemporaries. We study his American associations only so that we may subsequently discount them. And we may well think that in the future we shall have to do the same with other English poets besides Bunting. *Technically,* surely Anglo-American is what our poetry will be henceforth, but at levels more profound than technique — to which however only technique gives us access — the English poet will remain as English as ever, the American as American.

In 1966 the American poet and declared 'Objectivist', George Oppen, was explaining himself to his French translator[1]: 'Several dozen commentators and reviewers have now written on the assumption that the word 'Objectivist' indicated the contributors' objective attitude to reality. It meant, of course, the poets' recognition of the necessity of form, the objectification of the poem.' With that 'of course' Oppen is too sanguine, as he is again when he goes on to say: 'The point may seem rather obvious today...' The point is so far from obvious that what is meant, by 'the objectification of the poem', is a question not even debated, let alone resolved. As Hugh Kenner has said[2], '*That* history is still unwritten'. History in the first place, not theory... For Oppen in 1966 was a veteran harking back nearly forty years to the initial formulation of a conviction that had governed his writing over the years since. Thus when he speaks of 'the contributors', he means the contributors to *An 'Objectivists' Anthology*, which appeared in 1932, edited by Louis Zukofsky and published by Oppen and his wife on a small press of their own in a French provincial town. The anthology is dedicated to Ezra Pound, and it includes two poems by Pound, but the contributors that Oppen has in mind are Basil Bunting, Robert McAlmon, Carl Rakosi, Kenneth Rexroth, Charles Reznikoff, William Carlos Williams, Louis Zukofsky. This group had good reason to be grateful to Pound because a year before he had donated to them space allotted to him in the magazine *Poetry* (Chicago). And the interesting and affecting thing is that in 1966 Oppen still aligns himself with these men: '. . . it remains my opinion that Reznikoff, Rakosi, Zukofsky, Bunting of Briggflats *(sic)* the most considerable poets of my own generation.' How wide of the truth it is, to say that the point these poets were making 'may seem rather obvious today', is apparent in the fact that most of these names are still unknown or go largely unregarded — the most flagrant case being that of Zukofsky, originally the spokesman and theorist of the entire group.

For our purposes, the intriguing feature is that all these names are American, save one — Basil Bunting, a name that figures along with Zukofsky's and Oppen's in Pound's own *Active Anthology* of 1933. But in the first place it's precisely Pound's patronage of this group that may cause misunderstandings. There is a general notion abroad that as it were the Poundian scriptures were promulgated, the tablets of the Poundian law were handed down, once and for all in the Period of Imagism and Vorticism, and that thereafter Pound would patronize only poets who hewed very close to the line thus laid down. This is quite untrue. Some years before 1930, in his ill-advised campaign on behalf of Ralph Cheever Dunning, Pound had irritably exclaimed against those who took statements appropriate to the particular circumstances of 1914 as if they were injunctions binding upon all poets at all times; and in a few years' time he was to be forced to the same exasperated protest when he wanted to applaud Binyon's translation of Dante. And so it should come as less of a surprise, to find Oppen beginning his case for Objectivism by attacking a central Imagist document:

> We could say — surely *I* would say —: The image for the sake of the poet, not for the sake of the reader. The image as a test of sincerity, as against (tho I may quote inaccurately here): 'The sun rose like a red-faced farmer leaning over a fence', which last is a 'picture' intended for the delectation of the reader who may be imagined to admire the quaintness and ingenuity of the poet, but can scarcely have been part of the poet's attempt to find himself in the world — unless perhaps to find himself as a charming conversationalist.

Of course Oppen *does* misquote. What he has in mind is T. E. Hulme's
'Autumn', the first of five poems which Pound printed provocatively (as
'The Complete Poetical Works of T. E. Hulme') at the end of his *Ripostes*
in 1912.

> A touch of cold in the Autumn night—
> I walked abroad,
> And saw the ruddy moon lean over a hedge
> Like a red-faced farmer.
> I did not stop to speak, but nodded,
> And round about were the wistful stars
> With white faces like town children.

Yet Oppen's misremembering does not destroy the point he is making.
For it is surely quite true that in Hulme's piece there is indeed a great deal
of self-regarding and yet cajoling whimsy, which does indeed point quite
away from what Oppen goes on to call 'the strength of Imagism', 'its
demand that one actually *look*.' And thus, however aptly Hulme may have
come to Pound's hand in 1912, when Pound wanted to assert that 'As for
the future, *Les Imagistes* . . . have that in their keeping', none the less, by
elevating this trivial and dubious piece to the status of a central Imagist
exhibit (for this is what it has since become), Pound opened the way to
whimsical trivia as well as to the 'demand that one actually *look*.'
Zukofsky and Oppen were right in 1932 to want to purge the Imagist
inheritance of this weakness, and Pound by giving them his blessing virtually admitted as much.

It can still be said of course that the purge 'went too far'. Readers of
Oppen's own poems — exhilaratingly sparse and 'purged' as they are —
may well feel so. And those who remember and endorse Wordsworth's
definition of the poet as 'a man speaking to men' may well feel that
Oppen's sneer at the 'charming conversationalist' is not quite so con-
clusive as he means it to be. When Basil Bunting says, 'Pound has had a
great influence on me of course but Wordsworth has had a steady, solid
one all my life on everything' [3], he declares an allegiance that none of his
American associates, not excluding Pound, would subscribe to. And it is
somewhere here that one starts differentiating this English 'objectivist'
from the Americans, and envisaging the possibility of a distinctively
English version of this otherwise all-American movement. But first it
must be emphasized that 'objectivist' is certainly what Bunting is, that he
undoubtedly endorses most of the positions taken up by Zukofsky and
Oppen more than forty years ago. And this is something that his English
readers have not taken account of. They know him as a Poundian poet —
as one has been in the habit of saying, 'the only card-carrying English
Poundian'. But in the preface to his *Loquitur* (1965) Bunting acknowledged 'a continual debt to the two greatest poets of our age, Ezra Pound
and Louis Zukofsky.' The italics are mine; and in what follows I shall

enquire what Bunting meant by those italicized words — not principally
so as to get Bunting into perspective, but rather, as an English poet
addressing other English poets, to see where English poetry has got to,
and where it may go to next (at our hands, if we so choose).

And so we must go back to 'the necessity of form, the objectification of
the poem' — 'as against', so Oppen goes on to say, 'the liquidation of
poetry into the sentimentalism of the American so-called Imagists of the
late twenties and early nineteen-thirties'. (Who *they* were, we need not
now enquire, we need only note once again that Objectivism defines itself
as what Imagism — at any rate, one sort of Imagism — is not) William
Carlos Williams in 1944 was talking about 'the necessity of form, the
objectification of the poem', when he defined a poem as 'a small (or large)
machine made of words.' And twenty years later Bunting is saying the
same thing when he declares: 'A work of art is something constructed,
something made in the same way that a potter makes a bowl. A bowl may
be useful but it may be there only because the potter liked that shape —
and it's a beautiful thing. The attempt to find any meaning in it would be
manifestly absurd.'[4] For most readers, I dare say, Williams's 'machine'
will seem to point one way — towards *agitprop*, perhaps, and Bunting's
pot will point almost the opposite way — back towards the nineties and
Oscar Wilde. But the perception of the poem as artifact rather than com-
muniqué is not a monopoly of aestheticism; any more than 'form' is a
monopoly of those who write triolets and villanelles, or verses that can be
scanned:

> The lines of this new song are nothing
> But a tune making the nothing full
> Stonelike become more hard than silent
> The tune's image holding in the line.

That is Zukofsky's way of putting it, and exemplifying it too. And those
for whom the analogy with the musician comes easier than the analogy
with the potter may set beside Zukofsky's lines Bunting's from *Briggflatts:*

> It is time to consider how Domenico Scarlatti
> condensed so much music into so few bars
> with never a crabbed turn or congested cadence,
> never a boast or a see-here; and stars and lakes
> echo him and the copse drums out his measure. . .

Bunting's 'never a boast or a see-here' corresponds, at least in part, to
Oppen castigating Hulme's 'Autumn' for 'the falsity of ingenuity, of the
posed tableau, in which the poet also, by implication, poses.'

And yet 'It is time to consider. . .' Wouldn't Oppen have to object to
that? Wouldn't he think that it established the poet merely as
'a. . . conversationalist'? Perhaps not. But it does strike a note that we sel-

dom find in the American objectivists: a note that is social and public,
where theirs is characteristically intimate and private. In their poems the
addressee is usually in the singular: the poet is a man who speaks not to
men but to *a man*. Or, to a woman — as Oppen does, touchingly:

> To find now depth, not time, since we cannot, but depth
>
> To come out safe, to end well
>
> We have begun to say goodbye
> To each other
> And cannot say it

This is from Oppen's *Seascape: Needle's Eye* (1972), in which the only
punctuation stops that appear — and those sparsely — are comma, dash,
and inverted comma. The punctuation is as sparse or sparser in *North
Central* (1968) by Lorine Niedecker, who was for Bunting at that time 'the
best living poetess'. (Though she never published with the Objectivists,
Mrs Niedecker, an exquisite poet since dead, was as surely of their company as, *avant la lettre*, Marianne Moore was.) And throughout the ten
poems of Williams's sequence 'Pictures from Brueghel', in his *Selected
Poems* (1969), there is not a single punctuation stop. On the other hand,
merely to turn the pages of Bunting's volumes is to see the full range of
punctuation stops sown at least as thickly as in normal prose; and a closer
inspection will show that for the most part they have the same function as
in prose, clarifying the articulate structure of sentences. This points to an
acknowledgment by Bunting of the social and public institution that
grammar is — an acknowledgment that his American peers (though not,
incidentally, Zukofsky) mostly, or often, refuse to make.

It will be clear what these comments are tending to — to the suggestion
that for the English poet the writing of poems is a public and social
activity, as for his American peers it isn't. Considering that until the
publication of *Briggflatts* in 1966, when the poet himself was 66, Bunting
had been ignored by the British public as totally as Oppen and Zukofsky
and Niedecker had been by the American, this contrast is very striking.
And I'm prepared to argue that this is, and should continue to be, a distinctive feature of English poetry of our time, as against American.

But this, though it is true, is something one must beware of saying at all
loudly or at all often, to the English reading-public. For the sad fact is that
English readers of contemporary poetry — few as they are, and perhaps
just *because* they are so few — have got used to being cajoled and coaxed,
at all events sedulously *attended to*, by their poets. Teachers in English
classrooms have for decades now persuaded school-children and students
to conceive of the reading of a poem as a matter of responding to nudges
that the poet, on this showing debased into a rhetorician, is supposedly at
every point administering to them. And accordingly English readers have
taken to their bosoms a poet like the late John Berryman who, though an

American and at times a very affecting writer indeed, does indeed nudge
and cajole and coax his readers, in a way that one can be sure Americans
such as Oppen and Zukofsky are offended and incensed by. Oppen flies to
the other extreme when he declares, 'The image for the sake of the poet,
not for the sake of the reader'; and so does Bunting when he declares, of
his poem like a pot, 'The attempt to find any meaning in it would be
manifestly absurd.' Neither of these declarations is worded with care, and
neither is defensible as it stands. But behind them both is a conviction
that is wholesome, which the English reader needs to hear about even
more than the American does: the conviction that a poem is a transaction
between the poet and his subject more than it is a transaction between the
poet and his readers. This is to make the poet once again more than a
rhetorician; and on this showing the reader, though the poet cannot be
oblivious of his presence, nevertheless is merely 'sitting in on' or 'listening in to' a transaction which he is not party to. That Bunting is more
social, more public, than Oppen — this is true and significant and important; but what is more salutary for the English reader is to realize that
Bunting none the less shares the Objectivists' determination to cut the
reader down to size, by making him realize that he is only as it were a bystander.

The same lesson, incidentally, can be read out of Hardy. As John Bayley
has said[5], though 'his need for praise was as great as or greater than that of
other artists', yet 'Hardy's anthropomorphic imagination is a substitute
for. . . the direct intercourse of writer and reader', and accordingly, 'the
way to appreciate Hardy best in his poems is to resign oneself to being cut
off from him'. Because of this the current vogue for Hardy's poetry in
England, though it certainly has its unfortunate sides — as when it nour-
ishes Little Englandism, or contrives to be at once idolatrous of Hardy
and condescending to him — none the less is welcome. What needs to be
said — what one wishes John Bayley had said — is that in this respect
Hardy is not an odd man out: that 'being cut off from' the poet one is reading is a normal experience; that it is Berryman's intimacy with his reader
that is exceptional.

How intransigently Bunting holds to the poem as artifact, as verbal
machine, appears in an interview he gave about *Briggflatts*. This is a very
out-of-the-way document [6] — which is a great pity, since it is indispensable for penetrating that poem, however much the author might
want to pretend otherwise. Here Bunting insists that his poem came to
him in the shape of a schematic diagram, which he proceeds to draw for
his interviewers. They cannot believe their eyes: 'Well. . . when you
started, or say at this stage, this piece of paper, this outline, did you know
that it was Briggflatts, that that was the title, that the village was the. . .'
And Bunting interrupts: no, he knew nothing of that, the poem was there
before him in its schematic blueprint 'before there was a line written or
thought of'. The actual wording of the poem, it seems, actually and quite

literally its *content*, was merely the filling of the outline thus determined
in advance. And yet the writing that 'fills in' is — in cadence and
orchestration of sound, no less than in the associations of images — as far
from aestheticism as this:

> Cobweb hair on the morning,
> a puff would blow it away.
> Rime is crisp on the bent,
> ruts stone-hard, frost spangles fleece.
> What breeze will fill that sleeve limp on the line?
> A boy's jet steams from the wall, time from the year,
> care from deed and undoing.
> Shamble, cold, content with beer and pickles,
> towards a taciturn lodging amongst strangers.

I will show my hand without more equivocation, and assert that it is writing of this quality — so compact, having no syllables to spare for nudges or
tipping the wink — that English poetry needs to assimilate and build on.
Only when we have done that shall we be able to deny Oppen's and
Kenner's contention that the whole Objectivist endeavour is 'an American movement'. Why should we want to do that? For our own good, I
think. And, heaven knows, the matter that Bunting packs into *Briggflatts,*
the content of it, the experience that it re-creates and celebrates, is
indelibly and specifically English enough to satisfy anybody. He has
shown us that the achievement is abundantly possible, if only we choose to
emulate it. To emulate him does not mean abandoning metre; it does not
mean, in his Poundian fashion, peppering our pages with the names of
Catullus and Firdausi, Dante and Villon; least of all does it mean taking
over his maddening habit of supplying notes that only tease. But it does
mean writing like this, about autumn twilight over an ancient battlefield
in the Yorkshire dales:

> Grass caught in willow tells the flood's height that has subsided;
> overfalls sketch a ledge to be bared tomorrow.
> No angler homes with empty creel though mist dims day.
> I hear Aneurin number the dead, his nipped voice.
> Slight moon limps after the sun. A closing door
> stirs smoke's flow above the grate. Jangle
> to skald, battle, journey; to priest Latin is bland.
> Rats have left no potatoes fit to roast, the gamey tang
> recalls ibex guts steaming under a cold ridge,
> tomcat stink of a leopard dying while I stood
> easing the bolt to dwell on a round's shining rim.
> I hear Aneurin number the dead and rejoice,
> being adult male of a merciless species.
> Today's posts are piles to drive into the quaggy past

on which impermanent palaces balance.
I see Aneurin's pectoral muscle swell under his shirt,
pacing between the game Ida left to rat and raven,
young men, tall yesterday, with cabled thighs.
Red deer move less warily since their bows dropped.
Girls in Teesdale and Wensleydale wake discontent.
Clear Cymric voices carry well this autumn night,
Aneurin and Taliesin, cruel owls
for whom it is never altogether dark, crying
before the rules made poetry a pedant's game.

That this passage about killing comes from a poem named after a Quaker
meeting-house, written by a Quaker poet who went to prison for his
pacifism in the First World War, is, as they say, relevant. But this is
information that we may or may not bring to the poem; it is not *in* the
poem, nor necessary to it. For this poet eschews the sort of intimate relation with us in which consideration of his personal history would be to the
point. Instead he aims for and achieves the hieratic tone of epic and lament, in which his own voice is indistinguishable from that of the ancient
Cymric poet, Aneurin. We are as little aware of the historical identity of
Basil Bunting as we are of that of Thomas Gray, the valetudinarian Cambridge don, when Gray makes over the same Cymric poem (the *Gododdin*)
into eighteenth-century heroic idiom:

> To Cattraeth's vale in glittering row
> Twice two hundred warriors go;
> Every warrior's manly neck
> Chains of regal honour deck,
> Wreath'd in many a golden link:
> From the golden cup they drink
> Nectar, that the bees produce,
> Or the grape's ecstatic juice.
> Flush'd with mirth and hope they burn:
> But none from Cattraeth's vale return,
> Save Aeron brave, and Conan strong,
> (Bursting thro' the bloody throng)
> And I, the meanest of them all,
> That live to weep, and sing their fall.

Bunting's achievement is greater than Gray's, because he achieves the
hieratic tone not by archaic diction but by ramming his words so hard,
one on the heel of the other (object on verb on subject), that no interstices
are left through which his eye on the thing to be said can be deflected towards the reader, the person he is saying it to. Though it is unthinkable
that George Oppen could, or would ever want to, address himself to this
subject, yet this writing answers to his stringent prescriptions for
Objectivist poetry; and we have seen Oppen admit as much. Elevated

though it is, this passage is all poetry, there is no point at which it strays into the rhetorician's persuasive wooing of an audience. This is where English poetry has got to, it is what English poets must assimilate and go on from.

NOTES

[1] See George Fauchereau, 'Three Oppen Letters with a Note', *Ironwood* 5, Tucson, Arizona, 1975, pp. 78-85.

[2] Hugh Kenner, *The Pound Era,* Faber, 1971, p. 406.

[3] *Multi: Basil Bunting from the British Press,* (Octaroon Book). A flyer distributed at Bunting's San Francisco reading, 1976.

[4] Bunting, *loc. cit.*

[5] 'Separation and Non-communication as Features of Hardy's Poetry', *Agenda* 14.3 (Autumn 1976), pp. 45-62.

[6] *Georgia Straight,* Vancouver, British Columbia. Writing Supplement 6.

CHRISTOPHER MIDDLETON

Notes on a Viking prow

TO RECAPTURE poetic reality in a tottering world, we may have to revise, once more, the idea of a poem as an expression of the 'contents' of a subjectivity. Some poems, at least, and some types of poetic language, constitute structures of a singularly radiant kind, where 'self-expression' has undergone a profound change of function. We experience these structures, if not as revelations of being, then as apertures upon being. We experience them as we experience nothing else.

Yet we say that a poetic text is not this or that thing out there. We say that such a virtual thing as a text is not an actual thing, that it is not even thing-like at all. Or we say that this or that text occupies an interface between things and persons, but has its ontological status only c/o the addressee, who is itinerant and anonymous. Look at the problem this way: Might it be that we are forgetting what a thing as artifact firstly is and secondly signifies? We might be forgetting, in particular, about the intrinsic virtues of preindustrial artifacts, not only ones that had explicitly sacred value.

Lace, icons, hand-blown glass, hand-struck Greek coins, bone implements, masks, figurines, old books, paintings, carts and bedspreads and ploughs — such hand-made things are real, did become real, because they were brought to life by currents of formalized energy, desire crystallizing as it passed from imagination to skilled hands, through to treasured materials, and back again in a circuit never broken. Some artifacts were charged with a 'spirit' which, as in Kwakiutl masks, formalized itself while the skill of the artificer conducted it, like lighting, and crystallized it into a socially significant object illuminating the whole time/space context of the artificer and his tribe. Such an artificer is not confessing, not foregrounding his own subjective compulsions, not cataloguing impressions, not hanging an edict from an anecdote. There is nothing random which is not absorbed into the structure of the artifact. The artificer fashions a group wisdom in the thing which speaks for itself.

That is, at least, one way of viewing, now, certain objects and practices older and other than ours. We may dismiss such practices as fetishism. Seldom do we recognize the watery fetishism, or idolatry, that we ourselves bring to bear on cars, washing machines, cigarette lighters, a glittering host of technoid commodities. The older practices were informed by vigorous, even fierce animistic feeling about the materials at hand, the wood, the jade, the bronze, to which people could relate as once to animals and to the gods in animals. The animism may not have been always lucid. At least it resourcefully furnished knowledge through the conduit of the material, as we can still see in old cathedrals. Our practices are evidently less animate. We fetishize commodities on a basis of yawning indifference — or tight-lipped hostility — toward a world of objects that confuse perception and multiply signs of our alienation. Yet worse, faced with this forbidding world, bothered by it, we finally cease to care. The profit motive, blunted by high taxation, sees to it that we seldom take joy in putting body and soul into things we make for sale or even for our own consumption. A tiny fraction of the mass world, West or East, can still find gratification in hand-making perfect things in leisure time stolen from money time. Artisanal work is coming back, yes, and in the USA, of all places, a little good cooking. But the mainline production mechanisms keep these changes peripheral, for an élite. For the rest: plastics and apathy, sinister twins. Plastix & Apathy — twin *croquemorts* stuffing the corpse of Western Civilization.

The old animistic practices, the old view of *things,* had a great range of vital significance: from witchcraft to Rilke, from soothsaying to apparel, from Viking ships to the most delicate French and German portrait-miniatures of the later eighteenth century. The artifact as icon: if you lived in that world, an icon actually contained for you the soul-substance of the person portrayed. Portrayal was not descriptive or derived. It was presentation, immediate and precise, of the being resonantly invoked by the image and stored in the image. There was more to this than idolatry. By the image the viewer was freed from some snags in the circuitry of response to the world, snags which for us stop growth in two general ways: one is the opacity, compounded of dread and habit, which bottles subjectivity up, the other is the NOHOW feeling which liquefies subjectivity. No wonder that, throughout the 1840s, hundreds of thousands of American people rushed into the daguerreotype studios, hoping to achieve structure, in the form of a perfect and detailed image.

I must edge away from this frame of reference to approach another question. It may be impossible to reconstruct exactly an older world's quasi-magical reality, the texture of its beliefs. But we can do so conjecturally, in this case, by asking how artifacts behaved, or else were thought to reach out and touch the boundaries of space, physical and social space, which defined them. First I shall outline a conjecture, then trace correspondences between that touch-relation (artifact/environment) and poems experienced as apertures upon specific spaces, or places.

Artifact and environment: a dramatic example is the prow of the Oseberg Viking ship. The photo I'm looking at as I write shows a curved piece of wood, elaborately carved, sweeping up out of the rocks and mud which buried the ship for eleven centuries. Placed in receding layers behind the carved wooden curve, secured by wooden plugs, are eight boards, quite slender, the front of the hull, their own curve following the axe-edge upward curve of the prow. Then comes another carved board, as if to reinforce the significance of the prow board. The leading edge of the prow board is about as wide as a matchbox; it is blank and is parallelled by another blank, the trailing edge. Inside this frame come the carved figures.

The figures are carved in low relief, curlings and weavings and interlacings, dragonlike designs. On what is left of the prow board you can count seven major areas, interlocking. The anterior reinforcing board, eight boards back, has a similar but not identical configuration of interlaced and interlocking squirls, tendrils, stick-like ligaments, and broader body areas — again dragon-like. This figuration is not representational. It is something else, but what? The body areas are cross-hatched all over, with striations less deep than the squirl outlines: little elevated rectangles, like those which are reversed ('coffered') in a waffle — dragon scales, if dragons were intended at all. But nowhere does this intricate ornamentation obliterate the woody nature of the wood. You can see the grain. Nowhere, either, does the carving weaken the wood. You see what they mean, the etymologists who derive from the word *cosmos* the word *cosmetic*. Essential virtù explicit in accented palpable form.

People say that the dragons, whose claws invariably point outward to the sea, were meant to protect the oarsmen from evil spirits. I would go further. The dragons are sea foam formalized into (mythic) animal shapes. They are animal formalizations of the sea foam that crashes against the prow or lies briefly on the ocean surface. At the same time, the dragons in no way deform the wood. They are realized directly out of the wood and its grain. The carver carved the protoforms of sea substance into the wood, because then, he thought, even if portrayed as dragons, these protoforms, at home in the wood, know also how to deal with the sea, they being made of the sea, while sharing too the life of the wood.

The ship was protected and guided by marine protoforms carved — into symbols — out of the wood whose axe-edge shape cut through the salty matter of the sea. The symbols worked a magical substitution. The substitute, as symbol, participates communicatively in the brute life, sea, from which it is extracted. Because of that communicative participation, because it knows its double origin, the dragon wood knows how to grip the sea, cope with it, deflect its onslaughts, and how not to be smashed. That was how the carver of wood served his fellow-beings, with capable hands. Enormous muscles on the backs and arms of the oarsmen would otherwise have been helpless. They needed these delicate and incisive woodcarver's hands, needed this information, and they needed the dragons as helpers, to anticipate and disperse the horrors of the sea.

The carving which induces the magical substitution has not only a sheltering (or passive) role to play. Its role is transitive too. The carving acts in and upon the sea, cuts into the sea the shape of the human journey. Finally, the carving is a model of order, good energy in good order. It signified — even if it did not always achieve — a conquest of randomness.

By its transitive action this model made sense of the hazardous sea. To the oarsmen's muscles it signalled orientation among the whirling cross-currents, the heaving labyrinthine web of high tensions between order and chaos, ship and ocean.

Thinking about artifice of this kind — the prow system is not isolated, nor need we lose sight of social implications for ourselves — one comes to have doubts about poems which conform to the scripts of subjective expression; doubts also about anecdotal or confessional poems, poems that catalogue impressions additively, and so forth. I say doubts, but the key to value in any text is the character (quality) of the writing; so perhaps I have simply crept a long way around in order to concede an obvious distinction. This would be a distinction between two kinds of text, the configural and the confessional. Either may appeal to sound aesthetic judgement. If my doubts apply at all, it would be because the (broadly) confessional mode is more apt to encourage limp, self-indulgent, and haphazard writing, also because it makes room for what is fake.

The scripts for self-expression are not all formulae, not by any means. The liberating force of poetry as we know it today derives much from volcanic expressions of the recent past. From Whitman to Artaud — crises in the guts, psyche and voice, oceanic feeling, democracy, elaborate invention of human interiors, not excluding the anguish of Artaud's anus. The great confessional crowing, at its most intense, can show what savage stuff a creative individual is made of. But the artificer poets, who contend with their seas on other levels, at disparate angles, have different ways of making that stuff luminous. Many of the artificer poets, unlike the unwinders of intestines or excavators of the void, are connected with historic places. At the very roots and altogether transparently they are connected with specific places, solid scenes. I wonder if their sense of dwelling along a particular time/space axis implies an imagination akin to that of the prow-carver.

Propertius, Musil, Lorca, Kafka, Baudelaire, Mandelstam, Balzac, Fontane, Joyce, Mörike, Proust, Leopardi, Pindar, and Ladislas Nowak in Trebic today, or Fritzi Mayröcker in her Zentagasse room — they are anything but milieu writers. They all wrestle, respectfully, with arbitrariness. Their cities, landscapes and rooms are not photographically literal. Never frontal reportage about apparent localities, their writings are formal creations which enshrine and radiate poetic space. A particular time/space axis, as 'world of appearance', may be recognized, certainly, in the words and the imagination words embody. But that embodiment includes a crucial moment of change. Nothing is neutral any more, all is transvalued and animated by the rhythms of a unique formal vision grounded in an original sensibility. (There are many women among such writers; their keen and rich sense of space, oddly, is less mixed with artifice.)

Mörike's Swabia, Propertius' Rome, René Char's Vaucluse, all are structures — or I should say structurings — which relate transitively to the extraneous world whose form they gaily enshrine. Hence we experience these places as *world*, as *cosmos*, once we have experienced them in these forms of words. The inaugural word-forms are distinct from expression in the usual sense; they are vocal, but not thought/feeling arbitrarily vociferated. Almost they put us in perceptual contact with being; almost we perceive, in their organization, being as most subtle and integral form. It does not matter much whether the point of contact is a gutter or a fountain, a 'ship under sail' or 'a hog in a high wind,' as Byron said. Perhaps the actual place, in all its dense psychic variety, was in the last analysis a focus for the creation of a vision: a vision of being as an enigmatic and deep structuring, a structuring full of conflict, but pervasive.

At which point I hear my academic hat whistling through the air, aiming to clamp itself back on my head. Yet, if I emphasize structure as a radical linguistic happening, if I consider that some structurings imply magic, I do not advocate making structure conspicuous or exclusive. No neo-parnassian frigidity. Any doctrinaire purism repels me, even that of Gerhard Rühm. I do admire some French poets who are working intelligently to deregulate the sentence-mechanism, who have a fine sense of fragmentariness, and who rid a text of random feeling. But keep at arm's length, I tell myself, the attractive idea of a non-discursive, trans-reflexive poetry which, as it presents complex lyrical experience, is said to be a disclosure of being. At arm's length — partly because this idea lends itself to academic word-spinning, partly because conscious effort so to write results in an esotericism both vacant and prim.

All I have tried to do in these notes is propose, as one possible model for the poem, the significant and useful ancient artifact. In doing so, I stand by figurative speech, as a time-tested access to truth in finite existence, and more, as speech which tells of the impact of the world upon the body. Figures offer an access — to truth and to death — which might be called physiognomical, because it does not shear away feeling and randomness, but admits them, whatever the pain, in a purged and dynamic condition. Purged and dynamic: it is the evolving structure which, as you write your artifact into life, tests and tempers this or that feeling, this or that random particle. The testing and tempering is what eventually makes a text radiant, polysemous, and redeems it from the flat modes of confessional anecdotage or impression-cataloguing.

It is understandable that in the Bundesrepublik younger poets should place imagination, the source of figures, under suspicion (or arrest?), because of its erratic tonal flights and its deceptiveness. Understandable too, but less so for me, that in England not only younger poets seem to regard imagination much as their forebears regarded sex, as a release not often permitted, and then only if it helps you to feel better. Imagination, precisely because it is deceptive and demonic, needs artifice, needs the pressure of craft, the pleasure of artistry, for a dialectical counterpart. As another set of controls one can practise the critique of imagination suggested by Wen I, the Chinese Ch'an (Zen) master of the 10th century: 'All appearances lack in essence and all names arise from that which is nowhere.'

So the world is tottering and still you do what you can to make the prow that shall make sense of the sea, with all the times of your life and of your fellow-beings to propel the ship it guides and shields. Let subjectivity rip, in a poetry of panic and egomaniacal delirium — and the volatile, animated word, the figural form, as an aperture upon being, will very likely be splintered.

Poetry and myth

I

THE assertion about the myth-kitty with which Philip Larkin astonished the world some years ago is perhaps better understood as a piece of auto-biography than as a statement about poetry at large. The young man be-mused by Yeats had the impression of being relieved of his load of dreams by Thomas Hardy, whose dreams were certainly of a different kind. One might leave it at that, had not the author of this dramatic announcement added glosses which suggested that he was putting forward a critical prin-ciple. You 'have to be terribly educated, you have to read everything, to know these things', and that would not do for a man from St John's College, who has spent most of his life in libraries.

> As a guiding principle I believe that every poem must be its own sole freshly-created universe, and therefore have no belief in 'tradition' or a common myth-kitty or casual allusions in poems to other poems or poets, which last I find unpleasantly like the talk of literary understrappers letting you see they know the right people.

This last, rather spiteful little point, must be one to which Larkin attaches some importance, for he makes it again elsewhere: 'you've got somehow to work them' — your bits of reading — 'in to show that you are working them in'. These asides are probably meant to be read as the apologia of a poet who had evaded the impact of Eliot and Pound, and wished to make this a matter for congratulation. It is, however, hardly possible to ignore major innovations, made by one's seniors, without paying a penalty — which some think Larkin has paid.

  Larkin's contention seems to be that he has exemplified a higher form of originality than that of the mere literary innovator. 'Its own sole freshly-created universe' — there must be some exaggeration in that, surely! It suggests a dynamic which puts to shame the hero of the first chapter of *Genesis*. In any age other than ours the phrase would have been re-garded as mere wind; but that, perhaps, shows how truly original and — at the same time — of the age, it is. It is one step beyond that originality of the 'individual' expressing 'himself' ('herself') of which we hear so much. But of course it is only rhetoric, or nonsense. A poem can have meaning only in terms of words other people use, and which we have from our ancestors. It is a part and not a whole or, if one allows it to be a whole, it can be so only in the sense in which individual people may be 'wholes', as members of a company.

When, therefore, Larkin says, 'But to me the whole of the ancient world, the whole of classical and biblical mythology means very little', it must be taken either as confessing, how properly it is not for me to say, to intellectual and imaginative limitations of asphyxiating narrowness, or as a boast of staggering proportions. For he goes on, 'and I think using them today not only fills poems full of dead spots but dodges the writer's duty to be original.' Why 'today'? How does it differ from other days? Because the reader cannot be expected to know anything of the things of which he must know something if he is to read any of the European masters from Homer to — up to but not including — Philip Larkin.

The truth is, one must know something, in order to read anything. Knowing less does not increase one's chances of being original, though it may increase one's chances of imagining that one is. Certainly, if one can attach no meaning to 'the whole of the ancient world, the whole of classical and biblical mythology', better keep clear of those subjects in one's poetry. None the less, it is proper to concede that these are matters about which every literate person — including Larkin — has some knowledge. Nobody could pursue his reading of English poetry very far without picking up a smattering, and a more intensive reading is likely to take one deeper in. Better understand something about the Christian religion if you want to read Herbert or Dr Johnson, let alone such a damned foreigner as Dante, who by the way seems to have been incapable of distinguishing between pagan and Christian mythology, for he speaks of 'il sommo Giove,/Che fosti in terra per noi crucifisso'. There is however the other question, of 'the writer's duty'. Clearly a man may *write* poems without much consciousness of Christianity or of pagan mythology, though of course he will, in the west, not have escaped their influence entirely, for our languages are full of it. If he does use this material overtly, he will make 'dead spots' — lucky if they are only *spots* — unless his understanding, however fragmentary, reaches to a grasp of some contemporary significance it might have, which can only appear in the language in which he speaks of it. So, unless one is to say *a priori* that references to this material are banned, which would be a political, not a critical principle, then we are back at the most solid of all critical dogmas, That the proof of the pudding is in the eating. Yet the problem of mythology is deeper than this. It has to do, precisely, with the standing of that 'experience' of which the twentieth century makes so much. Of course we all have experience; it would be difficult to avoid, as one knocks around the world, or even if one stayed in one place, behind drawn curtains. It is the conscious — though, maybe, not the most important — part of this beastly business of living that we all engage in. The question is, are our feelings about things some sort of absolute? Or can they be checked against some wider reference? And if so, how? It is certainly essential to the possibility of any sort of civilization that the answers to these latter questions should not be entirely negative. It is essential to any communication, to human life itself which, whatever it may be, is certainly not that of any individual floating in space. Mythology is one of the vehicles by which the human being can escape from his solipsism. Through it, one stands for all, as in the Christian religion, or for some of all, or for part of all, as in the pagan mythologies. The old gods were put to flight, but not altogether chased off the scene, by Christ, and if he could be erased from men's apprehension it would not be in favour of a vacuum.

The subject, like any of the fundamental questions which can be asked about art, takes one beyond the frontiers of literary criticism, and deep into it. Is a girl called Sue less a figure of mythology than one called Diana? The question in each case is the reach of her typicality, which is a measure of her significance for other people. Perhaps Larkin should read Hardy again, and consider this question.

II

Sir Philip Sidney, who says he 'slipped into the title of a poet', and that it was for him an 'unelected vocation', was driven to *An Apologie for Poetry* by the silly things that were said about it. His explanations creak a little, because of the Platonic machinery, which we do not handle very well in our century, but they contain a remarkable amount of sense and observation. With a wholesome emphasis on what is *made*, for all to see, as against the modern emphasis on what is alleged to have been felt, he says that the poet, 'lifted up with the vigour of his own invention, doth grow in effect another nature, in making things either better than nature bringeth forth, or, quite anew'. It is the Aristotelian *mimesis*, an imitation of the processes of nature, rather than a copying from her. So, in place of Larkin's 'prime responsibility. . . .to the experience itself', which he is 'trying to keep from oblivion for its own sake', we have the invention of 'forms such as never were in Nature, as the Heroes, Demigods, Cyclops, Chimeras, Furies, and such like'. That might bring a laugh of triumph to the lips of all who can make nothing of 'the whole of the ancient world'. A large claque can be organized, at any moment, for doing without the heraldic beasts. But Sidney can restate his argument in a manner which makes it less easy to set aside. For 'right poets', he says, 'be they which most properly do imitate to teach and delight, and to imitate borrow nothing of what is, hath been, or shall be; but range, only reined with learned discretion, into the divine consideration of what may be, and should be.' That is to say, the party of the hippogriff is the party of invention, which takes its stand on bringing something new into the world, as against the party of preservatism, which thinks, with Larkin, that 'the impulse to preserve lies at the bottom of all art'.

Sidney's conception of poetry has to be considered in relation to a vatic function, of those 'that did imitate the inconceivable excellencies of God'.

That language may not suit, but it is important to realize that the imitation in order to set examples, of which Sidney and other older writers make so much, is a doctrine of *creation*. It is easy to read as a mere bit of school moralism, Sidney's summary: 'whatsoever the philosopher saith shall be done, he' — the peerless poet — 'giveth a perfect picture of it in some one by whom he presupposeth it was done'. In fact, Sidney emphasizes 'a perfect picture', and says that the poet 'yieldeth to the powers of the mind an image of that whereof the philosopher bestoweth but a wordish description'. It is a process which involves a 'purifying of wit', an 'enriching of memory, enabling of judgment, and enlarging of conceit' — precisely, the rewards of a humane education, as they ought to be. And so it is that such a figure as Sue Bridehead enabled readers of *Jude the Obscure* to understand better what was happening to themselves and others. The image did undoubtedly 'strike, pierce' and 'possess the sight of the soul' more than any mere theory, defined the type and, for good or ill, gave it followers. It is not for the poet to follow, but to invent.

That leaves us with the problem — a whole range of problems — about the relationships of what is invented to the world supposed real. Bacon, who had, no doubt, read the *Apologie*, took this matter up in *The Advancement of Learning*, with less sureness of touch, it may be, because he was not himself of the 'unelected vocation' of poet. For him poetry was 'nothing else but FEIGNED HISTORY'; the use of it was

> to give some shadow of satisfaction to the mind of man in those points wherein the nature of things doth deny it. . . because true History representeth actions and events more ordinary and less interchanged, therefore Poesy feigns them with more rareness and more unexpected and alternative variations.

We are approaching the realm of half-truth which confuses art with sentimentality, art with ingenuity, and art with mere vicarious sexual satisfaction, and cuts it off from reality. That was not Sidney's notion. For him it was a form of reality, which was invented. But Bacon goes on, with a sentence which seems to sweep away both the poetical and the divine: 'And therefore Poesy was ever thought to have some participation of divineness, because it doth raise and erect the mind, by submitting the shows of things to the desires of the mind, whereas reason doth buckle and bow the mind unto the nature of things.' The coming thing was not poetry but the inductive method.

III

With Shelley the unkillable spirit of Platonism is with us again, to bedevil our understanding of his formulations. But, in one respect at least, we are better off than with the author of *The Advancement of Learning*. For Shelley was undoubtedly a poet, though he is an unfashionable one. So he occupies the essential common ground with Sidney, and states his claim in a more unmistakable manner than the modest soldier, who merely 'slipped into' being a poet. 'Poetry... differs in this respect from logic, that it is not subject to the control of the active powers of the mind, and that its birth and recurrence have no necessary connexion with the consciousness or will.' So much for recording that moment when Philip Larkin got up for a piss. The claim that it is with the recording of some such precious moment of consciousness that poetry is primarily concerned is implicit in acres of journalistic verse produced in our time, but it is a fiction of the critics, not unrelated to the attempt made by I. A. Richards, in *Principles of Literary Criticism,* to establish a positive basis for the valuation of literature. In practice the poet finds himself with a poem, which cannot be checked, by the poet or anyone else, against the golden moment which is to be kept from oblivion 'for its own sake'.

Despite Shelley's manic tone, and his much greater facility in handling abstractions, the poetic function as he defines it is recognizably the same as that of which Sidney speaks. In neither is a mere copying of the everyday world what is in question; for Shelley poetry 'strips the veil of familiarity from the world, and lays bare the naked and sleeping beauty, which is the spirit of its forms'. Again, it 'transmutes all that it touches, and every form moving within the radiance of its presence is changed by wondrous sympathy to an incarnation of the spirit which it breathes'. He is, decidedly, of the party of the hippogriff. Yet all the poet's inventions have their origin in a human faculty, which is 'a going out of our own nature, and an identification of ourselves with the beautiful which exists in thought, action, or person, not our own'. To 'imagine intensively and comprehensively', a man 'must put himself in the place of another and of many others; the pains and pleasures of the species must become his own.' Sidney makes more of the example, Shelley more of abstract laws, but for both what gives the poet's images their significance is the generality perceived in and through the sensible presentation.

Mere Platonism! But not at all. Both Sidney and Shelley are observers of a process in which they have participated. The involuntary element in composition, of which both speak, is that which 'defeats the curse which binds us to be subjected to the accident of surrounding impressions', in Shelley's words. 'It makes us the inhabitants of a world to which the familiar world is a chaos... It creates anew the universe, after it has been annihilated in our minds by the recurrence of impressions blunted by iteration.' Precisely; what we have seen and felt, over the years, establish their own relationships, among themselves, and the poem which emerges is a piece of stuff torn from that pattern.

But what is that pattern? No one can say exactly. But the figures which appear in it — which move in it, for nothing is stable — are the giants and heroes of the world, as far as we have made them our own, as far, that is, as our nature has been capable of 'going out', and so far as 'the pains and pleasures of the species' have become our 'own'. Such figures, half-figures, ghosts, fragments, are, of their nature, mythological, whether or not they bear, for us, a name you could find in Lemprière.

Bibliography

This select bibliography was compiled by Carcanet New Press from the collection in the Arts Council Poetry Library. It concentrates on books and anthologies printed between 1970 and 1980 and excludes translations, criticism, memoirs and other related writings.

Abbott, Kathleen, *Where the sun began*, Enitharmon 1970; *Masks and Ikons*, Enitharmon 1973.

Abse, Dannie, *Funland and other poems*, Hutchinson 1973; *Selected Poems*, Hutchinson 1973; *Collected Poems*, Hutchinson 1977.

Ackland, Valentine, *The nature of the moment*, Chatto 1973.

Ackroyd, Peter, *Country life*, Ferry Press 1978.

Adams, Sam, *The boy inside*, C. Davies 1973.

Adcock, Fleur, *High tide in the garden*, Oxford University Press 1971; *The scenic route*, OUP 1974; *The inner harbour*, OUP 1979; *Below Loughrigg*, Bloodaxe 1979.

Aitchison, James, *Sounds before sleep*, Chatto 1971; *Spheres*, Chatto 1975.

Aitken, Michael, *The school*, Aquila 1976.

Aldiss, Brian W., *Pile*, Cape 1979.

Alexander, Michael, *Twelve poems*, Agenda 1978.

Allen, Graham, *Out of the dark*, C. Davies 1974.

Allott, Kenneth, *Collected poems*, Secker & Warburg 1975.

Alvarez, A., *Apparition*, University of Queensland Press 1971; *Autumn to autumn* and *Selected poems*, Macmillan 1978.

Amis, Kingsley, *Collected poems*, Hutchinson 1979.

Andrews, Lyman, *Kaleidoscope*, Calder & Boyars 1973.

Annand, J. K., *Twice for joy*, Macdonald 1973; *Songs from Carmina Burana*, Macdonald 1978.

Arden, Jane, *You don't know what you want, do you?* Polytantric 1978.

Ash, John, *Casino*, Oasis 1978.

Ashby, Cliff, *The dogs of Dewsbury*, Carcanet 1976; *Lies and dreams*, Carcanet 1980.

Atik, Anne, *Words in hock*, Enitharmon 1974.

Auden, W. H., *Academic Graffiti*, Faber 1971; *Epistle to a Godson*, Faber 1972; *Thank you, fog,* Faber 1974; *Collected poems*, ed. Edward Mendelson, Faber 1976; *Selected poems*, ed. Edward Mendelson, Faber 1979.

Baldwin, Michael, *Hob and other poems*, Chatto Poets for the Young 1972; *Double image: five poems* by Michael Baldwin, John Fairfax and Brian Patten, Longman 1972; *Buried god*, Hodder 1973.

Bantock, Gavin, *Eirenikon*, Anvil 1972; *Gleeman*, Second Aeon 1972; *Dragons*, Anvil 1979.

Barker, George, *To Aylsham Fair*, Faber 1970; *Poems of places and people*, Faber 1971; *The alphabetical zoo*, Faber 1972; *In memory of David Archer*, Faber 1973; *Dialogues etc.*, Faber 1976; *Villa Stellar*, Faber 1978.

Barker, Sebastian, *On the rocks*, Martin Brian & O'Keeffe 1977; *Epistles*, Martin

Brian & O'Keeffe 1980.

Bartlett, Elizabeth, *A lifetime of dying*, Peterloo 1979.

Barton, Joan, *The Mistress and other poems*, Sonus 1972.

Baybars, Taner, *Narcissus in a dry pool*, Sidgwick & Jackson 1978.

Beckett, Samuel, *Not I*, Faber 1973; *Footfalls*, Faber 1976; *Collected poems*, Calder 1977.

Bedford, William, *The hollow landscapes*, Hippopotamus 1977; *Whatever there is of light*, Mandeville 1975.

Beer, Patricia, *The estuary*, Macmillan 1971; *Driving west*, Gollancz 1975; *Selected poems*, Hutchinson 1980.

Bellerby, Frances, *Selected poems*, Enitharmon 1970; *The first-known*, Enitharmon 1975.

Bennett, Roy, *Phases of memory*, Hippopotamus 1973.

Beresford, Anne, *Footsteps on snow*, Agenda 1972; *The curving shore*, Agenda 1975.

Betjeman, John, *A nip in the air*, Murray 1974; *The best of Betjeman*, selected by John Guest, Murray 1978; *Collected poems*, 4th edn, Murray 1979.

Bidgood, Ruth, *The given time*, C. Davies 1972; *Not without homage*, C. Davies 1975; *The print of miracle*, Gomer 1978.

Birtwhistle, John, *The conversion to oil of the Lots Road London Transport Power Station*, Anvil 1972; *Tidal models*, Anvil 1980.

Black, D. M., *The old hag*, Akros 1972; *The happy crow*, Macdonald 1974; *Gravitations*, Macdonald 1979.

Blackburn, Thomas, *The fourth man*, MacGibbon & Kee 1971; *The devil's kitchen*, Chatto Poets for the Young 1975; *Selected poems*, Hutchinson 1975; *Post mortem*, Rondo 1977.

Boland, Eavan, *The war-horse*, Gollancz 1975.

Bold, Alan, *A pint of bitter*, Chatto 1971; *A century of people*, Academy Editions 1971.

Bond, Edward, *Theatre songs and poems*, Eyre Methuen 1978.

Bosley, Keith, *Stations*, Anvil 1979.

Bottrall, Ronald, *Day and night*, London Magazine Editions 1974; *Poems, 1955-1973*, Anvil 1974; *Reflections on the Nile*, London Magazine Editions 1980.

Bowden, R. H., *Poems from Italy*, Chatto 1970.

Bowman, Ian, *Orientations*, Akros 1977.

Boyle, Charles, *Affinities*, Carcanet 1977.

Broadie, Frederick, *My findings*, Chatto 1970.

Brock, Edwin, *A cold day at the zoo*, Rapp & Whiting 1970; *The portraits and the poses*, Secker & Warburg 1973; *The blocked heart*, Secker 1975; *Here. Now. Always.*, Secker 1977; *Song of the battery hen*, Secker 1977; *The river and the train*, Secker 1979.

Brophy, Michael, *A tired tribe*, Blackstaff 1974.

Brown, Christy, *Come softly to my wake*, Secker & Warburg 1971; *Background music*, Secker 1973; *Snail and skylarks*, Secker 1977.

Brown, George Mackay, *A spell for green corn*, Hogarth Press 1971; *Fishermen with ploughs*, Chatto 1971; *Winterfold*, Chatto 1976; *Selected poems*, Chatto 1977.

Brown, Wayne, *On the coast*, Deutsch 1972.

Browne, Michael D., *The wife of winter*, Rapp & Whiting 1970.

Brownjohn, Alan, *Brownjohn's beasts*, Macmillan 1970; *Warrior's career*, Macmillan 1972; *A song of good life*, Secker & Warburg 1975.

Bruce, George, *Collected poems*, Edinburgh University Press 1971.

Buchanan, George, *Annotations*, Carcanet 1970; *Minute-book of a city*, Carcanet 1972; *Inside traffic*, Carcanet 1976; *Possible being*, Carcanet 1980.

Burn, Michael, *Out on a limb*, Chatto 1973; *Open day and night*, Chatto 1978.

Burns, Richard, *Avebury*, Anvil 1972; *Double flute*, Enitharmon 1972.

Caddel, Richard, *Quiet alchemy*, Ceolfrith 1976.

Caird, Janet, *Some walk on a narrow path*, Ramsay Head 1977.

Callow, Philip, *Bare wires*, Chatto 1972.

Campbell, Donald, *Rhymes 'n reason*, Reprographia 1972.

Campbell-Kease, John, *Second chorus*, Enitharmon 1978; *On the third day*, Enitharmon 1979.

Carson, Ciaran, *The new estate*, Blackstaff 1976; *The lost explorer*, Ulsterman 1978.

Carter, Sydney, *Love more or less*, Galliard 1971; *The two-way clock*, Stainer & Bell, 1974.

Cassidy, John, *An attitude of mind*, Hutchinson 1978; *Charges of light*, Bloodaxe 1979; *The fountain*, Bloodaxe 1979.

Causley, Charles, *Figgie Hobbin: poems for children*, Macmillan 1970; *Collected poems*, Macmillan 1975; *The hill of the fairy calf*, Hodder 1976; *Gift of a lamb*, Robson 1978.

Cavaliero, Glen, *The ancient people*, Carcanet 1973; *Paradise stairway*, Carcanet 1977.

Cayley, Michael, *Moorings*, Carcanet 1971; *The spider's touch*, Carcanet 1973.

Chiari, Joseph, *Lights in the distance*, Enitharmon 1971; *The time of the rising tide*, Enitharmon 1975; *Collected poems*, Enitharmon 1978.

Clark, Leonard, *Walking with trees*, Enitharmon 1970; *Secret as toads*, Chatto Poets for the Young 1972; *Singing in the streets*, Dobson 1972; *The broad Atlantic*, Dobson 1974; *The hearing heart*, Enitharmon 1974; *Collected poems and verse for children*, Dobson 1975; *Four seasons*, Dobson 1975; *Silence of the morning*, Enitharmon 1978.

Clarke, Gillian, *Snow on the mountain*, C. Davies 1971; *The sundial*, Gomer 1978.

Cleary, A. A., *Men homeward*, Ceolfrith 1977.

Clemo, Jack, *The echoing tip*, Methuen 1971; *Broad autumn*, Eyre Methuen 1975.

Clifton, Harry, *Null beauty*, Ulsterman 1975.

Clucas, Humphrey, *Small comfort*, Hippopotamus 1975.

Cluysenaar, Anne, *Nodes*, Dolmen 1971.

Cobbing, Bod, *Concrete*, Writers Forum 1979.

Cole, Barry, *The visitors*, Methuen 1970; *Vanessa in the city*, Trigram 1971; *Pathetic fallacies*, Eyre Methuen 1973.

Cole, David, *This and other worlds*, C. Davies 1975.

Conn, Stewart, *An ear to the ground*, Hutchinson 1972; *Under the ice*, Hutchinson 1978.

Connor, Tony, *In the happy valley*, Oxford University Press 1971; *The memoirs of Uncle Harry*, OUP 1974.

Conquest, Robert, *Forays*, Chatto 1979.

Conran, Anthony, *Spirit level*, C. Davies 1974.

Cook, Stanley, *Signs of life*, Morten 1972; *Form photograph*, Peterloo 1976; *Staff photograph*, Peterloo 1976; *Alphabet*, Peterloo 1976.

Cookson, William, *Dream traces*, Hippopotamus 1975.

Costley, Ron, *see* Ian Hamilton Finlay.

Cotton, John, *Old movies*, Chatto 1971; *Kilroy was here*, Chatto 1975.

Creagh, Patrick, *To Abel and others*, Bodley Head 1970; *The lament of the border-guard*, Carcanet 1980.

Crossley-Holland, Kevin, *Norfolk poems*, Academy Editions 1970; *The rain-giver*, Deutsch 1972; *The dream-house*, Deutsch 1976.

Cruikshank, Helen, *Collected poems*, Reprographia 1971; *More collected poems*, G. Wright 1978.

Cumberlege, Marcus, *Poems for Quena and Tabla*, Carcanet 1970; *Running towards a new life*, Anvil 1972; *Firelines*, Anvil 1977.

Curtis, Simon, *On the Abthorpe road*, Davis-Poynter 1975; *Mrs. Paine*, NW Arts 1978.

Curtis, Tony, *Album*, C. Davies 1974.

Cutler, Ivor, *Many flies have feathers*, Trigram 1973; *A flat man*, Trigram 1977.

Dale, Peter, *Mortal fire*, Macmillan 1970, 1976; *Cross channel*, Hippopotamus 1977; *One another*, Agenda/Carcanet 1978.

Daryush, Elizabeth, *Verses, Seventh Book*, Carcanet 1971; *Selected poems from verses I-VI*, Carcanet 1972; *Collected poems*, Carcanet 1976.

Davie, Donald, *Six epistles to Eva Hesse*, London Magazine Editions 1970; *Collected poems*, Routledge 1972; *The Shires*, Routledge 1974; *In the stopping train*, Carcanet 1977.

Davie, Ian, *Roman Pentecost*, Hamish Hamilton 1970.

Davies, Elwyn, *Words across the water*, C. Davies 1970; *A lifting of eyes*, C. Davies 1974.

Davies, Gloria E., *Her name like the hours*, Chatto 1974.

Davies, Idris, *Collected poems*, Gomer 1972.

Davies, John, *Strangers*, C. Davies 1974; *At the edge of town*, J. Jones 1980.

Dav s, Dick, *In the distance*, Anvil 1975.

Dawe, Gerald, *Heritages*, Aquila 1976; *Sheltering places*, Blackstaff 1978.

Day, David, *Brass rubbings*, Carcanet 1975.

Day Lewis, C., *The whispering roots*, Cape 1970; *Poems*, Cape/Hogarth 1977; *Posthumous poems*, Whittington 1979.

Dennis, Nigel, *Exotics*, Weidenfeld 1970.

Dickinson, Patric, *More than time*, Chatto 1970; *A wintering tree*, Chatto 1973; *The bearing beast*, Chatto 1976; *Our living John and other poems*, Chatto 1979.

Digby, John, *The structure of bifocal distance*, Anvil 1974; *Sailing away from night*, Anvil 1978.

Downie, Freda, *A stranger here*, Secker & Warburg 1977.

Duffy, Maureen, *The Venus touch*, Weidenfeld 1971; *Evesong*, Sappho 1975; *Memorials of the quick and the dead*, Hamish Hamilton 1979.

Dugdale, Norman, *Corncrake in October*, Blackstaff 1978.

Dunn, Douglas, *Backwaters*, The Review 1971; *The happier life*, Faber 1972; *Love or nothing*, Faber 1974; *Barbarians*, Faber 1979.

Durrell, Lawrence, *Vega*, Faber 1973; *Selected poems*, Faber 1977; *Collected poems*, Faber 1980.

Dutton, Geoffrey Fraser, *Camp One*, Macdonald 1978.

Dyment, Clifford, *Collected poems*, Dent 1970.

Earle, Jean, *A trial of strength*, Carcanet 1980.

Earley, Tom, *The sad mountain*, Chatto 1970; *Rebel's progress*, Gomer 1979.

Edwards, Mary S., *Before and after*, Enitharmon 1978.

Edwards, Michael, *To kindle the starling*, Aquila 1972; *Where*, Aquila 1975; *The ballad of Mob Conroy*, Aquila 1977.

Edkins, Anthony, *Worry beads*, Peterloo 1976.

Elliot, Alistair, *Contentions*, Ceolfrith 1977; *Kisses*, Ceolfrith 1978.

Enright, D. J., *Daughters of earth*, Chatto 1972; *The terrible shears*, Chatto 1973; *Rhyme Times Rhyme*, Chatto Poets for the Young 1974; *Sad ires, and others*, Chatto 1975; *Paradise illustrated*, Chatto 1978; *A Faust book*, Oxford University Press 1979.

Evans, Stuart, *The function of the fool*, Hutchinson 1977.

Ewart, Gavin, *Twelve apostles*, Ulsterman 1970; *The Gavin Ewart show*, Trigram 1971; *An imaginary love affair*, Ulsterman 1974; *Be my guest*, Trigram 1975; *No fool like an old fool*, Gollancz 1976; *Or where a young penguin lies screaming*, Gollancz 1977; *All my little ones*, Anvil 1978; *The Collected Ewart*, Hutchinson 1980.

Fainlight, Ruth, *The region's violence*, Hutchinson 1973; *Twenty One Poems*, Turret 1975; *Another full moon*, Hutchinson 1976; *Sybils*, Hutchinson 1980.

Fairfax, John, *Adrift on the star brow of Taliesin*, Phoenix 1974; *Bone harvest done*, Sidgwick & Jackson 1980; *see also* Michael Baldwin.

Falck, Colin, *Backwards into the smoke*, Carcanet 1973; *In this dark light*, TNR 1978.

Fanthorpe, U. A., *Side effects*, Peterloo 1978.

Faulkner, Pete, *Rats dance by candlelight*, Aquila 1976.

Fearn, Susan, *Marking time*, Aquila 1976.

Feinstein, Elaine, *The magic apple tree*, Hutchinson 1971; *The celebrants*, Hutchinson 1973; *Some unease and angels*, Hutchinson 1977.

Fekete, Irene, *Time elsewhere*, Chatto 1971.

Fenton, James, *Terminal moraine*, Secker & Warburg 1972; *A vacant possession*, TNR 1978.

Fiacc, Padraic, *Nights in the bad place*, Blackstaff 1977; *The selected Padraic Fiacc*, Blackstaff 1980.

Ffinch, Michael, *Voices round a star*, Latimer 1970; *The beckwalker*, Latimer New Dimensions 1977; *Selected poems*, Titus Wilson 1979.

Finch, Peter, *Whitesung*, Aquila 1972; *Blats*, Second Aeon 1972.

Finlay, Ian Hamilton, *Poems to hear and see*, Collier-Macmillan 1971; *The boy's alphabet book*, Coach-house, Toronto, 1976; *Heroic emblems*, with Ron Costley, Z Press 1978.

Fisher, Roy, *The cut pages*, Fulcrum, 1971; *Matrix*, Fulcrum 1971; *The thing about Joe Sullivan*, Carcanet 1978; *Comedies*, Pig Press 1979.

Foley, Michael, *True life love stories*, Blackstaff 1976; *The Irish frog: adaptations from Rimbaud, Corbière, Laforgue*, Ulsterman 1978.

Fortuna, Blackie, *Twilight song*, Mid-day 1979.

Fowler, Alastair, *Catacomb suburb*, Edinburgh University Press 1976.

Fraser, Douglas, *Rhymes o' auld reekie*, Macdonald 1973; *Where the dark branches part*, Macdonald 1977.

Fuller, Jean Overton, *Darun and Pitar*, Fuller d'Arch Smith 1970; *Conversations with a captor,* d'Arch Smith 1973.

Fuller, John, *Cannibals and missionaries,* Secker & Warburg 1972; *Epistles to several persons,* Secker 1973; *Squeaking crust,* Chatto Poets for the Young 1974; *The mountain in the sea,* Secker 1975; *Lies and secrets,* Secker 1979.

Fuller, Roy, *Seen Grandpa lately?* Deutsch 1972; *Tiny tears,* Deutsch 1973; *An old war,* Tragara 1974; *From the joke shop,* Deutsch 1975; *An ill-governed coast,* Ceolfrith 1976; *Poor Roy,* Deutsch 1977; *A reign of sparrows,* London Magazine Editions 1980.

Fulton, Robin, *Quarters,* Castlelaw Press 1971; *The man with the surbahar,* Macdonald 1971.

Furnival, Christine, *Prince of sapphires,* Aquila 1976; *Towards praising,* C. Davies 1978.

Gardner, Donald, *For the flames,* Fulcrum 1973.

Garfitt, Roger, *Caught on blue,* Carcanet 1970; *West of elm,* Carcanet 1974.

Garioch, *The big music,* J. Humphries 1971; *Doctor Faust in Rose Street,* Macdonald 1973; *Collected poems,* Macdonald 1977, Carcanet 1980.

Garlick, Raymond, *A sense of time,* Gomer 1972; *Incense,* Gomer 1976.

Gershon, Karen, *Legacies and encounters,* Gollancz 1972; *My daughters, my sisters,* Gollancz 1975; *Coming back from Babylon,* Gollancz 1979.

Gibbon, Monk, *The velvet bow,* Hutchinson 1972.

Gibson, Miles, *The guilty bystander,* Methuen 1970; *Permanent damage,* Eyre Methuen 1973.

Gillies, Valerie, *Each bright eye,* Canongate 1977.

Gittings, Robert, *American journey,* Heinemann 1972; *Collected poems,* Heinemann 1976.

Glen, Duncan, *In appearances,* Akros 1971; *Clydesdale,* Akros 1971; *Feres,* Akros 1971; *Mr and Mrs J. L. Stoddart at home,* Akros 1975; *In place of wark,* Akros 1977; *Of philosophers and tinks,* Akros 1977; *Gaitherings,* Akros 1977.

Goodridge, Frank, *The raw side,* Peterloo 1978.

Gowrie, Grey, *A postcard from Don Giovanni,* Oxford University Press 1972.

Graham, Henry, *Passport to earth,* Rapp & Whiting 1971.

Graham, W. S., *Malcolm Mooney's land,* Faber 1970; *Implements in their places,* Faber 1977; *Collected poems,* Faber 1979.

Graves, Charles, *Collected poems,* Ramsay Head 1972; *The warming pan.* Ramsay Head 1975.

Graves, Robert, *Poems 1968-1970,* Cassell 1970; *Poems 1970-1972,* Cassell 1972; *Collected poems,* Cassell 1975; *Poems,* selected by Robert Graves and Anthony Thwaite, 5th edn, Penguin 1978.

Green, F. Pratt, *The old couple,* Peterloo 1976.

Green, J. C. R., *By weight of reason,* Aquila 1974; *A beaten image,* Aquila 1977.

Greene, James, *Dead-man's-fall,* Bodley Head 1980.

Grieg, Andrew, *Men on ice,* Canongate 1977.

Griffiths, Bryn, *The survivors,* Dent 1971; *The dark convoys,* Aquila 1974.

Grigson, Geoffrey, *Discoveries of bones and stones,* Macmillan 1971; *Sad grave of an imperial mongoose,* Macmillan 1973; *Angles and circles,* Gollancz 1974; *The fiesta,* Secker & Warburg 1978; *The history of him,* Secker 1980.

Gruffyd, Peter, *The shivering seed,* Chatto 1972.

Guest, Harry, *The cutting room,* Anvil 1970; *A house against the night,* Anvil 1976.

Gunn, Thom, *Moly*, Faber 1971; *Touch*, Faber 1974; *Jack Straw's castle*, Faber 1976; *Selected poems*, Faber 1979.
Gutteridge, Bernard, *Old damson face*, London Magazine Editions 1975.

Hall, D. J., *Journey into morning*, Chatto 1972.
Hall, J. C., *A house of voices*, Chatto 1973.
Hamburger, Michael, *Ownerless earth*, Carcanet 1973; *Real estate*, Carcanet 1977.
Hamilton, Ian, *The visit*, Faber 1970.
Hamilton-Paterson, James, *Option three*, Gollancz 1974.
Harrison, Tony, *The loiners*, London Magazine Editions 1970; *Newcastle is Peru*, Northern House 1974; *Bow down*, Collings 1977; *From the school of eloquence*, Collings 1978.
Harsent, David, *After dark*, Oxford University Press 1973.
Harvey, Andrew, *Masks and faces*, Deutsch 1978; *Evidence*, Mid-day 1979.
Harvey, W. J., *Descartes' dream*, Carcanet 1973.
Harwood, Lee, *The sinking colony*, Fulcrum 1970; *HMS Little Fox*, Oasis 1975; *Boston-Brighton*, Oasis 1977.
Havins, Peter J. Neville, *The matchbox*, C. Davies 1975.
Haynes, John, *Sabon Gari*, London Magazine Editions 1974.
Heaney, Seamus, *Wintering out*, Faber 1972; *North*, Faber 1975; *Stations*, Ulsterman 1975; *Field work*, Faber 1979.
Heath-Stubbs, John, *Artorius*, Enitharmon 1973; *A parliament of birds*, Chatto Poets for the Young 1975; *The watchman's flute*, Carcanet 1978; *The mouse, the bird and the sausage*, Ceolfrith 1978.
Hendry, J. F., *Marimusa*, J. Humphries 1978.
Henri, Adrian, *Poems for Wales and Six landscapes for Susan*, Arc 1970; *Autobiography*, Cape 1971; *The best of Henri*, Cape 1975; *One year*, Arc 1976; *City Hedges*, Cape 1977; *From the loveless motel*, Cape 1980.
Hesketh, Phoebe, *A song of sunlight*, Chatto Poets for the Young 1974; *Preparing to leave*, Enitharmon 1977.
Hewitt, John, *Out of my time*, Blackstaff 1974; *Time enough*, Blackstaff 1976; *The rain dance*, Blackstaff 1979; *Kites in spring*, Blackstaff 1980.
Hewlings, Michael, *The release*, Anvil 1972.
Hill, Geoffrey, *Mercian hymns*, Deutsch 1971; *Tenebrae*, Deutsch 1978.
Hobsbaum, Philip, *Women and animals*, Macmillan 1972.
Hoida, Pete, *Lips*, Allison & Busby 1972.
Holbrook, David, *Chance of a lifetime*, Anvil 1978.
Holden, Molly, *Air and chill earth*, Chatto 1971; *The country over*, Chatto 1975.
Holloway, Geoffrey, *To have eyes*, Anvil 1972; *Rhine jump*, London Magazine Editions 1974; *All I can say*, Anvil 1978.
Holloway, John, *Planet of winds*, Routledge 1977.
Holmes, Philip, *A place to stand*, Anvil 1977.
Hooker, Jeremy, *The elements*, C. Davies 1972; *Soliloquies of a chalk giant*, Enitharmon 1974; *Landscape of the daylight moon*, Enitharmon 1978; *Solent shore*, Carcanet 1978; *Englishman's road*, Carcanet 1980.
Horovitz, Michael, *The Wolverhampton Wanderer*, Latimer New Dimensions 1971; *Growing up*, Allison & Busby 1979.
Houston, Libby, *Plain clothes*, Allison & Busby 1971.
Howden, Keith, *Marches of familiar landscape*, Peterloo 1978.

Howell, Anthony, *Imruil,* Barrie & Jenkins 1970; *Oslo: a Tantric ode,* Calder &
  Boyars 1975.
Howell, Jim, *Survivals,* Peterloo 1976.
Hughes, Glyn, *Neighbours,* Macmillan 1970; *Rest the poor strugglers,* Macmillan
  1972; *Alibis and convictions,* Ceolfrith 1978.
Hughes, Ted, *Crow,* Faber 1970; *Selected poems,* Faber 1972; *Season songs,* Faber
  1976; *Gaudete,* Faber 1977; *Moon-bells and other poems,* Chatto 1978; *Cave birds,*
  Faber 1978; *Remains of Elmet,* Faber 1979; *Moortown,* Faber 1979.
Hunt, Irvine, *Tyson,* MidNAG 1978.
Huws, Daniel, *Noth,* Secker & Warburg 1972.
Hyland, Paul, *Riddles for Jack,* Northern House 1978; *Domingus,* Mid-day 1978.

Jackson, Dawson, *Ice & the orchard,* Carcanet 1973.
Jay, Peter, *Lifelines,* Satis 1977; *Shifting Frontiers,* Carcanet 1980.
Jennings, Elizabeth, *Lucidities,* Macmillan 1970; *Relationships,* Macmillan 1972;
  Growing points, Carcanet 1975; *Consequently I rejoice,* Carcanet 1977; *After the
  ark,* Oxford University Press 1978; *Moments of grace,* Carcanet 1979; *Selected
  poems,* Carcanet 1979.
John, Roland, *Report from the desert,* Hippopotamus 1973.
Johnson, B. S., *Poems two,* Trigram 1972.
Johnstone, Robert, *Our lives are Swiss,* Ulsterman 1977.
Jones, Bramwell, *Cadence notes,* C. Davies 1977.
Jones, Brian, *For mad Mary,* London Magazine Editions 1974; *The Spitfire on the
  Northern Line,* Chatto Poets for the Young 1975; *The island normal,* Carcanet
  1980.
Jones, David, *The sleeping lord,* Faber 1974; *The Kensington Mass,* Agenda 1975.
Jones, Glyn, *Selected poems,* Gomer 1974.
Jones, Peter, *The peace and the hook,* Carcanet 1972; *The garden end,* Carcanet 1977.
Jones, Richard, *Love suite,* Aquila 1976.
Jones, Sally Roberts, *The forgotten country,* Gomer 1977.
Jones, T. Harri, *Collected poems,* Gomer 1977.
Joseph, Jenny, *Rose in the afternoon,* Dent 1974; *The thinking heart,* Secker &
  Warburg 1978.

Kavanagh, P. J., *About time,* Chatto 1970; *Edward Thomas in heaven,* Chatto 1974;
  Life before death, Chatto 1979.
Kazantzis, Judith, *Minefield,* Sidgwick & Jackson 1977.
Keene, Dennis, *Surviving,* Carcanet 1980.
Kell, Richard, *Heartwood,* Northern House 1978; *Humours,* Ceolfrith 1978.
Kendrick, George, *Erosions,* Phoenix 1971; *Bicycle tyre in a tall tree,* Carcanet 1974.
King, Patrick, *Still running,* Ulsterman 1977.
Kirkup, James, *White shadows, black shadows,* Dent 1970; *A Bewick bestiary,* Mid
  NAG 1971; *The body servant,* Dent 1971.
Knowles, Susanne, *The sea-bell,* Dent 1974.
Kops, Bernard, *For the record,* Secker & Warburg 1971.

Laing, R. D., *Knots,* Tavistock 1970; *Do you really love me?* Allen Lane 1976;
  Sonnets, M. Joseph 1979.
Larkin, Philip, *High windows,* Faber 1974.

Levi, Peter, *Life is a platform,* Anvil 1971; *Death is a pulpit,* Anvil 1971; *Collected poems,* Anvil 1976; *Five ages,* Anvil 1978.

Lindop, Grevel, *Fools' paradise,* Carcanet 1977.

Lindsay, Frederic, *And be the nation again,* Akros 1975.

Lindsay, Maurice, *Comings and goings,* Akros 1971; *Selected poems,* R. Hale 1973; *Walking without an overcoat,* Hale 1977; *Collected poems,* Paul Harris 1979.

Littlechild, Frank, *An Easter legend,* R. Hale 1974.

Lloyd, Theodora, *Song of the iron hoop,* Gomer 1976.

Lochhead, Liz, *Memo for spring,* Reprographia 1972.

Logue, Christopher, *Twelve cards,* Lorrimer 1971; *Abcedary,* Cape 1977.

Lomas, Herbert, *Private and confidential,* London Magazine Editions 1974.

Longley, Michael, *An exploded view,* Gollancz 1973; *Man lying on a wall,* Gollancz 1976; *The echo gate,* Secker & Warburg 1979.

Lowbury, Edward, *Green magic,* Chatto Poets for the Young 1972; *The night watchman,* Chatto 1974; *Troika,* by Edward Lowbury, John Press and Michael Riviere, Daedalus 1977; *Selected poems,* Celtion 1978.

Lowenstein, Tom, *The death of Mrs Owl,* Anvil 1977.

Lowy, Simon, *Melusine and the Nigredo,* Carcanet 1979.

Lucie-Smith, Edward, *The well-wishers,* Oxford University Press 1974.

Macbeth, George, *The burning cone,* Macmillan 1970; *Collected poems,* Macmillan 1971; *The Orlando poems,* Macmillan 1971; *Lusus,* d'Arch Smith 1972; *A poet's year,* Gollancz 1973; *Shrapnel,* Macmillan 1973; *In the hours waiting for the blood to come,* Gollancz 1975; *Poems of love and death,* Secker & Warburg 1980.

MacCaig, Norman, *Selected poems,* Hogarth Press 1971; *The white bird,* Chatto 1973; *The world's room,* Chatto 1974; *Tree of strings,* Chatto 1977; *Old maps and new,* Chatto 1978; *The equal skies,* Chatto 1980.

McCarthy, Shaun, *Places,* Hippopotamus 1973.

MacCrimmon, Patrick, *Deirdre,* Akros 1971.

MacDiarmid, Hugh, *More collected poems,* MacGibbon & Kee 1970; *The Hugh MacDiarmid anthology,* eds. Michael Grieve and Alexander Scott, Routledge 1972; *Complete poems,* Martin Brian & O'Keeffe 1978; *The Socialist poems,* eds. T. S. Law and Thurso Bewick, Routledge 1978.

McDuff, David, *Words in nature,* Ramsay Head 1971.

McFadden, Roy, *The Garryowen,* Chatto 1971; *Verifications,* Blackstaff 1977; *A watching brief,* Blackstaff 1978.

McGough, Roger, *After the merrymaking,* Cape 1971; *Gig,* Cape 1973; *Sporting relations,* Eyre Methuen 1974; *In the glassroom,* Cape 1976; *Holiday on Death Row,* Cape 1979.

Mackinnon, Rayne, *The spark of joy,* Caithness 1970; *The blasting of Billy P.,* Enitharmon 1978.

Maclean, Alisdair, *From the wilderness,* Gollancz 1973; *Waking the dead,* Gollancz 1976.

Maclean, Sorley, *Poems to Eimhir,* translated from the Gaelic by I. Crichton Smith, Gollancz 1971; *Spring tide and neap tide,* Canongate 1977.

Macleod, Joseph, *An old olive tree,* Macdonald 1971.

McLoghlen, Diana, *The last headlands,* Chatto 1972.

Magee, Wes, *Urbane Gorilla,* University of Leeds, 1972; *No man's land,* Blackstaff

1978; *Aberlefenni: at the quarry,* Xenia 1979.

Mahon, Derek, *Beyond Howth Head,* Dolmen 1970; *Lives,* Oxford University Press 1972; *The snow party,* OUP 1975; *Light music,* Ulsterman 1977; *Poems,* OUP 1979.

Manning, Hugo, *Madame Lola,* Enitharmon 1974; *Modigliani,* Enitharmon 1976; *Dylan Thomas,* Enitharmon 1977.

Marshall, Douglas, *Upstairs neighbours,* Ulsterman 1977.

Marshfield, Alan, *Mistress,* Anvil 1972; *Dragonfly,* Oasis 1972.

Massingham, Harold, *Frost-gods,* Macmillan 1971.

Mathias, Roland, *Absalom in the tree,* Gomer 1971; *Snipe's castle,* Gomer 1979.

Mayer, Gerda, *The knockabout show,* Chatto 1978.

Mead, Matthew, *The administration of things,* Anvil 1970; *The midday muse,* Anvil 1979.

Merchant, Moelwyn, *Breaking the code,* Gomer 1975.

Middleton, Christopher, *The lonely suppers of W. V. Balloon,* Carcanet 1975; *Pataxanadu,* Carcanet 1977; *Carminalenia,* Carcanet 1980.

Middleton, Kate, *Into the wind,* Ulsterman 1974.

Mills, Paul, *North carriageway,* Carcanet 1976; *Herod,* Collings 1978; *Third person,* Carcanet 1978.

Millward, Eric, *Dead Letters,* Peterloo 1978.

Milne, Ewart, *Cantata under Orion,* Aquila 1976; *Drift of pinions,* Aquila 1976.

Mitchell, Adrian, *Ride the nightmare,* Cape 1971; *Tyger,* Cape 1971; *The apeman cometh,* Cape 1975.

Mitchell, Elma, *The poor man in the flesh,* Peterloo 1976; *The human cage,* Peterloo 1979.

Mole, John, *The love horse,* Morten 1973; *A partial light,* Dent 1975; *Our ship,* Secker & Warburg 1977; *From the house opposite,* Secker 1979.

Moore, Hubert, *Down by a bicycle,* Hippopotamus 1979.

Morgan, Edwin, *Twelve songs,* Castlelaw Press 1970; *The horseman's word,* Akros 1970; *Instamatic poems,* McKellar 1972; *From Glasgow to Saturn,* Carcanet 1973; *The whittrick,* Akros 1973; *The new divan,* Carcanet 1977.

Morgan, Pete, *The grey mare being the better steed,* Secker & Warburg 1973; *The spring collection,* Secker 1979.

Morgan, Robert, *The storm,* C. Davies 1974.

Morris, Brian, *Tide race,* Gomer 1976; *Stones in the brook,* Gomer 1978.

Morris, Stephen, *Born under Leo,* Aquila 1972; *The revolutionary,* Aquila 1972; *Death of a clown,* Aquila 1976; *The moment of truth,* Aquila 1976.

Morrison, Vincent, *The season of comfort,* Bloodaxe 1979.

Motion, Andrew, *The pleasure steamers,* Carcanet 1978.

Muldoon, Paul, *New weather,* Faber 1973; *Names and addresses,* Ulsterman 1978.

Mulrine, Stephen, *Poems,* Akros 1971.

Munro, Robin, *The land of the mind,* Dent 1975.

Murphy, Richard, *High island,* Faber 1974; *Selected poems,* Faber 1979.

Neill, William, *Poems,* Akros 1970; *Despatches home,* Reprographia 1972.

Nicholson, Norman, *A local habitation,* Faber 1972; *Stitch and stone,* Ceolfrith 1975; *The shadow of Black Combe,* MidNAG 1979.

Norris, Leslie, *Ransoms,* Chatto 1970; *Mountains Polecats Pheasants,* Chatto 1974; *Water voices,* Chatto 1980.

Nuttall, Jeff, *Poems,* Fulcrum 1970; *Objects,* Trigram 1976.
Nye, Robert, *Divisions on a ground,* Carcanet 1976.

Oakes, Philip, *Married/Singular,* Deutsch 1974.
Oliver, Douglas, *The diagram poems,* Ferry Press 1979.
Olivier, W. H. L., *Out of season,* Oxford University Press 1980.
Ormond, John, *Definition of a waterfall,* Oxford University Press 1973.
Ormsby, Frank, *A store of candles,* Oxford University Press 1977; *Being walked by a dog,* Ulsterman 1978.

Pacey, Philip, *Charged landscapes,* Enitharmon 1978.
Patten, Brian, *The irrelevant song,* Allen & Unwin 1971; *Vanishing trick,* Allen & Unwin 1976; *Grave gossip,* Allen & Unwin 1979.
Paulin, Tom, *Theoretical locations,* Ulsterman 1975; *A state of justice,* Faber 1977; *Personal column,* Ulsterman 1978; *The strange museum,* Faber 1980.
Perrie, Walter, *A lamentation for the children,* Canongate, 1977; *Surge Aquilo,* Akros 1977.
Perry, Alan, *Live wires,* C. Davies 1970; *Fires on the common,* C. Davies 1975.
Peskett, William, *Cleaning stables,* Ulsterman 1974; *The nightowl's dissection,* Secker & Warburg 1975; *A killing in the grove,* Ulsterman 1977; *A more suitable terrain,* Ulsterman 1978.
Phillips, Douglas, *Beyond the frontier,* C. Davies 1972.
Pickard, Tom, *The order of chance,* Fulcrum 1971; *Hero dust,* Allison & Busby 1979.
Pilcher, Barry Edgar, *Liberty Cape from the coast,* Aquila 1976.
Pinter, Harold, *Poems and prose,* Eyre Methuen 1978.
Pitter, Ruth, *End of drought,* Barrie & Jenkins 1975.
Plomer, William, *Celebrations,* Cape 1972; *Collected poems,* Cape 1973.
Poole, Richard, *Goings,* C. Davies 1978.
Porter, Peter, *The last of England,* Oxford University Press 1970; *After Martial,* OUP 1972; *Preaching to the converted,* OUP 1972; *Living in a calm country,* OUP 1975; *The cost of seriousness,* OUP 1978.
Power, Kevin, *Work in progress,* Trigram 1977.
Powell, Neil, *At the edge,* Carcanet 1977.
Pownall, David, *Another country,* Peterloo 1978.
Press, John, *see* Edward Lowbury.
Prince, F. T., *Memoirs of Oxford,* Fulcrum 1970; *Drypoints of the Hasidim,* Menard Press 1975; *Afterword on Rupert Brooke,* Menard Press 1976; *Collected poems,* Anvil/Menard 1979.
Prynne, J. H., *Brass,* Ferry Press 1971; *Into the day,* Ferry 1972; *News of warring clans,* Trigram 1977; *Down where changed,* Ferry 1979.
Prys-Jones, A. G., *Valedictory verses,* Gomer 1978.
Pudney, John, *Take this orange,* Dent 1971; *Selected poems,* Dent 1973; *Living in a one-sided house,* Shepherd-Walwyn 1976.
Pugh, Sheenagh, *Crowded by shadows,* C. Davies 1977.
Purcell, Sally, *The holly queen,* Anvil 1971; *Dark of day,* Anvil 1977.
Purser, John, *The counting stick,* Aquila 1976.

Pybus, Rodney, *In Memoriam Milena*, Chatto 1973; *Bridging loans*, Chatto 1976; *At the stone junction*, Northern House 1978.

Radice, William, *Eight sections*, Secker & Warburg 1974.

Raine, Craig, *The onion, memory*, Oxford University Press 1978; *A Martian sends a postcard home*, OUP 1979.

Raine, Kathleen, *The lost country*, Dolmen/Hamish Hamilton 1971; *On a deserted shore*, Dolmen/Hamish Hamilton 1973; *The oval portrait*, Enitharmon 1977.

Raworth, Tom, *Lion lion*, Trigram 1970; *Moving*, Cape Goliard 1971; *Act*, Trigram 1972.

Rawson, Nicholas, *Shards*, Calder & Boyars 1973.

Reading, Peter, *For the municipality's elderly*, Secker & Warburg 1974; *The prison cell and barrel mystery*, Secker 1976; *Nothing for anyone*, Secker 1977; *Fiction*, Secker 1979.

Redgrove, Peter, *The mother, the daughter and the sighing bridge*, Sycamore Press 1970; *Love's journeys*, Second Aeon 1971; *Dr. Faust's sea-spiral spirit*, Routledge 1972; (with Penelope Shuttle) *The hermaphrodite album*, d'Arch Smith 1973; *Sons of my skin*, Routledge 1975; *From every chink of the ark*, Routledge 1977; *The weddings at Nether Powers*, Routledge 1979.

Reed, Jeremy, *Count Bluebeard*, Aquila 1976; *The isthmus of Samuel Greenberg*, Trigram 1976; *Saints and psychotics*, Enitharmon 1979. *Bleecker Street*, Carcanet 1980.

Reeves, James, *Poems and paraphrases*, Heinemann 1972; *Complete poems for children*, Heinemann 1973; *Collected poems*, Heinemann 1974; *More pre-fabulous animals*, Heinemann 1975; *Arcadian ballads*, Heinemann 1978.

Reid, Alastair, *Weathering*, Canongate 1978.

Reid, Christopher, *Arcadia*, Oxford University Press 1979.

Rhydderch, William, *A necessary simplicity*, Gomer 1975.

Richards, I. A., *Internal colloquies*, Routledge 1972; *New and selected poems*, Carcanet 1978.

Rickword, Edgell, *Fifty poems*, Enitharmon 1970; *Behind the eyes*, Carcanet 1976.

Riddell, Alan, *Eclipse*, Calder & Boyars 1972.

Ridler, Anne, *Some time after*, Faber 1972.

Ritchie, Crae, *Confrontation*, Caithness 1973.

Riviere, Michael, *see* Edward Lowbury.

Robin, Ian, *Round circles*, Weidenfeld 1977.

Robson, Jeremy, *In focus*, Allison & Busby 1970.

Rodgers, W. R., *Collected poems*, Oxford University Press 1971.

Ross, Alan, *Tropical ice*, Covent Garden Press 1972; *The Taj express*, London Magazine Editions 1973; *Open sea*, London Magazine Editions 1975; *Death Valley and other poems in America*, London Magazine Editions 1980.

Rowse, A. L., *Strange encounter*, Cape 1972; *The road to Oxford*, Cape 1978.

Rudolf, Anthony, *The manifold circle*, Carcanet 1971; *The same river twice*, Carcanet 1976.

Rumens, Carol, *A strange girl in bright colours*, Quartet 1973; *A necklace of mirrors*, Ulsterman 1978.

Russell, Peter, *Paysages légendaires*, Enitharmon 1971; *The elegies of Quintilius*, Anvil/Routledge 1975.

190

Sail, Lawrence, *Opposite views,* Dent 1974; *The drowned river,* Mandeville 1978.

Sale, Arthur, *Under the war,* Hutchinson 1975.

Scammel, William, *Yes and no,* Peterloo 1979.

Scannell, Vernon, *Selected poems,* Allison & Busby 1971; *The winter man,* Allison & Busby 1973; *The apple raid,* Chatto Poets for the Young 1974; *The loving game,* Robson 1975; *New and collected poems,* Robson 1980.

Schmidt, Michael, *Desert of the lions,* Carcanet 1972; *It was my tree,* Anvil 1972; *My brother Gloucester,* Carcanet 1976; *A change of affairs,* Anvil 1978.

Scott, Alexander, *Greek fire,* Akros 1971; *Double agent,* Akros 1972; *Selected poems,* Akros 1975.

Scott, Hardiman, *When the words are gone,* Chatto 1972.

Scupham, Peter, *The snowing globe,* Morten 1972; *The small containers,* Phoenix 1972; *Prehistories,* Oxford University Press 1975; *The hinterland,* OUP 1977; *Natura,* Gruffyground Press 1978; *Summer palaces,* OUP 1980.

Searle, Chris, *This new season,* Calder & Boyars 1973; *Mainland,* Calder & Boyars 1974.

Seddon, Alexandra, *Sparrows,* Carcanet 1970.

Selzer, David, *Elsewhere,* Peterloo 1973.

Seymour-Smith, Martin, *Reminiscences of Norma,* Constable 1971.

Shepherd, W. G., *Sun, oak, almond, I,* Anvil 1970; *Evidences,* Anvil 1979.

Silkin, Jon, *Amana grass,* Chatto 1971; *The principle of water,* Carcanet 1974; *The little time-keeper,* MidNAG/Carcanet 1976; *The psalms with their spoils,* Routledge 1980.

Sillitoe, Alan, *Barbarians,* Turret 1973; *Storm,* W. H. Allen 1974; *Snow on the north side of Lucifer,* Allen 1979.

Simmons, James, *Energy to burn,* Bodley Head 1971; *The long summer still to come,* Blackstaff 1973; *West Strand visions,* Blackstaff 1974; *Memories of a tour in Yorkshire,* Ulsterman 1975; *Judy Garland and the cold war,* Blackstaff 1976; *Selected poems,* ed. Edna Longley, Blackstaff 1978; *Constantly singing,* Blackstaff 1980.

Simpson, Matt, *Letters to Berlin,* Driftwood 1971; *A Skye sequence,* Driftwood 1972; *Water colours from an Approved School,* Toulouse Press 1975.

Singer, Burns, *Collected poems,* Secker & Warburg 1970; *Selected poems,* ed. Anne Cluysenaar, Carcanet 1977.

Sisson, C. H., *In the Trojan ditch,* Carcanet 1974; *The corridor,* Mandeville 1975; *Anchises,* Carcanet 1976; *Exactions,* Carcanet 1980.

Skelton, Robin, *The hunting dark,* Deutsch 1971; *Remembering Synge,* Dolmen 1971; *Timelight,* Heinemann 1974.

Smart, Elizabeth, *A bonus,* Polytantric 1977.

Smith, Cara L., *Riding to Canonbie,* Hamish Hamilton 1972; *Old Merlaine,* Heinemann 1975.

Smith, Iain Crichton, *Selected poems,* Gollancz 1970; *Love poems and elegies,* Gollancz 1972; *Hamlet in autumn,* Lines Review Editions 1972; *Poems for Donalda,* Ulsterman 1974; *Orpheus and other poems,* Akros 1974; *The notebooks of Robinson Crusoe,* Gollancz 1975; *The permanent island,* Macdonald 1975; *In the middle,* Gollancz 1977; *River, river,* Macdonald 1978; *An end to autumn,* Gollancz 1978.

Smith, John, *Entering rooms,* Chatto 1973.

Smith, Ken, *Frontwards in a backwards movie*, Arc 1975; *Tristan Crazy*, Bloodaxe 1978.

Smith, Stevie, *Scorpion and other poems*, Longman 1972; *Collected poems*, Allen Lane 1975.

Smith, Sydney G., *Gowdspink in reekie*, Macdonald 1974; *Collected poems*, Calder 1975.

Snow, John, *Contrasts*, d'Arch Smith 1971; *Moments and thoughts*, Kaye & Ward 1973.

Spender, Stephen, *The generous days*, Faber 1971; *Recent poems*, Anvil 1978.

Squires, Geoffrey, *Figures*, Ulsterman 1978.

Stallworthy, Jon, *The apple barrel*, Oxford University Press 1974; *Hand in hand*, Chatto 1974; *A familiar tree*, Oxford University Press/Chatto 1978.

Stanford, Derek, *The traveller hears the strange machine*, Sidgwick & Jackson 1980.

Stephens, Meic, *Exiles all*, C. Davies 1973.

Stevenson, Anne, *Correspondences: a family history in letters*, Oxford University Press 1974; *Travelling behind glass*, OUP 1974; *Enough of green*, OUP 1977.

Storey, Edward, *A man in winter*, Chatto 1972.

Syms, Jeremy, *Child of air*, Aquila 1976.

Symes, Gordon, *Names for shadows*, Peterloo 1978.

Szirtes, George, *The slant door*, Secker & Warburg 1979.

Tarn, Nathaniel, *Lyrics for the bride of God*, Cape 1970; *A nowhere for Vallejo*, Cape 1972.

Taylor, I. P., *The grip*, Oasis 1978.

Thomas-Ellis, Aeronwy, *Later than Laugharne*, Celtion 1976.

Thomas, D. M., *Logan stone*, Cape Goliard 1971; *Lilith prints*, Second Aeon 1974; *Love and other deaths*, Elek 1975; *The honeymoon voyage*, Secker & Warburg 1978.

Thomas, Donald, *Welcome to the Grand Hotel*, Routledge 1975.

Thomas, Peter, *The trailing chord*, C. Davies 1972.

Thomas, R. S., *H'm*, Macmillan 1972; *Young and old*, Chatto Poets for the Young 1972; *Selected poems*, Hart-Davis MacGibbon 1973; *What is a Welshman?* C. Davies 1974; *Laboratories of the spirit*, Macmillan 1975; *The way of it*, Ceolfrith 1977; *Frequencies*, Macmillan 1978.

Thomas, Stanley, J., *November man*, Aquila 1975.

Thwaite, Anthony, *Points*, Turret 1972; *Inscriptions*, Oxford University Press 1973; *New confessions*, OUP 1974; *A portion for foxes*, OUP 1977.

Tibble, Anne, *Labyrinth*, Oriel 1972.

Tiller, Terence, *That singing mesh*, Chatto 1979.

Tipton, David, *Millstone grit*, Second Aeon 1972; *Pachacamac*, Rivelin 1974; *Black Clough*, Rivelin 1975.

Tomlinson, Charles, *Written on water*, Oxford University Press 1972; *The way in*, OUP 1974; *In black and white*, Carcanet 1976; *Selected poems*, OUP 1978; *The shaft*, OUP 1978.

Tong, Raymond, *Crossing the border*, Hodder 1978.

Tower, Christopher, *Firuz of Isfahan*, Weidenfeld 1975; *A distant fluting*, Weidenfeld 1977; *Oultre Jourdain*, Weidenfeld 1980.

Traynor, Shaun, *The hardening ground*, Martin Brian & O'Keeffe 1974; *Images in winter*, Martin Brian & O'Keeffe 1979.

Tremayne, Sydney, *Selected and new poems,* Chatto 1973.

Trevor, Stan, *World in action,* Hippopotamus 1975.

Tripp, John, *Bute Park and other poems,* Second Aeon 1971; *The province of belief,* C. Davies 1971; *The inheritance file,* Second Aeon 1973; *Collected poems,* C. Davies 1978.

Turnbull, Gael, *Scantlings,* Cape Goliard 1970.

Turner, Raymond, *The garden of Cain,* Aquila 1973.

Turner, W. Price, *The moral rocking horse,* Barrie & Jenkins 1970.

Vanson, Frederic, *Spring at Llyn Ogwen,* Gomer 1972.

Vidler, John, *Interludes,* Aquila 1973.

Vince, Michael, *The orchard well,* Carcanet 1978.

Wain, John, *The shape of Feng,* Macmillan 1972; *Feng,* Macmillan 1975; *Poems 1949-1979,* Macmillan 1980.

Wainwright, Jeffrey, *Heart's desire,* Carcanet 1978.

Walker, Ted, *The night bathers,* Cape 1970; *Gloves to the hangman,* Cape 1973; *Burning the ivy,* Cape 1978.

Walters, Bryan, *Cloud flowers,* Aquila 1973; *Images of stone,* Aquila 1974; *We haven't done it lately,* Celtion 1976; *From the Welsh,* Celtion 1977.

Walton, Peter, *Out of season,* NW Arts/Carcanet 1977.

Walton, Robert, *Workings,* Gomer 1979.

Ward, Donald, *The dead snake,* Allison & Busby 1971; *A few rooks circling trees,* Mandeville 1975.

Ward, J. P., *The line of knowledge,* C. Davies 1972; *From alphabet to logos,* Second Aeon 1973.

Warner, Val, *These yellow photos,* Carcanet 1971; *Under the penthouse,* Carcanet 1973.

Waterman, Andrew, *Last fruit,* Mandeville 1974; *Living room,* Marvell 1974; *From the other country,* Carcanet 1977; *Over the wall,* Carcanet 1980.

Watkins, Vernon, *I that was born in Wales,* University of Wales 1976; *Unity of the stream,* Gomer 1978; *The ballad of the outer dark,* Enitharmon 1979.

Webb, Harri, *A crown for Branwen,* Gomer 1974; *Rampage and revel,* Gomer 1977.

Weissbort, Daniel, *The leaseholder,* Carcanet 1971; *In an emergency,* Carcanet 1972; *Soundings,* Carcanet 1977.

Wells, Robert, *The winter's task,* Carcanet 1977.

Wheway, John, *The green table of infinity,* Anvil 1972.

Whigham, Peter, *Astapovo, or What are we to do?* Anvil 1970.

White, Jon Manchip, *The mountain lion,* Chatto 1971.

Whittaker, Patricia, *The flying men,* London Magazine Editions 1971.

Wilkins, Paul, *Pasts,* Carcanet 1979.

Williams, Evan G., *The clown,* C. Davies 1971.

Williams, Gwyn, *Inns of love,* C. Davies 1970; *Foundation stock,* Gomer 1974.

Williams, Hugo, *Sugar Daddy,* Oxford University Press 1970; *Some sweet day,* OUP 1975; *Love-life,* Whizzard/Deutsch 1979.

Williams, John S., *Dic Penderyn,* Gomer 1970; *Banna Strand,* Gomer 1975.

Wilmer, Clive, *The dwelling-place,* Carcanet 1977.

Winter, Joe, *A miracle and the tree,* Anvil 1972.

Woodcock, George, *The kestrel,* Ceolfrith 1978.

Wright, Adrian, *Waiting for Helen*, Carcanet 1970; *The shrinking map*, Carcanet 1972.
Wright, David, *A view of the north*, Carcanet 1976; *To the gods the shades*, Carcanet 1976; *Metrical observations*, Carcanet 1980.
Wright, Edmond L., *The Horwich hennets*, Peterloo 1976.
Wright, Kit, *The bear looked over the mountain*, Salamander 1978.

Young, Augustus, *A tapestry of animals*, Menard Press 1977.

Anthologies

Anthology of contemporary poetry: post-war to the present, ed. John Wain, Hutchinson 1979.
Cambridge Book of English verse 1939-1975, ed. Alan Bold, Cambridge University Press 1976.
Corgi modern poets in focus, 1, 3 and *5*, ed. Dannie Abse 1971-3; *2* and *4*, ed. Jeremy Robson, 1971.
Faber book of 20th century verse, 3rd edn eds. John Heath-Stubbs and David Wright, Faber 1975.
Green horse: anthology of young poets of Wales, eds. Meic Stephenson and Peter Finch, C. Davies 1978.
Here and human, compiled by F. E. S. Finn, Murray 1976.
Living poets, eds. Michael Morpurgo and Clifford Simmons, Murray 1974.
Made in Scotland, ed. Robert Garioch, Carcanet 1974.
23 modern British poets, ed. John Matthias, Swallow Press, Chicago, 1971.
Modern poets four, revised edn, ed. Jim Hunter, Faber 1979.
Modern Scottish poetry, ed. Maurice Lindsay, Carcanet 1976.
New poems 1973, ed. Charles Osborne, Poetry Book Society 1973.
New poems 1970-71, eds. Alan Brownjohn, Seamus Heaney, Jon Stallworthy; *1971-72*, ed. Peter Porter; *1972-73*, ed. Douglas Dunn; *1973-74*, ed. Stewart Conn; *1975*, ed. Patricia Beer; *1976-77*, ed. Howard Sergeant; *1977-78*, ed. Gavin Ewart; PEN/Hutchinson .
New poetry 1, eds. Peter Porter and Charles Osborne;
New poetry 2, eds. Patricia Beer and Kevin Crossley-Holland;
New poetry 3, eds. Maureen Duffy and Alan Brownjohn;
New poetry 4, eds. Fleur Adcock and Anthony Thwaite;
New poetry 5, eds. Peter Redgrove and Jon Silkin; Arts Council/Hutchinson 1975-9.
Oxford book of twentieth century English verse, chosen by Philip Larkin, Oxford University Press 1973.
Penguin modern poets:
16 (Jack Beeching, Harry Guest, Matthew Mead) 1970.
17 (David Gascoyne, W. S. Graham, Kathleen Raine) 1970.
18 (A. Alvarez, Roy Fuller, Anthony Thwaite) 1970.
19 (John Ashbery, Lee Harwood, Tom Raworth) 1971.
20 (John Heath-Stubbs, F. T. Prince, Stephen Spender) 1972.
21 (Iain Crichton Smith, Norman MacCaig, George Mackay Brown) 1972.
22 (John Fuller, Peter Levi, Adrian Mitchell) 1973.
23 (Geoffrey Grigson, Edwin Muir, Adrian Stokes) 1973.

24 (Kenward Elmslie, Kenneth Koch, James Schuyler) 1974.

25 (Gavin Ewart, Zulifkar Ghose, B. S. Johnson) 1975.

26 (Dannie Abse, D. J. Enright, Michael Longley) 1975.

27 (John Ormond, Emyr Humphreys, John Tripp) 1979.

Peterloo anthology, Harry Chambers/Peterloo Poets 1979.

Poems '70, ed. Wyn Binding; *'71,* ed. Jeremy Hooker; *'72,* ed. John Ackerman; *'73,* ed. Gwyn Ramage; *'74,* ed. Peter Elfred Lewis; *'76,* ed. Glyn Jones; *'78,* ed. Graham Allen; Gomer Press 1970-78.

Poetry dimension annual 1, ed. Jeremy Robson; *2-6,* ed. Dannie Abse; Robson Books 1973-9.

Poetry introduction 1-4, Faber 1969-74.

A Poetry quintet, Gollancz 1976.

Poetry supplements, compiled annually for the Poetry Book Society, by various editors.

Poets from the North of Ireland, ed. Frank Ormsby, Blackstaff 1979.

Scottish poetry 5 and *6,* eds. George Bruce, Maurice Lindsay, Edwin Morgan, Edinburgh University Press, n.d.; *7, 8* and *9,* eds. Maurice Lindsay, Alexander Scott, Roderick Watson, Glasgow University Press 1974; Carcanet/Scottish Arts Council 1975, 1976.

Ten Anglo-Welsh poets, ed. Sam Adams, Carcanet 1974.

Ten English poets, ed. Michael Schmidt, Carcanet 1976.

Ten Irish poets, ed. James Simmons, Carcanet 1974.

Ten North-East Poets, ed. Neil Astley, Bloodaxe 1980.

Treble poets One, Two, Three, Chatto, 1974-7.

Trio poetry 1, Blackstaff 1980.

Twelve modern Anglo-Welsh poets, eds. Don Dall-Jones and Randal Jenkins, University of London Press 1975.

The wearing of the black: contemporary Ulster poetry, Blackstaff 1974.

Widening circles: five Black Country poets, ed. Edward Lowbury, W Midland Arts 1976.

The young British poets, ed. Jeremy Robson, Chatto 1971.

MICHAEL SCHMIDT

A short anthology

This anthology draws largely on poems published in *PN Review* or in Carcanet New Press collections. Most of the work was composed in the latter part of the decade. My intention is not to be broadly 'representative': such an aim in so short a space would be impracticable. Some of the poetry chosen complements the essays in this book; some of it makes up for gaps in the comment and appraisal, and all of it is work I value highly. It is a small display of the formal and thematic variety of work by both new and well-established writers. It also reflects the editorial policy of a serious literary journal and a small independent publishing house founded in the 1970s.

C. H. SISSON

THE BADGER'S TRAIL

animula, vagula, blandula,
hospes comesque corporis

Direct across the moor
The badger's trail ran from far distant fields
To where the wood hung like a wrinkled brow
And is one now. For in a hollow I
Consider conscience, what it is, and how.

So much for winter. But when summer comes,
As it must come, over my bones perhaps,
There will be laughing there between the trees
And, where the blue sky pours itself out for us,
Not a thought in the mind or in the blue.

Wind, winter, summer, all is over now
And nothing waits for nothing, at a point
Poised midway in the blue, or on the eye.
—Now goes, animula, animalcule,
Pure is not, is, or suspect, written on
The glass, the phial of the blue universe
That shatters into darkness. *Hospes, comes.*

BURRINGTON COMBE

Not what I think but any land beside
Hidden from human speech, is where I go
As that dark leaf of thyme pushes its way
Into the empty world, and so speak I

Blackdown and Burrington and the deep combe
Which was my land, is also what shall be
Arraigned by time. I make my way only
Backwards, where I may look indulgently

And yet the indulgent land, where silence is
Is not my friend nor ever was before
The great ferns held terror as well as love
Who was lost on the heather-covered moor?

If I could climb out of this bitter combe
Into a lucid world, nothing there said
Could equal now the silence of your grief
Or the exchanges of the recorded dead.

The word stands still upon the frozen lip
The eye is glazed that should have danced with love
For such days as are uneaten by the years
A nod, a commonplace will be enough.

**

O Light, I do not want you
The years have taken away
Whatever there was lovely
In the day

The land stretches to doomsday
The rivers to the sea
And nothing done and nothing said
Matters to me

The age laughed in its hollow skull
And strove to be polite
But how can the dazzling fingers equal
The shepherd with his pipe?

Travel across the lips you bones
And do not stop for me
If there is nothing but death in the whistle
It will do for me.

* * *

So I address the musing mind
Which has no mind to speak
Which can hear nothing, see nothing
And has no heart to break.

The key of the kitchen is frenzy
And the cook stands by the door
Pobble-de-hope fair stranger
What is the ladle for?

A fortune for your porridge
The hope of a transitive verb
Is only to find its object
But the best word here is, Starve.

* * * *

But this is where I came
And where I wish to be
Burrington Combe, half in the dark
Half in the light of the moon

Ellick Farm you are buried
Deep in your greenery
And there is nothing miraculous left
Under the sky.

* * * * *

Cry up the pastures of the moon
They stretch from here to nowhere else;
A weed grows on a mossy bank
Its roots go down and down and down

Down to the dark the dark the dark
Forget the light it is ending soon;
A cloud scuds over the face of the grass-land
Down-a-down and a hurrying moon.

I stood exactly over the valley
Looking down on the changing light.
What vixen cries in the hollow?
What owl passes the barn tonight?

I am not caught in the falling thunder
I am not pierced by the spits of rain;
Six foot long and six foot under
Never to speak on earth again.

Yet the mind hovers like a falcon
A bird of daylight and of dreams
Over the meadows and over the willows
But only hears the nightjar scream.

******

I came to speak to her
It was no good
No sign in the bushes
Or in the wood.

No sign on her lips
When I found her
There was nothing nothing nothing
But the chill around her.

The willows, she did not see
Or the ditch
Her eyes stared as if the day
Were black as pitch.

Me it may be she saw
As I were any thing
Stoned and stoned and stony
Not living

And scarcely I am
Or I would not stay here
Walking, talking, proferring
And cannot break her fear.

****

If night falls, there is nothing more
If night falls, there is nothing more
If night falls, there is nothing more.

And it does fall, it is falling now
The light is less already, see how it goes
Smaller, smaller, smaller, the circle of light;
But the scent of the rose

The scent of the wallflower, the night-scented stock
The scent of thyme, never off my hands
Except when rue chases it, or fennel, or sage
—Whose hands?—

Except when the bonfire that I have tended
Leaves me with nothing but its acrid air
In my clothes, in my finger-nails
In my hair.

Wherever I sit, as night falls
A last blackbird, perhaps, such things are
The moving night, and I awaiting it
And the first star.

It should be enough, but it is not
When night falls, it will take away
All I wanted and all that I did not
With the last day.

Patience, it is all that is required
Night is patience itself, when it falls
Not even memory disturbs its dream
Loser takes all.

****

When I walk out there will be nothing missing
That I can see;
The pond will be there with its fish,
The rosemary

Spreading itself over the garden
As if still aided by my hand;
The mulberry-tree I planted, and the cherry,
The old apple-trees and

The plums stretching up against the wall
Over which the church-tower still looks;
Starlings and swallows, the swans flying over,
And always the rooks.

And that distance into which I shall have vanished
Will still be there;
It was always dear to me, is now
In the thickening air.

No distance was ever like this one
The flat land with its willows, and the great sky
With the river reflecting its uncertainty
But no more I.

ALISON BRACKENBURY

FOUR POEMS

1

Strange sea: sudden sea: no thing can be the same.
I think of snowdrops and lit hedgerows which
may never have been there.
What lay in that drink that we should stare,
the birds shout salt and harsh, black ways
gape between the water and your eyes?
I burn and my bones melt to gold.
And as I grip your hard wrist and we rise
I understand how our love lies:

not in waves' green light but light's great cold

2

By the king's trees I walked afraid.
You spoke your riddles tenderly:

Is not the moon's cold rising made
To lure the salt sea from the land?

Is not the horse which bolts with you
Gentle in stall, to brush your hand

And the amazing cherry tree
Rooted in possibility?

Silence. The dazzling boughs above
Dance white belief I dare not prove.

3

I am the maid who slept with you
to cheat you on your wedding night.
Mine is the mouth that parts on you
questing, till the birds cry light.
You the dark shape on the cliff,
my dreaded lord, my lovely man
no maid or woman in the world
can hate or take you as I can.
My feet crush thyme. The fluid lark
Fuses your voices, Tristan, Mark.

4

It could go on for ever so; the giving
As the sea melts into the autumn haze
I could wear out my weariness with love
Not knowing yet which shadow cools my days
Black king; a young man on a sunlit deck.
Fearing the wrecks where seas in winter break
I walk the garden's walks alone and plant
Two autumn crocuses the tall winds shake
To shivered blue of eyes. You wrote to me
We might at least 'preserve intensity'.
Not quite Isolde; but the crocus lit
To stranger flame. Through fear and work's ache we
Read the dark's story; risk; since one forgot
To change the heavy sails from black to white
Another died. As in an older story
The grieved man leapt from cliffs, crashed down in light.
The lark lifts struggling but she frees her voice.
Our business is avoiding tragedy.
My double flower: give me no choice
Between black ships and empty sea.

DERBY DAY: AN EXHIBITION

The great Stubbs' picture of the great Eclipse
Hangs in the corner it defies
Effortless. The great are luminous.
Orbed flanks shine solid, amber, having won.
A gold-red horse called Hermit won, and broke

The wild Earl of Hastings, who had flung
Woods and fields against. What can Eclipse
Comfort those eclipsed, who never won?

The young Fred Archer with a boy's sad face,
Shot himself, sick dizzy on the edge.
He won six flaring Derbys. Not that one
In which a woman sprang beneath the rail.
In thudding dark, pain tore all colours; died.

And yet a brilliant day. Do not mistake:
That which we do best kills us. Horse and man
Amber in the mist of downs, sea-shore,
The spring of wave, glow greatly. They survive.

AN ORANGE OF CLOVES

Clove-scent: the dark room where the lovers lie
A closet smelling both of must and musk,
Which makes the head faint: rawer and more old
Than pale-flowered stocks which scent the dusk.

Caverns of dark I entered first: I thought
I have danced here, and to a golden lute.
Branched velvet, rushes, gallows in the sunlight—

Sense shudders till it glimpses in a space
The great sharp-scented tree, its flowers, its fruit
All of a season, beating in the rain;
The orange, cloves cross-cleft; and past the pain,
A dark tree fading, seeding in each face.

SUMMER FRUIT

Inviting me, the peach lies on the plate,
Sliced dripping gold, and roughly veined with red.
The stone is broken from its bed
The soft skin curls. I hesitate.
Hot waves of summer's scent
It holds: a glowing world, where day is spent
In orchards with the juice-stained pickers' gang
Sweating, longing for the winter's tang;
While perfect, undesired, the peaches hang.

JEREMY HOOKER

RICE GRASS   (*Spartina Townsendii*)

Praise one appearing
lowly, no man's rose,
but with roots far-reaching
out and down.

Give homage to a spartan cross,
native and American,
hardier and more adaptable
than those; nearly a newcomer
but one that, by staying put
has made itself a home;
also a traveller east and west.

Celebrate the entertainer
of sea aster, sea lavender,
thrift and nestling gulls;
lover of mud and salt;
commoner and useful colonist,
converter from ooze
of land where a foot may fall.

AT THE STATUE OF ISAAC WATTS

   1.
Image set
Among sticky buds:

Dated, the marble
Establishes a prodigal
Home for good.

Clear through traffic,
Trains and horns
The Civic Centre chimes
'Our God, our help . . .'

   2.
The measured tide
Moves congregations;
Its undertow sways
Outside the walls.

Across the narrow sea
From Western Shore
(Refinery hazy
Under the Forest)
An impure land delights.

Against sluggard wit
And muddy spirit,
Dr Watts stands proof.

At his granite base,
Place tributary strands
Of living wrack.

ON SPEDE'S MAP ANNO DOMINI 1611

Four craft ride light
off West Key, two
by the Water Gate,
an easterly fills the sails
of a merchantman.
Castle and churches stand out
inside the walls,
houses press together
in the form of hieroglyphs.
On Gods house grene
two citizens play at bowls
with a watchman.
Empty, the streets appear
neither plagued nor decaying.
Waves crawl in
like water snakes, or eyebrows
raised—a child's gulls.
Halted at rush hour
on the roof of a carpark,
smoky cloud hailing
where the sea was, on acres
of containers, the image
reappears—unreadable
except by one for whom
the sky not on the map
existed quite ordinarily.

SHINGLE-SPIT

Where the next moment
wiped out the last impression
the sea had raised
a wall of shingle.
Slippery reefs of kelp
blotched the water; sandbars
barely covered, shone like bullion.
The Island showed plainly
what it was: the splintered foot
of a bridge, and on a surface
backed into crests
the chalk blue waves reflected it.
They broke, of course,
and a slow, dark pulse
beat rhythmically in the sand.
It will not be like that now,
and was not then.
I expected to hold nothing visible,
and did not, though my steps
remade the pattern they had long become.

ROBERT WELLS

AFTER HAYMAKING

The last bale placed, he stretched out in the hay.
    Its warmth and his were one.
He watched the fields beneath the weakening day
And felt his skin still burning with the sun.

When it was dusk, he moved. Between his skin
    And clothes the sweat ran cold.
He trembled as he felt the air begin
To touch and touch for what it could not hold.

THE AXEHANDLE

Calling my eyes back from the sea
—With adoration I watched the horizon lift

Above the headland, far up against the sky—
And looking instead for a human token
Even at this distance, to hold me back,
I noticed the axe where I had put it aside
—How the balanced ashwood handle
Was like a limb with its muscle shaped to use,
An arm graceful and certain with hillside labour
Evidencing the generations of hands.

THE ICKNIELD WAY

He wakes to the sky's first pallor,
Has shed the sickness of sleep
Before gold hits the cloud.

Summer is the heavy hedgerow
By the path. At his shoulder
He carries its weight of green.

THE POOL

There is no reflection on the dusted surface.
An edge of lime crusts the steep rock. Some leaves
Lie on the water. A frog leaps from your tread.
A trickle spills and seeps away through gravel.

Come back in spring to bathe here.
Winter will bring the pool back to its shape.

FOR PASOLINI

Vecchio ragazzo di Casarsa, dear protagonist,
Where shall we find the like of your intelligence?
The hunters who come here on Sunday with their dogs and guns
Are not enough to keep the forest paths open.
Two years untrodden, and bramble will cover the track,
The broom lean across. They were paved once with stones
Packed in together to make rough and narrow highways,
Loosened now, a rubble, a watercourse, except
For some short stretches where the old work has held.
If someone climbs up between the crests of the ridge,

Pushing through bracken that drenches his boots and clothes,
He will guess perhaps that this was the charcoal-burners' place:
But who can imagine now what their lives were, find more
Than that if he scratches the surface of the mounded green
He turns up blacker earth—their trace? O early bodies
Moving amid the dark as it thins. O quiet voices.
When ignorant beauty chances to conjure back to life
The shape present in the air, who will be here to know it?

THE LAST CALIPH*

1

Quietly he watched the weighed eyes close
And the unhallowed presence intrude.
When the boy fell on the rug, he rose
In silence, his anger dispossessed

By kindness that took as its disguise
Ironic leave of each kingly mood;
Then stared at the scheme of paradise
In woven silk, and the limbs at rest.

2

The masterful whirls seemed metal grills
Of a great window, at which he stood
For a breeze from the spare-featured hills
To sting his eyes like a hint of dust.

But its life was fixed like summer air
Till he assented with gratitude
To the grace that broke the pattern there
In sleep's unthinking perilous trust.

3

Taking your challenge, one from their line
Is drawn, as flies by the smell of blood,
To feed his quickness on your design;
And hovers, thin-bearded, empty-faced.

*'The Last Caliph' is concerned with the sack of Baghdad in 1258 by the Mongols and
the end of the Abbasid Caliphate. The first two sections refer to an anecdote told of the
last Caliph. When a young servant waiting on him in his library had fallen asleep and acci-
dentally rolled on to the carpet where he was sitting, he signed to the librarian to wait till
he had left the room before waking the boy. Thus the boy was spared fear and confusion
at his mistake. The third section describes an incident of single combat which preceded
the defeat of the Arab army. The fourth section reflects on the subsequent destruction.

Gentle warrior, accoutred knight,
Whose field is mired by a stream in flood,
You mock his coming; as if to fight,
That too, were an exercise of taste.

4

What reason is there? Each perfect shape
Rebuts its devil and is pursued,
Turns at a promise, half-wills the rape;
Then feels the unclaimed impulse burst

Its random confines, until that drive
Is the one proof that is understood,
With no thought but panic left alive,
No art except to believe the worst.

JEFFREY WAINWRIGHT

THOMAS MÜNTZER

for David Spooner

Thomas Müntzer was a Protestant reformer in the early years of the German
Reformation. He was a radical and a visionary both in theology and
politics for whom religious thought and experience became integrated with
ideas and movements towards social revolution.

  Travelling through Germany, preaching and writing, continually in trouble
with the authorities, he came to support and lead struggles by common
people against the monopolies of wealth and learning. In 1525, in the
Peasant War, he led an army against the princes which was heavily defeated
at Frankenhausen. Müntzer was subsequently captured and executed.

> *Doubt is the Water, the movement to good and evil. Who swims on
> the water without a saviour is between life and death.*   —Müntzer

> *I have seen in my solitude
> very clear things
> that are not true.*   —Machado

I

Just above where my house sits on the slope
Is a pond, a lodge when the mine was here,
Now motionless, secretive, hung in weeds.

Sometimes on clear nights I spread my arms wide
And can fly, stiff but perfect, down
Over this pond just an inch above the surface.

When I land I have just one, two drops of water
On my beard. I am surprised how quick
I have become a flier, a walker on air.

II
I see my brother crawling in the woods
To gather snails' shells. *This is not
A vision*. Look carefully and you can tell

How he is caught in the roots of a tree
Whose long branches spread upwards bearing as
Fruit gardeners and journeymen, merchants

And lawyers, jewellers and bishops,
Cardinals chamberlains nobles princes
Branch by branch kings pope and emperor.

III
I feel the very earth is against me.
Night after night she turns in my sleep
And litters my fields with stones.

I lie out all summer spread like a coat
Over the earth one night after another
Waiting to catch her. And then

She is mine and the rowan blooms—
His black roots swim out and dive to subdue her—
His red blood cracks in the air and saves me.

IV
How many days did I search in my books
For such power, crouched like a bird under
My roof and lost to the world?

Scholars say God no longer speaks with us
Men—as though he has grown dumb, lost his tongue,
(Cut out for stealing a hare or a fish?)

Now I explode—out of this narrow house,
My mind lips hands skin my whole body
Cursing them for their flesh and their learning—

V

dran dran dran we have the sword—the purity
Of metal—the beauty of blood falling.
Spilt it is refreshed, it freshens also

The soil which when we turn it will become
Paradise for us once rid of these maggots
And their blind issue. They will seek about

And beg you: 'Why is this happening to us?
Forgive us Forgive us', pleading now for
Mercy a new sweet thing they've found a taste for.

VI

So you see from this how I am—Müntzer:
'O bloodthirsty man' breathing not air
But fire and slaughter, a true phantasist—

'A man born for heresy and schism',
'This most lying of men', 'a mad dog'.
And all because I speak and say: God made

All men free with His own blood shed.
Hold everything in common. Share evil.
And I find I am a god, like all men.

VII

He teaches the gardener from his trees
And the fisherman from his catch, even
The goldsmith from the testing of his gold.

In the pond the cold thick water clothes me.
I live with the timorous snipe, beetles
And skaters, the pike smiles and moves with me.

We hold it in common without jealousy.
Touch your own work and the simple world.
In these unread creatures sings the real gospel.

VIII

I have two guilders for a whole winter.
I ask for company and food from beggars,
The very poorest, those I fancy most

Blessed . . . I am in love with a girl
And dare not tell her so . . . she makes me
Like a boy again—sick and dry-mouthed.

How often have I told you God comes only
In your apparent abandonment. This is
The misery of my exile—I was elected to it.

IX
My son will not sleep. The noise
And every moving part of the world
Shuttles round him, making him regard it,

Giving him—only four years old!—no peace.
He moves quietly in his own purposes
Yet stays joyless. There is no joy to be had,

And he knows that and is resigned to it.
At his baptism we dressed him in white
And gave him salt as a symbol of this wisdom.

X
I am white and broken. I can hardly gasp out
What I want to say, which is: *I believe in God* . . .
At Frankenhausen His promised rainbow

Did bloom in the sky, silky and so bold
No one could mistake it. Seeing it there
I thought I could catch their bullets in my hands.

An article of faith. I was found in bed
And carried here for friendly
Interrogation. They ask me *what I believe*.

XI
Their horsemen ride over our crops kicking
The roots from the ground. They poison wells
And throw fire down the holes where people hide.

An old woman crawls out. She is bleeding
And screaming so now they say they are sorry
And would like to bandage her. She won't

Go with them. She struggles free. *I see it
I see it*—she is bound to die . . .
This is the glittering night we wake in.

XII

I lie here for a few hours yet, clothed still
In my external life, flesh I have tried
To render pure, and a scaffold of bones.

I would resign all interest in it.
To have any love for my own fingered
Body and brain is a luxury.

History, which is Eternal Life, is what
We need to celebrate. Stately tearful
Progress . . . you've seen how I have wept for it.

ANDREW MOTION

HULL PARAGON

The mind is its own place,
so what should I see here—a city
where important centuries survive
with lesser uses? The inland docks
contain their waste of sky, and lamps
along the Humber illustrate a map
I cannot recognise as home tonight.

Though will, in time. I watch you
vanish on the last train south
through districts no one visits.
Wrecked by bombing first, then
dereliction, all they show is love
and work fanned up as dust before
it smothers their abandoned lives.

Absence will replace us—so we said
and yet cannot believe. I turn away
imagining already how that room
we shared will greet me: silent
as you left it, with the vague
imperfect loneliness of shadows
leaning over empty chairs and plates.

And you? you're lost in darkness,
still remembering that once, where

now the river narrows undisturbed,
were fishing fleets at anchor—
till they took their cold direction
past these sunken hills, towards
the whales' exhausted fading call.

A NATURAL PERSPECTIVE

Though more beautiful and reflective
you are not the first to stand by me,
close on this grey pier, for what
I can hardly explain. Part guide

and part inquisitor, I point out
docks for you, the sunken barge, and there
the Humber ferry drawing near, flecked
with passengers who think this water

brings them to a different country.
Ourselves are all they find,
and round us, leavings of the same
deceptive century that fades behind—

its snug societies at rest, content,
while evening lasts, to contemplate
the random conversation of their dogs,
or sunlight angled into empty bars.

Though this is why we came: to make
believe a lost utopia which sold
community for silence will revive;
and not, as soon we must, admit

its derelict romance can give us
nothing but these useless wharves,
this black deserted beach, and prove
the natural perspective of our lives.

ANNE FRANK HUIS

Even now, after twice her lifetime of grief
and anger in the very place, whoever comes

to climb these narrow stairs, discovers how
the bookcase slides aside, then walks through
shadow into sunlit rooms, can never help

but break her secrecy again. Just listening
is a kind of guilt: the Westerkerk repeats
itself outside, as if all time worked round
towards her fear, and made each stroke die
down on guarded streets. Imagine it—

three years of whispering and loneliness
and plotting, day by day, the Allied line
in Europe with a yellow chalk. What hope
she had for ordinary love and interest
survives her here, displayed above the bed

as pictures of her family; some actors;
fashions chosen by Princess Elizabeth.
And those who stoop to see them find
not only patience missing its reward,
but one enduring wish for chances like

my own: to leave as simply as I do,
and walk where couples stroll at ease
up dusty tree-lined avenues, or watch
a silent barge come clear of bridges
settling their reflections in the blue canal.

BRIAN JONES

UPON CRAPPLETON HOUSE
'The Beasts are by their Dens exprest'—Marvell

          i
And now, they said, there must be a Centre.
And they toiled three years.
Those who remembered proportions
drew thin blue plans

by night under cowled lamps.
The hefty wielded pickaxe
and shovel, gouging
troughs through strata.

The rogue toughs churned
mushes of concrete, and the more
precise laid level lines
of brick. And from the ranks

a plasterer came, and a strange
remote man with the secret of glass.
Out of the woods
chimed the strike of axes,

and, tall, fine-fingered, one
ruled and planed and stacked
sweet resinous planks.
Another, finicky, herringboned a floor.

And just as, in a hive
rolls a murmur, confused yet harmonious,
as creatures skilled in one skill
pursue their blind genetic stars

and miraculously the tiny
strictures of self merge
to elaborate concordance,
so the tappings, thuds, chink-chinks,

clanks, squeals and slithers
subsumed themselves at last
into the singing silence of completion.
And they stood back to see that it was good.

   ii
It was disastrous.
The high-hung concave dish urinals
splashed piss back accurately. The tiles,
pinned arsey-versey,

fell like leaves at the first big wind.
The elaborate concertina-sliding
partition slid once only,
jumped a crooked rail

and fell, scoring irreparably
a floor already found to be
susceptible to hard-soled shoes.
The elegant all-round clerestory,

lacking panes of like dimension,
made impossible the installation
of the cheap blackout required
for the inauguration of film-shows

envisaged to establish
the Centre as a place of pleasure.
The heating system irregularly
launched spasms of percussion

driving away a Yoga class that found
contemplation and the development
of inner harmony impossible
in such conditions.

No door
complied with the half-hour
burning specifications.
No cupboard was large enough.

No vision that they had of man
could be accommodated in
this bleak and bald
reverberating barn,

even the letters of whose name
sunk in a hunk of porage concrete
appeared slowly like slugs
only in rain.

   iii
Something had crossed
oceans with them,
tougher than nostalgia
or recurrent dreams.

So many leagues of emptiness
travelled, such pain
endured; and still incompetence
flowered from design.

The ashes were cold now
on the distant shore.
For this new beginning
they had come so far

to an earth untrammelled.
The journey stopped here.
And the Centre proclaimed
they had reached Nowhere

to gaze in horror
at their fresh start—
a Centre, sprung crooked
straight from the heart.

JEAN EARLE

BOXES

As we grow older
We should acquire these boxes,
Of which the sides invisible but strong
Hold divided time, to be lived in pieces
Separately keen as steel, flashing like winter stars,
Scarce to be borne, so immediate and intense.

For this box, the day's grief—oh, how the concentration hurts me!
But in this other box I look at flowers
As at first seeing or the very last . . .

Yet another box cooks the dull dinners,
Chops upon chops.

And then again, I strive through the bright wind
With all my strength and the dog—ageing.
Nothing in that box, nothing
Save the dog and I, homing against the wind.

So no life spills from one box into another.

All the day's pieces sharp,
The colours adamant at last and true,
Saying, '*This*, this I am and not that universal gold
You thought I was when you were young.'

WHAT DO I STAND FOR?

When I consider the night battles and the day cries
Out of my strings, corebones: the one luminous drop
From the distilled dreams—now they seem sorrowful as rejected seeds,
Sharper than samphire tasted in storm salt,
Sadder than monkeys' eyes—these flares out of my heart.

And yet I glow, I burn with the best leaves
In the gold-shouting wood. When children laugh
All the blood blooms in my amaze of pipes
True as a rose. I am made well with love,
And colours tell me their real names, their secret names,
Complimenting my stand in the world of lights.

Why, then—since I wear joy for a shroud—
Must all my shinings celebrate the dark?

THE BIRCH TREE

Long ago, wrapped in my coats walking,
Under my coats, deep in my coats me—
A frozen birch I saw was attacked by the sun,
Suddenly set shining,
Winterset strings, trailers and weepers loosened, singing
An ice-knocker, a glass tune, a preparation
To free off cases of dead bark,
The cold shimmer-coat and the hard shine,
And be that simple, wind-responding statement,
A birch tree.

My coats are of wool from the sea islands,
Over my mind my thick cap,
Over my lips my scarf—
Nothing has told me yet the way to shed coats—
Only I walk in hope, noting that such things happen
As the ice sliding at the true signal, from the birch tree.

No, it would not do. I have to be so careful!
These coats are something other than the sleep of a birch tree.

THE PICTURE OF THE TIGER HUNT

I did not wince because the tiger is pinned by spears,
Stuck and lifted on the elephant's tusk,
Nor for the blood too bright
Nor for the forest leaves
Streaming to blaze the scene
As in frightening dreams.

No—what moved me was the tiger's hands
Hands, not paws—
Past all powerful dealing,
Sprawling out wide, loose,
Asking astounded of the light off the continuing spear,
Of the red workday gleam in the elephant's eye.

So do all creatures, peaceful or tiger, lift hands—
Not paws—
At the flash of death.

This picture was done by a 'naive' painter:
'Naive' we call him—and we look for truth.
Hands open and shape no. Hands, not paws,
Two or four hands—or one, as in a dying flower.

Towards light is the last appeal
And should evoke tears.

PATRICK CREAGH

from EPISTULARIUM

[*After nine years without writing verse, Patrick Creagh—now living in Italy—
was engaged in a verse correspondence with George d'Almeida. These poems
are part of Creagh's side of this correspondence.*]

6

Yes, the isle you speak of: in a small boat
Even in the stillest night, you know you are close,
For the air is full of spices, and along the shore,
However sleepy, the daughters of the waves are white.

And noon is a pestle bruising the corianders
On terraces high above each little village
Splayed on hills like pebbles flung at the sand.
Fishermen, pirates, murderers of Turks:
It is a fragrant, dangerous land.

But I came to another island, a slag reef
Where no gull risks a wing, but dwarfish gorse
Clings to the flat cold dunes like a curse.
Gunmetal molluscs suck at the scum tide.

Your foot once prints that ossuary beach
And you have to be born again, or die and die
On the steel island of self and grief.
Hard to be born, for the child who has once died.

The sorrow was not of words, not just an absence
Of still-dropped syllables and beloved tongues,
But silence of the heart and soul, as absolute
As the void where God should be.
                                        Yet, far out,
Where the foolish virgins float white belly upwards
Cramming the dead lagoon, I heard your shout.

We are born again, we are born again through tears,
Terrors of memory laving our charred façades,
Tears of loss and the cross of the lost years.
So I walk in a wintry landscape. Plenty of robins
Don't make a summer, even the weeds are sparse,
Shudder to think what the new year may bring.
But fragrant and dangerous still is the dream we dream,
And even the dead, the dead tree on the hill
Is a sacred thing.

   18 *A se stesso*
Hold the tall candle in the dark and wait
Here at the window,
For now it is almost night.
Maybe someone will notice, some late boat,
Someone out there mistake himself for a pirate
Mistaking this for a message, maybe.
A small flame can cry out, on a dark night.

You have been too much alone. Your wretched books,
That fretting from cover to cover, the lovely dead,

The lonely—who are also dead.
Does it scare you: 'Where are the living fingers?'
Your blood is sad and terrible: cowardly blood
Fretting from cover to cover, dead and lovely.

Are you ready to come to the window? Come to the window.
Hold the tall candle in the dark, and wait.
And if no answering hail, no yell for help,
Don't give up: the night is long,
The need is endless.

20

A long time since I stood and stared,
But just this morning
Way down by Val di Pesa, and beyond
The city lying low,
A paragon of white peaks, wondrous Appenines.

I saw Olympus there, holy Parnassus,
Places remote from men, a light
Clear as Apollo's eye; and then
Friezes of love and war, the white
Hearts of hills rebuked and taught to rise,
The wrack of columns, capitals:
I think one time they touched the skies.

I forgot the road over the birdless moor
Where the days whisper together to our ruin
And the soul longs for mortality.

22

A man is coming towards, he is in the distance
Still, but something familiar . . .
Down by the old wall, moving, coming towards me.

A syllable of wind and he sweeps back his hair,
Easy unhurrying pace, a path before him,
Something familiar, and a hand half-raised,
Gentlest of salutations, motionless almost.

It is like a tune I knew.

He has passed the stream and my golden-wanded willow,
Threshold of utterance; in his open palm

He is bringing me something,
Something grieved and grieved for, not forgotten,
Lost long ago, and in another country.

   24 *A Picture of Little T. C.*
The education of dreams:
A phrase once used for a dead man that I loved
Beyond reckoning, as beyond recall.
What did he bring me?

A pillow in the long night? A light? A coverlet?
A laden cherry-branch, earliest gift of summer?
Loukoum and roses? Argosies? Anodynes?
Fables to sail in to unforethought-of shores?

What did he bring me then?

Some cold iron artichokes, hedging Golgotha,
A knife at work in a cork, grinçant, grinçant,
Toad under stone, his ugliness . . .
Merciless cough, phlegm thick as chicken-fat
—Fertilized yolk: look at the spot of death—
Spittle of rancour, prayerless, unappeased,
His sheep's heart flung at a well-wisher:
Faker on a bed of nails—Ugh . . .
Splintered as his legs, his lines—useless—

He showed me the way to die, for me to know it,
And the education of dreams,
That dead man on a headland scanning the Atlantic
For a love that never came.

It is the bringing, the making, and the bringing.
Not an ambrosial word. Beautiful Tristan!

VAL WARNER

OUTDOOR RELIEF

But for the grace: an eye for pretty things,
royal blue blooms in window boxes, tubs.
They huddle on a lintel, eat their day

their loud bonhomie stinks, their bodies high
don't notice what across the pavement crawls
chasing the shade, the interregnum, that
the bottles end, black nails scratch broken light.

Our brutish good-looking, just lording it,
Mediterranean tan, speedwell eyes;
beside an also-ran in any walk,
the third man, I didn't see, eyes biting dust.
All day nasties and pip of their tone
shorten against the clean and blurring panes
of houses owned or multi-occupied.

ROUND THE CORNER

Vying a pillar-box, the salvias
in pink and white window-boxes explode,
fire next door's balcony, where hyacinths
sent the air—spring earthed April, the day's promise

cut by the angle of the masonry
glancing the other way through the light's puzzle,
cracked vision, bloody salvias, blue things
stringing eyes round the corner, urns trail green.

Under the warder eyes of tenements
a derelict is sitting in the sun,
the tenant on the balcony sucks up
the sun watering skin exhumed in sweat;
the afternoon through glittering traffic slurs
tomorrow and tomorrow round the bend.

ACROSS THE YARD

It is the moment of the lighting of
the lamps, whose flair and of the Lares flared,
flaming switch is homecoming and Laura's theme:
dusk falls at six, the lighting of the year
standing a while while dark creeps up on us
whose homecoming's across the royal parks,
departures nothing all over Europe.

the lights go up, dusk falling down again.
Chance of illumination like the sun
picks out a rainbow chequering among
day's rows of warder eyes of tenements
keeping the day, their window on their world
twilit, whose salmon, peaches, oranges
glowing against a donkey coat, dun dusk

darkened to yellow and white panes of light
against the night we watch, I'm framed against
the long window, uncurtained, open sash
giving on low roofs, builder's yard once mews
between the houses in between, eyes get
across tomorrow with the hopes and fears
of all the years that met in yesterday.

A DEATH

September 1977

All this world's beauty blinds
my eyes and mind's
eye. I walk on on colour
mouldered to soil,
even the iris.

Sometimes the evening light's too much
beyond any vision
in the split hair-
lines of dazzle.

Looking back's like looking
the wrong way through a glass
they focused on the Ratio
observed and illumined
curves of their Nature:
a spider's thread catching

the light and tears,

perception's membrane, loom
of a leaf
under the greenwood tree.
Light dyes an open book.

DAVID DAY

CAVE PAINTING

Well into a grey winter afternoon
and working at a pile of documents
I came on a sketch
of Prehistoric Man collecting honey.

The desk was in a gloomy place
between partitions. The man was a thin streak
high on a bent ladder. I put it out,
self-portrayal being far from common.

Also the bees were scarcely evident,
and by variation in the pressure
of a stroke a woman seemed to turn
as she looked up in anticipation.

The mark made a graceful body.
Often returning to the picture as I worked
I thought about a library
round which a manor had been built.

The daughters were all famous for their looks.
I had been led up through the several levels
out into the air to see the colours
and how far the garden spread.

The shelves were packed with books of flowers.

AT ANCHOR HERE

At anchor here and after their shore leave
the crew are still asleep below.
A coaxing breeze is straight along the reach.
The morning tide will take us out.

Till then the waves will lap
beside their heads, go with
their dreams, full sounds coming
to appease the ripples, detail. I woke early,

noticing the colour swaying slightly
in the tumbler holding
down a corner of the shaded chart.
I rose to work. Because my cabin is so near

the water-line reflections enter
even in the dark. I slid my last night's drink
aside and ruled some angles
over shoals, then climbed the narrow ladder,

coming down directly underneath the Plough
and Pole Star. None of the stars are strong now
dawn approaches. This is only a small fishing craft,
and there is time to put the compasses

still in my hand about the sky, from place
to place. One constellation has a mouth.

IN THE SPACE

In the space through which I operate
the constellations do not seem to make

the figures in the myth
about the person rescued
by the Gorgon's head, yet they have the names
that cold observers gave them.

My head is close
below my leafless apple tree. The October air
is cool and limpid. Black twigs hide some stars.
Without any aid

Perseus' hand is unmistakable
on Algol. I look about
and know that soon the frost will rib
the fences, marking out my garden

in the starlight. The obscured fields are bare.
No one else is here,
so that I am absolutely without interruption
in the silence. Such is the phase.

of 'The Bad Star' on which I concentrate
its magnitude is strong. The man who found
its long-spanned pulse was deaf
and dumb and was a good astronomer.

He watched hard and wrote it down.

PAUL MILLS

PROCRIS

Now she is wearing a blue gown
Covering her ankles
And red sandals
And a necklace
Decorated with shells. Now she is smiling
Wide, a twinkling ocean.

Now she is gazing out of the door.
Now her blank eyes slant to the side.
Now she is wearing a secret smile
Which sometimes she changes
For a secret numbness.

Now she is asleep, like Procris
Under the hands of Pan
Who has found a leopard
In the form of a young girl, asleep,
Pillowed on her hands.

But now she is trying to cover herself up
With sleep. Now trying
To struggle out of her dreams.
Now she is clenched.

The door opens and she comes into the room.
Not here. She sits down and smiles.
Not here. Now she is wearing a new face.

PAST STOKE

The car climbs up past Stoke.
Blue signs in the sun mark
Where we are, not what we
Each think. For this we look
Ahead towards the haze. A host
Of traffic on our right moves South.
Contented on my left you sit,
You smile. I see your mouth
Moving in the noise. You speak:
'It's beautiful,' as if wide sky
Hallowed our version of the previous night.

Onward stretched Cheshire:
A flat-topped level of oak,
And near to, always ten yards on,
Silver tarmac burnished after rain
Splayed before our faces, always ahead.
At a firing touch I increase pressure,
Ride the surge, drain into view new ground.

Now I ask if it were true, the world
Slid open briefly and we through
To a heroic world. But it is No,
Alas. There's less meaning in
The tale of me and you
Than in traffic driving day and night
As it must be now down this same road:
A mixed, contemptuous rush of hurtling steel,
Where you might pass me, going the other way.

THE STREET ARGUMENT

I wake to see you standing in the strange bedroom
And to hear a woman crying in the street.
You look down naked to the tree hung street
Of suburb London, listening, your face dim
And on your arms the street light's straddled amber,
            hot night's shade.
Eighty degrees of heat past midnight still:
Settled summer weather of the night.

'Bitch, bitch!' she cries. With running in the gloom
       obscure through leaves.
You stand still and hear as she groans and screams.
Two women and two men, he leaving her,
Aloud argue and shout in the night air:
Slammed steps and echoes in the road
       for good, good.
As if love grew teeth, nails, fists, she cries.
You could see nothing
But I knew just through her voice, you heard
What warm thing he murdered.

Myself waking. You by the open window
White skinned in the dark and your face hidden,
In the sleepless heat you turn your head
At her blind summary, absolute cause.
Where could your grip hold? Nothing
Had moved you to that pitch of loss.
Her statement thrust alive gave you no ground.

You turn and look at me.
You were thinking but I overheard.
Soft leaves fringed the leaded pane,
       half-wide:
On the lawn a table and four chairs
Grouped in moonshade, wait till long past dawn:
       and the street's silent.
It happened just beneath us out of sight
And by morning seemed a brief dream, nothing.

DENNIS KEENE

POETRY

The road mistaken at the turning which
Should not have been there, now leads to
This tunnel opening on the sea;

And opens on a lake those years ago,
The tunnel with its dripping roof,
The cloud-swept hills, the waterfall.

EXILE

The dead volcano puffs its cloud of snow.
Concrete façades the night will draw away.
Exile scatters its fragments on the lake.

Turning to grey before the sunset's green.
Fluorescent blighted trees; night's mask.
Rippling the steel hard surface of the lake.

A dazzling, cold tower in the morning.
The certainties of streets and hours and trains.
My body left in fragments on this lake.

ADVANCE

After the miles of orchards these torn fields
Lead to an empty space of silent walls.
The weather cannot hold: rain falls.

So this long line of tanks whose turrets move.
Someone comes from a doorway with no door.
One bird stops on a roof: then more.

It seems there should be people to come back:
Someone explains this as the engines die.
Beyond them earth lies black: then sky.

A universe is needed to hold this
So that it dwindles down and disappears;
Somewhere with spaces between stars.

TO THE SEA

All that it is must always be
Too much. We ride our horses to
        The sea, walking the shore.

Clouds hold the distance, lightning lays
Its sheets and lines: the broken roar
        Of what it is breaks here.

But no approaches made, no
Coming near: the horses' heads
    Shy at the straining hands.

BEHIND A GREEN HILL

Almost behind a green hill this
Concord of same days, these clouds that
Pass, the trains and people's faces.

A violet flute across grey water:
Almost behind a green hill these
Days that pass, the trains and faces.

Tell me of something else, walking
Down to the water's edge, the blue
Meridian and unmoving sky.

We look towards the hill, the music,
Dissolution of us almost
Now: music behind a green hill.

One grey sheet over the sky, one
Grey sheet almost over the hill, one
Violet flute across grey water.

Music behind a green hill, the
Dissolution of these days, these clouds:
A violet flute across grey water.

AUTUMN WIND

Grey arms in the tussle of night held in
By these fluorescent, concrete heights,
    Hold me, or let me fall.

Leaves burst and cloud the air, then rain down on
The silvered streets. We flow with them, we pass
    Under an opened sky

Which does not show the wind except as stars
Blown out or gathered into that bright hole
    The tortured trees would point to.

CLIFF ASHBY

LATTER DAY PSALMS

1

Somewhere there is Grace, Lord,
Was I not told it as a child
When the sound of the sparrow
Filled my heart with delight
And the rain fell like friendship on my head.
    Now the call of the cuckoo
Cannot calm my aching heart
And my soul is tormented with fear.
    Have mercy, Lord, for I have travelled far
Yet all my knowledge is as nothing.
My days are numbered. Time titters
As I stumble down the street.

Forgiveness, O forgive me, Lord,
Close my critical eye
Take me to your breast
For how else may I die.

2

The tree waves in the wind
But does not break unless
The bough is over-burdened.
When spring disrupts the dead days
Buds, leaves, and birds praise God
In song and silent sound.

    The dead dock, stiff
With last year's pride,
Leans unwillingly in the gale.

My heart, Lord, is unyielding.
My joints are stiff
The knuckles of my knees
Refuse to bend.
The knife is at my neck,
My back breaks.

    I will say my matutinal prayers
From a crippled position,
Perhaps the Lord will hear?

3

I lived among lewd men
Beneath the Crouch End clock
Waiting for God to speak.
But my ears were dull
And what my brain received
My mind misunderstood.
So I took my mean heart to the hills,
Beside the Palace of Alexandra
Gazed on Barbican and grieved.
   Lord speak to me in the morning
   Or the night will be everlasting.
Now all the dogs of Dewsbury
Bay about my heels
And the foul water of the Calder
Weeps into the sea.

4

On the estate, Lord, the people
Take counsel one with another
And in the public house
There is lamentation.
The cost of living soars
Like wild duck rising
After morning feed.
Man has neither means nor meaning.
The cry of the young in the street
Rouses a protest in the market place.
   What shall I do, Lord?
Though I bring my sad soul
And place it at Your feet,
My mouth is bitter, for fear
Infects my hand and heart.
The pit of hell yawns wide
Before my floundering feet,
I slip, I slide, I fall,
I try to grasp a skylark
But it flies south for summer.
   My mind is melancholic,
   I cannot praise my maker.

BITS OF BUSINESS

Reading this reference that I resurrect
To try and stem the sad drain on my self-respect
The one I have here has an innocent beauty,
'With honour and integrity do his duty'.
I can remember well the day you wrote me this,
A thin sun embraced 'Briggate' with bloodless kiss.
Afterwards, running down the stairs and feeling chuff
I heard you shout, 'The Police Force, Cliff, you're tall enough.'
'Tall enough', indeed, and big enough in the shoe,
And too big in the head for wearing navy blue.
My father knew you as a strong young man
Liked you before the slow decline began
Into that useful and highly respected friend
The one on whose Christmas cigars he could depend.
I used this testimonial thinking it true
For I was very young and not as wise as you,
I had not learnt dissimulation and the dread
Stage-fright and bits of business in the double bed.

OUT OF SEASON

I will sit in
The shade of this
Willow and watch
The water meander
Its thoughtless course
Passed Dewsbury.
          It means little
To me, who was
Baptized by an
Unknown man over
The kitchen sink
At Swaffham.
          Perhaps I cried
As I do now
The tears running
In rivulets through
The bearded mass
On my cheeks.
For a Man looked
For fruit in my heart

And nothing there
Could feed his appetite
So He cursed me
And went about
His business.
        Do not ask me
The way stranger
I have been lost
For longer than I knew.
        One could almost
Reach out one's hand
And stroke the sky.
Move a cloud around
With a twisted finger.

DESPERATION

Moving in desperation
Punching my shape through air
Moving by marking time.
     The kingdom sees violence
     A flowering of forget-me-nots
     A hedge of singing birds.
God of water and stone
All inanimate things
Beside the Jordan
Wind blows through my blood.
     God of all and the particular
     Beside the Calder
     Wind chills my marrow.
God of old men
The morning star
Hurricane and whisper
Speak louder, open my eyes.
     God of the desert
     Though I stand on barren land
     Tears running down my face
     Bring out the tiny flowers.
Permit me to remain by water, Lord.

ELIZABETH JENNINGS

WATCHER

He is the watcher underneath the stars.
He dresses the dome of night with strings of long
    Meditations. He seldom moves. If he does,
It is to become acquainted with nightly creatures
    And now with hibernators who are creeping
Out of their snowy sleep, their habitations
    Which, perilously, just kept them warm enough.
The watcher is hardy and burly but even he

    Rejoices in his own silence at the change
Apparent everywhere as the glacier winter
    Slides away, as the woken grass speaks
And a chorus of thrushes and blackbirds sings the hours.
    This watcher joins them in his meditations:
But he thinks of a shadow only just beginning
    To creep over grass dressed by the sun.
It is the encroachment of a gallows-tree.
    And the watcher waits for the torment in a garden,
Eden swept out, and a dark figure weeping.

ON ITS OWN

Never the same and all again.
Well, no same loss will tear me through
Or the same pain grip me if you
Go on your way. I yet shall gain
Knowledge and never wish unknown
The arguments that reach the bone,

The feelings which lay waste the heart.
No tidy place, no, I will have
All the destructiveness of love
If I can know, beyond the hurt,
Happiness waits or partly so
But not like once and long ago.

My world shall be dramatic then,
No repetitions, many acts,
A few hard treaties, broken tracts,

And peace made stronger yet by pain
Accepted but not chosen when
Love is its own and not again.

LOVE NEEDS AN ELEGY

Move over into your own secrecy.
The planet cools. Our bodies lie apart.
I am not part of you, nor you of me.

We have a separate and a wounded heart,
We hear the world, we see the kings go by
And men and children happy from the start.

Why are they so or is it all a lie?
Listen, a wind is rising. I think spring
Is skirmishing today. It feels nearby

Yet we are not affected. I hear wings
And flights. The birds need never heed the clock
Or hear a lonely summons. Such light sings

But we fit nowhere. What is it can break
Hearts while there's good faith still? I do not know;
We keep our promises but stay awake.

If love could be a matter of the will
O this would never be most sadly so.

INTO THE HOUR

I have come into the hour of a white healing.
Grief's surgery is over and I wear
The scar of my remorse and of my feeling.

I have come into a sudden sunlit hour
When ghosts are scared to corners. I have come
Into the time when grief begins to flower

Into new love. It had filled my room
Long before I recognized it. Now
I speak its name. Grief finds its good way home.

The apple-blossom's handsome on the bough
And Paradise spreads round. I touch its grass.
I want to celebrate but don't know how.

I need not speak though everyone I pass
Stares at me kindly. I would put my hand
Into their hands. Now I have lost my loss

In some way I may later understand.
I hear the singing of the summer grass.
And love, I find, has no considered end,

Nor is it subject to the wilderness
Which follows death. I am not traitor to
A person or a memory. I trace

Behind that love another which is running
Around, ahead. I need not ask its meaning.

CHILDHOOD IN LINCOLNSHIRE

Six years of a flat land.
Grasses cut your fingers on that shore.
People kept calling it Holland and a child
Thought this on some map somewhere
Linked it with that place
A Dutch doll came from.
So the sea trafficked with imagination
Which was more luminous even
Than the blazing tulips in formidable ranks
Or honeysuckle,
The first flower to be seen and smelt,
Tied to its own event and potent for that, therefore, always.

ANDREW WATERMAN

NORTH DERRY NOCTURNE

1
An unapologetic
Irish sky decays:
sunset, and Donegal's
ridge lies out on the water

crimson-rimmed, small clouds
like fluffs of ink above
on orange fading to blue.
I watch the embers burn

out.' Now only far
Greencastle's twinkle, where
boats nose from the land's shadow
to harvest a salt darkness.

2
I load the Bendix—round
and round all goes in the wash—
and walk down Prospect Road
to raise my glass in the Anchor:

the old familiar faces,
the University matters.
These horses of instruction!
Where are the wiser tigers

of wrath? Outside and headed
this way last evening, a car
blew up: they found an arm
tattooed 'for God and Ulster'.

3
We talk our last pints through;
your man here, blond, flush-faced,
degree in Greek and Latin,
grew up inside all this:

'But those were quieter days.
The big house was still owned
by mad aristocrats—
the goings-on up there,

locking each other in cupboards,
disowning heirs! I'd go
for chestnuts to the estate.
They chased me waving shotguns.'

4
Now the gun's outside
the plantation wall, and trigger

pulled. Our headlights catch
only a moving swathe

of scrubby verge, with bracken
smashed, and one dead hedgehog.
We pass the Bush round, sip
its thread of warmth. Unseen

the billowing hills pegged down
by stony farms attuned
to ancient disciplines,
bringing to growth, to market.

5

'My uncle's a country man',
says one. 'He's not been known
to construct an entire sentence.
But he could keep a farm.

He knew of just one way
with vermin: take the gun.
And so he'd keep the country.
But he couldn't hold his son.

Des married a go-go dancer
from Strabane, a Teague.
They've two wains now, in England.'
All's black outside the car.

6

As last month in the tube
before I came from England,
I watched straphanging faces
assuming some next station

and thought, What if we stopped
for ever in this tunnel,
or, not rising out
at Finchley Road, the train

dipped, and whooshed straight through?
So—we read the papers,
plan lectures, double-glazing;
now, coffee-time again.

7

Dropped back from which, indoors
I leave the curtains open:
set desk, the anglepoise's
glow, ringed mug, and dimmed

bookshelves—thus to cruise
night, the town's few roofs
heaving vague, subsumed
to the Atlantic groundswell;

precise in focused light
ink's strict notation charts
the spinning nebulae,
the labyrinthine self.

8

Where the Minotaur of soul
bellows darkly, ramps
mazed in intricacies,
gorges pale ideals.

All, killer in the night,
the poets, demagogues,
take as they find the world,
apotheosize these

confines. But mine those walls
with imagination's fuse—
poor souls in a rough field
adrift in stars and sea.

9

And I, returned, who hang
these blanched sheets to the moon,
feet tangling in wet grass?
I think three weeks back to

the girl in the Penge Chinese:
'They send you anywhere,
I see it all, meet friends.
But you know how it is.

It's like you're in the dark,
and strike match after match.

I could chuck the agency
I know . . . But it's not that . . .'

   10
And so, I wait for dawn's
pure green and silver, sea
calmed by soft arms of coast;
Portstewart clarifying

around me, white and frail
as shells these houses clasped
to rock, so rootless might
be gone with the next tide;

as when, in skins, men first
leant upon spears to see
dream-clear Donegal
sunlit across the water.

NEIL POWELL

AFTERNOON DAWN

for Rod Shand

They are felling the dead elms
to the west: the sidelong sun
surprises the room after
a hundred years of shadow.
The forgotten web and dust
on untouched books are sunstruck.
Clearly, something has begun.

Things that had been unspecial
are transmogrified, reborn
to *duende* and charisma.
Sun settles on faded spines;
crystals through a decanter;
chases spiders in this, its
perversely afternoon dawn;

lights upon Márquez: *through the
window they saw a light rain*

of tiny yellow flowers
falling. Through the window I
see a blue haze of woodsmoke
spiralling towards evening,
hovering, rising again.

The room begins to darken;
now, blood-coloured light splashes
across the page where the pen
labours towards conclusion.
An end to the beginning,
the web once more unnoticed;
the elms will soon be ashes.

AT THE EDGE

Far inland this late July,
I imagine those coastlines—
Caernarvon, Sussex, Suffolk—
and think of you at the edge
of a well-studied ocean
whose dirty secrets emerge
numbered in tomato pips.

Through a vocabulary
which does what it has to do
with ungraceful exactness,
you express about the sea
things I shall never fathom,
confronting those mysteries
whose gift is their remoteness.

And yet, awed, intransigent,
I too must question; concoct
in the kitchen of ideas
the approximate flavour
of some finely-charted coast;
season it with the right words.
Scientist and writer are

not so different, perhaps . . .
Men who live on their edges,
inhabit borders, margins,

embody the coasts they crave
and need the answering clash
of waves over the shingle,
no metaphor but design.

IN THE DISTANCE

First, the foreground. A class is reading,
Gratefully engrossed and undisturbed
By coughs or scraping metal chairs on wood.
Now is a time to watch unwatched, observe
The chin upon the wrist, the narrowed eyes,
The stifled yawn, the silence; and outside
An autumn bonfire flaring in the distance.

Consider this October close-up: hands
Clasped after the cold in new discovery
Of each other's throbbing warmth; a pen
Composing doodles no one understands;
A briefly broken train of thought; and then
The meditative meeting, nose with thumb.
Mist is blurring the horizon distantly.

The years are misting over. I recall
Something I didn't say a dream ago,
Return abruptly to the reading class.
The weeping condensation on a window
Becomes the image of another day,
A conversation in a different place,
Minutely glimpsed, and very far away.

What casual things define me! Clothes I wear,
Books I carry, a ballpoint on the desk
Upon a half-corrected essay: there
Is all the life I seem to have. The trees
Branch from the mist, their structures become clear:
The bonfire flashes sharply as I stare
Across a hundred yards, a hundred years.

In the distance, on a Kentish hillside,
A boy is writing a poem I know by heart.

MICHAEL VINCE

THE ORCHARD WELL

Water drawn from the well
Was cold, he says, and pure,
The orchard's underflow,
Its origin unsure.
Those with art would know
When it would sink or swell.

But chance created the spring.
Someone driving a post
Broke the water free,
The emergence of a ghost,
A clear inconstancy
Hidden in everything.

Nineteen seventeen:
Boys who splashed in the pool,
Ones who are old or dead.
The deep water was cool.
He touches his white head.
Time has been dipped clean.

Then it was tapped, one year,
And soon the well ran dry.
He sealed the shaft, the tomb.
Round it the trees die
Wasting for what might come,
Not quenched by what is here.

THE ART OF LIMNING

> 'It is sweet and cleanly to use, and it is a thing apart from all
> other painting or drawing.'   —Nicholas Hilliard

Your own face on a few inches of vellum;
The elaboration of lovers and personal dynasties,
Kings, merchants, all who endow themselves
From another's eyes and by the skill of a hand;
You touch posterity, the minute and accurate;
Queens and children of queens, fastidious jewellery;

The costume of state and the gravity of possession;
Court ceremony, a chain at a favourites neck;
A sword will fall there, your tiny images
Sail before to outpower time's armada.

You wrote of it: an exact art for gentlemen
With due precepts, and the first is cleanliness;
In act, the avoidance of anger in any wise,
The exclusion of questioners or busy fingers;
Welcome are discreet talk and quiet mirth,
Reading and music, they enliven the spirit
For sitter and painter, they shorten slow hours.
And after, though not subject to the market-place
Or common men's use, to be brought to great extremes,
Your house darkened by neighbours and much decayed.

Light, the open alley of a goodly garden;
A small space to illumine, the visible features
Ennobling the hidden and the impossible,
Flirtations of the Devil or of armed endeavour
Shadowed by the Tower and the blacker coastline
Of profit in the New World, contriving in the Old
And uncertain management in what may come.
Accordingly, all must be made as jewels.
Light curls in the ruff and holds in the hair;
A man clasps a hand out of a cloud.

BYZANTINE SAINTS

While Jesse sleeps, a tree
The painter never saw
Bears ancient bearded fruit,
Heads of the fathers; all
Grows here from the same root
To obey the maker's law
Of genesis, dream, and fall.
We wait and watch him see.

These walls are hung with a death,
The creator's awesome eyes
Having darkened and completed
The world inside the room.
His dream is posed and repeated

In gold and red, but dies.
Faces shine from the gloom,
The light stopping their breath.

And art must pall, the paints
Flaking their blood or pain;
Dim where the world was real,
They picture it at least,
Figures smiling to kneel
And meet the axe again,
Or humbling man and beast
In the wilderness, the saints.

Where the asses smile and suggest
Their affections, and twisting trees
Break into events and space,
An old man in a hood
Turns us his anxious face.
The shadows of what he sees
Have grained into the wood;
And we must dream the rest.

DONALD DAVIE

WILD BOAR CLOUGH

[*the second section of* 'Three for Watermusic']

1
A poet's lie!
            The boarhound and the boar
Do not pursue their pattern as before.
What English eyes since Dryden's thought to scan
Our spinneys for the Presbyterian,
The tusked, the native beast inflamed to find,
And rend the spotted or the milk-white hind,
The true Church, or the half-true? Long ago
Where once were tusks, neat fangs began to grow;
Citizen of the World and Friend to Man,
The presbyter's humanitarian.
The poor pig learned to flute: the brute was moved
By plaudits of a conscience self-approved;
'Self in benevolence absorb'd and lost'
Absorbed a ruinous Redemption's cost.

This too a lie; a newer zealot's, worse
Than any poet's in or out of verse.
These were the hunting-calls, and this the hound,
Harried the last brave pig from English ground;
Now ermine, whited weasel, sinks his tooth
Deeper than wolf or boar into the Truth.
Extinct, the English boar; he leaves a lack.
Hearts of the disinherited grow black.

2
When he grew up
in the England of silver
cigarette-cases and
Baptist chapel on Sundays,

long white flannels were still
worn, and the Mission Fields
ripe for the scything Gospel
cast him a weekly penny,

the Missionary box!
It rattled as he knocked it,
crouching nearer the wireless:
deuce, Fred Perry serving . . .

Doggedly he applies
himself to the exhumations:
those pre-war amateurs,
that missionary martyr.

As gone as Cincinnatus!
Still tongue-in-cheek revered, as
Republican virtue by
a silver-tongued florid Empire,

tired of that even, lately.

3
To Loughwood Meeting House,
Redeemed since and re-faced,
Once persecuted Baptists
Came across sixty miles
Of Devon. Now we ask
Our own good wincing taste
To show the way to Heaven.

But if under clear-glassed windows,
The clear day looking in,
We should be always at worship
And trusting in His merits
Who saves us from the pathos
Of history, and our fears
Of natural disasters,

What antiquarian ferrets
We have been! As idle
An excrescence as Ionic
Pilasters would be, or
Surely the Puritan poet:
Burning, redundant candle,
Invisible at noon.

We are, in our way, at worship;
Though in the long-deflowered
Dissenting chapel that
England is, the slim
Flame of imagination,
Asymmetrical, wavers,
Starving for dim rose-windows.

4
And so he raged exceedingly,
excessively indeed, he raged excessively
and is said to have been drunk, as certainly
in some sense and as usual he was;
lacking as usual, and in some
exorbitant measure, charity,
candour in an old sense. How
a black heart learns white-heartedness, you tell me!

Raged, and beshrewed his audience of one
without much or at all
intending it, having his eyes not on
her but on the thing to be hunted down;
or so he will excuse himself, without
much confidence. The rapist's plea:
not her but womankind. He has
the oddest wish for some way to disgrace himself.

How else can a pharisee clear the accounts, and live?

5

Wild Boar Clough . . . known to his later boyhood
    As the last gruelling stage before,
Feet and collar-bones raw, the tarmacadam
    Past unbelievable spa-hotels
Burned to the train at Buxton. Julian Symons,
    His poems, 'Confessions of X', reviewed
In *Poetry London* bought on Buxton station . . .

A nut-brown maid whom he cannot remember
    Sold him herb beer, a farmhouse brew,
One day above Wild Boar Clough, whose peat-sieved brown
    Waters were flecked below them. Legs
Were strong then, heart was light, was white, his swart
    Limbs where the old glad Adam in him,
Lissom and slim, exulted, carried him.

Somewhere that boy still swings to the trudging rhythm,
    In some brown pool that girl still reaches
A lazy arm. The harm that history does us
    Is grievous but not final. As
The wild boar still in our imaginations
    Snouts in the bracken, outward is
One steep direction gleefully always open.

So Lud's Church hides in Cheshire thereabouts
    Cleft in the moor. The slaughtered saints
Cut down of a Sunday morning by dragoons
    Grounded the English Covenant
In ling and peat-moss. Sound of singing drifts
    Tossed up like spume, persistently
Pulsing through history and out of it.

Index

This selective index includes page references to authors mentioned in the body of the book, to movements, small presses and magazines, and related entries. The titles of books and individual poems are not included.

252

A short anthology: contributors